1,000,000 Books
are available to read at

Forgotten Books

www.ForgottenBooks.com

Read online
Download PDF
Purchase in print

ISBN 978-1-330-65329-6
PIBN 10087843

This book is a reproduction of an important historical work. Forgotten Books uses
state-of-the-art technology to digitally reconstruct the work, preserving the original format
whilst repairing imperfections present in the aged copy. In rare cases, an imperfection in
the original, such as a blemish or missing page, may be replicated in our edition. We do,
however, repair the vast majority of imperfections successfully; any imperfections that
remain are intentionally left to preserve the state of such historical works.

Forgotten Books is a registered trademark of FB &c Ltd.
Copyright © 2018 FB &c Ltd.
FB &c Ltd, Dalton House, 60 Windsor Avenue, London, SW19 2RR.
Company number 08720141. Registered in England and Wales.

For support please visit www.forgottenbooks.com

1 MONTH OF FREE READING

at

www.ForgottenBooks.com

By purchasing this book you are eligible for one month membership to ForgottenBooks.com, giving you unlimited access to our entire collection of over 1,000,000 titles via our web site and mobile apps.

To claim your free month visit: www.forgottenbooks.com/free87843

* Offer is valid for 45 days from date of purchase. Terms and conditions apply.

English
Français
Deutsche
Italiano
Español
Português

www.forgottenbooks.com

Mythology Photography **Fiction**
Fishing Christianity **Art** Cooking
Essays Buddhism Freemasonry
Medicine **Biology** Music **Ancient Egypt** Evolution Carpentry Physics
Dance Geology **Mathematics** Fitness
Shakespeare **Folklore** Yoga Marketing
Confidence Immortality Biographies
Poetry **Psychology** Witchcraft
Electronics Chemistry History **Law**
Accounting **Philosophy** Anthropology
Alchemy Drama Quantum Mechanics
Atheism Sexual Health **Ancient History**
Entrepreneurship Languages Sport
Paleontology Needlework Islam
Metaphysics Investment Archaeology
Parenting Statistics Criminology
Motivational

Curiosities of Music

A Collection of Facts, not generally
known, regarding the Music of
Ancient and Savage Nations

By
LOUIS C. ELSON

Copyright, MDCCCLXXX, by J. M. STODDART & CO.

Copyright, MCMVIII, by OLIVER DITSON COMPANY

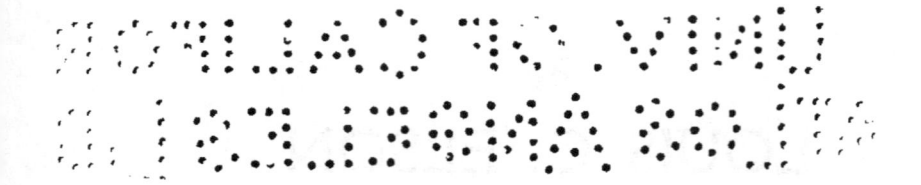

TO MY ESTEEMED FRIEND,

Dr. C. Annette Buckei,

THIS LITTLE WORK IS DEDICATED.

PREFACE.

In this work, I have endeavored to bring together the most curious points in the music of many nations, ancient and modern. As the work originally appeared in a magazine ("The Vox Humana") I was obliged to avoid any extended research into disputed points, such as Hebrew music, Greek music, water organs, etc., as being too abstruse for periodical reading. Yet many of the facts contained in its columns have not yet found their way into English literature. This was so entirely the case with Chinese music, that I was tempted to somewhat trangress my limits on this subject, it being, apparently, a neglected one. In all the other chapters I have merely sought out such facts as would interest, and present a comprehensive idea to the general reader, whether musical or not.

My hearty thanks are due to Col. Henry Ware, and Mr. J. Norton, of Boston, for many facilities afforded and suggestions offered, in the course of compiling this book. If it fills an unoccupied niche, however small, in musical literature, it will have fulfilled the desire of

THE AUTHOR.

CURIOSITIES OF MUSIC.

CHAPTER I.

Music has been broadly defined by Fetis as "the art of moving the feelings by combinations of sounds;" taken in this broad sense it may be considered as coeval with the human race.

Vocal music, in a crude form, is as natural in man, to express feelings, as it is for a cat to purr or a lion to roar ; as regards instrumental music, the primitive man might have found in every hollow tree a reverberating drum, and in every conchshell or horn of cattle, the natural beginnings of instrumental music; we shall find later that many nations ascribe the discovery of their music to the accidental appliance of some natural instrument; our surest guide in watching the rise of the art, should be the manner in which savage peoples, yet in a state of nature, produce music, and we shall find too, that even the lowest in the scale, even those beings who make the monkey tribe nearer and dearer to us, as possible relatives (the bushmen of Australia for example), have still a method of "moving the feelings by means of combinations of sounds."

It is therefore, really in barbarous nations, that we may, reasoning by analogy, find in what state music existed when our own ancestors were in a state of nature; but in order to give a more chronological character to our sketches we will begin with the *Music and Musical Mythology of the Ancients.*

THE HINDOOS.

With this people, and the Egyptians we find proofs of the existence of a musical system at a time which far antedates the earliest reliable Scriptural records.

Among the Hindoos especially, as far back as history extends, music has been treated not only as a fine art, but philosophically and mathematically. According to the oldest Brahminical records, in their all-embracing "Temple of Science," it belongs to the 2d chief division of Lesser Sciences, but its natural and philosophic elements, are, with a nice distinction, admitted into their holiest and oldest book, the *Veda.** Of course it has a divine origin ascribed to it, in fact the entire realm of Indian music is one tale of Mythology.

According to Brahminical accounts, when Brahma had lain in the egg three thousand billion, four hundred million of years (3,000,400,000,000) he split it by the force of his thought and made Heaven and Earth from the two pieces; then Manu brought forth ten great forces, which made

*Krause —Geschichte der Musik

Gods, Goddesses, good and evil spirits and Gandharbas (Genii of music), and Apsarasas (Genii of Dance), and these became the musicians of the Gods, before man knew of the art. Then Sarisvati, Goddess of Speech and Oratory, consort of Brahma, at Brahma's command brought the art to man and gave him also his finest musical instrument, the Vina, of which hereafter. Music then found a protector in the demi-god Nared, one of the chief Indian musical deities, while Maheda Chrishna helped it along by allowing five keys, or modes, to spring from his head (*a la* Minerva) in the shape of Nymphs, and his wife Parbuti, added one more; then Brahma added thirty lesser keys, or modes, and all these modes were also Nymphs.

The Hindoo scale has seven chief tones and these tones are represented as so many heavenly sisters.

In the Indian legends, music is represented as of immense might. All men, all animals, all inanimate nature listened to the singing of Maheda and Parbuti with ecstasy.

Some modes were never to be sung by mortals, as they were so fiery that the singer would be consumed by them. In the time of Akber, it is related, that ruler commanded Naik Gobaul, a famous singer, to sing the Raagni* of Fire; the poor singer entreated in vain, to be allowed to sing a less dangerous strain; then he plunged up

---

*The Raagni is the popular mode of singing in India; it is a free Fantasia, or improvisation.

to his neck in the river Djumna, and began: he had not finished more than half of his lay when the water around him began to boil; he paused (at boiling point) but the relentless, or curious Akber, demanded the rest, and with the end of the song the singer burst into flames and was consumed. Another melody caused clouds to rise and rain to fall; a female singer is said once to have saved Bengal from famine and drought in this manner. Another lay caused the sun to disappear and night to come at midday, or another could change winter to spring or rain to sunshine. All these typify beautifully the might of music with this race. Of the four chief tone systems, two also have divine origin, from Iswara and from Hanuman (the Indian Pan), the others come from Bharata Muni who invented the drama with music and dance, and from Calinath.

When Chrishna was upon the earth as a shepherd, there were sixteen thousand pastoral Nymphs or Shepherdesses who fell in love with him. — They all tried to win his heart by music, and each one sang him a song, and each one sang in a *different key*, (let us hope not all at once). Thence sprang the sixteen thousand keys, which according to tradition once existed in India.

In order that the full extent of Hindoo Musical Mythology may be conceived, we will now sketch the tones which are employed.

We have stated that there are seven chief tones; these tones have short monosyllabic names; as we give to our notes the syllables, *do, re, mi*, etc., the

Hindoos call their scale tones *sa, ri, ga, ma, pa, dha, ni, sa,* which are certainly as easy to vocalise upon as our *solfeggi;* in fact the language is very well adapted to music, as it has all the softness, elegance and clearness of the Italian. Von Dalberg says that Sanscrit unites the splendor of the Spanish, the strength of the German, and the singableness of the Italian.

With the resemblance of seven chief tones, however, the similarity ends, for while our scale has only half tones as smallest interval, the Hindoos have quarter tones, and not equally distributed either; thus:

whole tone	small whole	half tone	whole tone	whole tone	small whole	half tone
Sa	Ri	Ga	Ma	Pa	Dha	Ni	Sa
¼¼¼¼	¼¼¼	¼¼	¼¼¼¼	¼¼¼¼	¼¼¼	¼¼

In theory it will be seen that the octave is always a half tone flat, but practically they correct this by singing it on its proper pitch. On six of the above intervals they found their chief modes but they form various lesser modes on each interval, i. e., they could give ten different modes, or scales, starting from C alone.

These six chief styles, are, of course, six Genii, corresponding to the six Hindoo divisions of the year, these are each married to five Nymphs, the thirty lesser styles; each Genii has eight sons, who are each wedded, also to Nymphs, one apiece. There seem to be few celibates in Hindoo Mythology, therefore an exact census gives to this interesting family six fathers, thirty mothers, forty-eight sons, forty-eight daughters-in-law, or one hundred thirty-two in all, each of them being the God or Goddess of some particular key, and each of them, of course, having a distinctive name; we shall not give the various names, but to illustrate the relationship among them, the following will suffice; the four 1-4 tones beginning on the fifth tone of the scale, *Panchama* (or *Pa*) are the Nymphs *Malina, Chapala, Lola* and *Serveretna,* while the next full tone (*Dha*) is owned by Santa and her sisters; if *Dha* should be flatted 1-4 tone which would give it the same pitch as the highest 1-4 tone of *Pa*, (called Serveretna), the poetical Hindoo would not say " *Dha* is flat," but " *Serveretna* has been introduced to the family of *Santa* and her sisters."*

Although the musical art of the Hindoos had such an early existence, it seems not to have developed or receded much since ancient days; they possess airs to which the European ear instantly, and involuntary attaches harmony, (auxiliary voices), and yet they have not the slightest craving for harmony. They are completely satisfied to express all emotion by melody, sometimes combined with the dance, and yet do not feel the monotony, which would be obviated by additional voices.

But it must be said that, so far as melody goes, they have great taste and discrimination; the music often approaches the European in form and rhythm, and the Hindoo seems to feel instinctively

---

* Wm. Jones; Music of India.

the importance of the tonic, and dominant, and often finishes the phrases of a melody with a half cadence.*

Of the Hindoo instruments the Vina takes the lead; as before mentioned, they ascribe to it a divine origin; it has four strings and is incorrectly defined as a lyre by many commentators, but it is rather a guitar than lyre, and is made of a large hollow bamboo pipe, about 3 1-2 feet long, at each end of which are two large hollow gourds, to increase the resonance: it may be roughly compared to a drum major's *baton*, with a ball at *both* ends, while the strings extend along the stick; it has a finger-board like a guitar, and the frets are not fastened permanently on it, but stuck on by the performer with wax.

The tone is both full and delicate, sometimes metallic and clear and very pleasant. The music composed for it is usually brilliant and rapid, and the Hindoos seem to have their Liszts and Rubinsteins; in the last century Djivan Shah was known throughout all India as a *virtuoso*, on the Vina.

They ornament their Vinas sometimes very richly and there are paintings of their chief performers, sitting with magnificent Vinas leaning against their bodies, this being the attitude of the player. They also have possessed from time immemorial, a three-stringed violin, so that Raphael and Tintoretto may not have committed an anachronism in painting Apollo with a violin.†

* Ambros   † Krause.

A Guitar called Magoudi, finishes the list of characteristic stringed instruments.

The instruments of percussion and wind instruments are more numerous. They possess four kinds of drums, and their popular, secular dances are usually accompanied by the Vina, for the melody, and drums, bells and cymbals.

Flutes they have possessed from remotest antiquity, and a muffled drum called Tare for funeral occasions, and they also have a double flute with a single mouth piece. We will not dwell further upon their instruments; there is but one, the *Vina*, which is really fitted to produce beautiful music.

The Hindoos complain that their old music is deteriorating and such singers as Chanan or Dhilcook, two vocal celebrities of the last centuries, have passed away. When one inquires for the miracle-working Ragas, (improvised songs) in Bengal, the people say there are singers probably left in Cashmere who can give them; and should you inquire in Cashmere they would send you to Bengal for them, but in reality there seems to have been comparatively little change in the style of Hindoo music from its earliest days.

CHAPTER II.

ANCIENT EGYPTIAN.

The ancient Egyptians ascribed the origin of music to opposite causes, some legends giving its invention to beneficent Deities, while other legends are interpreted to give its origin to Satan, the evil principle, or at least the principle of sensuality, as represented by the buck Mendes. Hermes (or Mercury) is accredited with first having observed the harmony of the spheres, and the lyre also is represented as being his invention, in the following legend:

A heavy inundation of the Nile had taken place, and when the waters receded, there was left upon the banks a tortoise, who went the way of all tortoises, and after a time was completely dried up by the sun; the tendons however, which were attached to the shell, remained, and became tightly drawn by the expansion of the shell. Hermes, wandering upon the bank, accidentally struck his foot against it; the tendons resounded, and Hermes thus found a natural lyre.

This legend is however found also in Hindoo and Greek Mythology, and may be one of those tales, springing from Arian root, which belong to almost every race. We also find an Egyptian

Apollo and Muses in other musical legends, according to Diodorus Siculus.

"When Osiris was in Ethiopia,—the Egyptian God Osiris was a sort of blending of Bacchus and Apollo—he met a troupe of revelling satyrs, and being a lover pleasure and taking delight in choruses of music, he admitted them to his already numerous train of musicia s. In the midst of these satyrs were nine young maidens, skilled in music and divers scienc

The Egyptians also considered Horus, brother of Osiris, (equivalent to the Greek Apollo) as God of Harmony.

Thus three Gods have the honor of fostering Egyptian music, Osiris, Horus, and Hermes.

Hermes, or (by his Egyptian name) Thoth, was the especial God of many sciences, and is said to have written two books of song, or works relating to the song-art. According to Diodorus, the Lyre which he had invented had three strings, which represented the three seasons of Egypt; the deepest string was the wet season, the middle one the growing season, the highest the harvest season: the tones of Egyptian music seem to be taken from the seven heavenly planets, as known to the ancients, and from this circumstance Ambros hazards the conjecture that the diatonic scale was known to them.

Among the mythical musical personages of the earliest Egyptian music, may be mentioned Maneros, who was son of the first king of Egypt, who succeeded the second dynasty of demi gods.

He seems to be analogous to the Linus, (son of Apollo), of the Greeks; he died young, and the *first* song of the Egyptian music* was in his honor; it was a lament over his untimely end, the swift passing away of Youth, Spring, etc. The song was sung under various guises, for Maneros, Linus, Adonis, etc., among various ancient nations, and Herodotus was surprised at hearing it in Egypt. But in course of time the song itself, and not the king's son, was called Maneros, and gradually diffused its influence, (the warning of the passing away of Joy) through Egyptian social life; at their banquets a perfectly painted statue of a *corpse* was borne round and shown to each guest, and there was sung the following warning:

"Cast your eyes upon this corpse
You will be like this after Death,
Therefore drink and be merry now."†

The song also from being a mournful one, became in time joyous and lively,‡ Plutarch thinks that the words Maneros, became synonymous with "Good Health." The fashion was after the conquest of Egypt, imitated in Rome.§ The ancient Egyptian music was really a twofold affair and is well symbolized in being attributed by some to good, by others to evil gods; for it was used in the religious services of the highest gods, (except, according to Strabo, in the services of Osiris, at Abydos) and on the other hand was degraded as a pastime for the lowest orders.

* Plutarch, of Isis and Osiris. † Herodotus, Hist. ‡ Plutarch of Isis and Osiris. § Petronius.

The musicians were not held in any respect, and were not allowed to change their occupation, but were obliged to transmit it from father to son and were also probably compelled to live in a certain quarter of the cities wherein they dwelt.*

Of course there were celebrated singers and performers, and also leaders of the chants, and royal singers, who were exceptions to the foregoing rule, but according to Diodorus Siculus, the Egyptians not only considered music a useless art, but even a hurtful one, as it enervated the soul and made man effeminate. Yet for all this there are found among ancient sculptures many representations of singers and musicians evidently belonging to the higher classes, though we cannot but believe that these exceptions only prove the rule, and even to-day music is considered a sensuous and rather unmanly art, by Eastern nations.

Among the most ancient songs of Egypt there seem to have been little refrains sung by the working classes while at labor; there is here not conjecture but absolute certainty, for the words of part of one of these songs are preserved, on an ancient picture of threshers of grain, oxen, etc.; the threshers sing, according to Champollion's learned deciphering,

"Thresh for yourselves, oh oxen,
Thresh for yourselves;
Measures for your masters,
Measures for yourselves."

In a grotto at *El bersheh* there is also a **painting** of the transportation of a colossal statue from **the**

---

* Champollion.

quarry, and here also while one hundred and seventy-two men are laboring at the ropes, one is perched upon the statue and is giving the time of a refrain, which all are to sing.

The custom of singing while at work still exists in Egypt, as, for example, sailors sing a particular song when starting on a voyage, another when there is danger of a collision, another when the danger is past.

Music was a chief portion of the Egyptian funeral ceremonies, and on the walls of nearly all the tombs of ancient days, are found paintings of the funeral ceremonies; the greater part of what is known of their instruments comes from this source; the best singers and players were engaged for the purpose by the richer classes, and sang mournful chants, being similar to the professional mourners at present found in the East. The music was probably chiefly melodic, or one-voiced, though this subject has some ambiguity attached to it, our only guide as to their music being the representations in the tombs, etc., as not a scrap of actual music has been left to us; but when we consider the furious controversy about, and the different interpretations of the fragments of Greek music which time has left us, this may be an *advantage* rather than otherwise. There is one painting* left, which seems to confirm the idea that the Egyptians knew something of the effect of harmony. This painting represents **two**

---

* lepsius Abt. 2 Pl., 36 e

harpers at one side and three flute players at the other, while between them are two singers, one of whom seems to be following with his voice the melody of the harpers, while the otLer sings with the flutes; this seems to intimate that the Egyptians possessed, at least *two-voiced* harmony.

Chappell, in his admirable History of Music, says that it is mathematically impossible, that all of the instruments represented in their paintings should have been played in unison.

The music of Egypt was for a long time regulated by the Government, that is all innovations were punishable by law; probably this referred only to religious music, and did not affect popular music.

In all ages there seem to have been two distinct schools of music, the scientific, and popular. There is no doubt that while the early European theorists held that *only consecutive fifths and fourths* were musical, the populace had a less forced and more beautiful style, and it is more than probable that in Egypt the popular music was totally different from the sacred.

All the songs appear to have been accompanied by a clapping of hands, and therefore the rhythm was probably strongly marked. The effect of this clapping of hands is by no means unpleasant, and is still used by the negroes of America in some songs and dances, and among various barbarous nations. It seems curious to think, that in witnessing these lively dances, one may be beholding a counterpart of the enjoyments of four thousand years ago, or that in witnessing the *pirouettes* of a ballet dancer, we are amusing ourselves in the ancient Egyptian manner; the latter fact is proved by ancient paintings, however. Other ancient Egyptian dances were similar to the modern jigs, clog dances and breakdowns, as is amply shown by figures found both in Upper and Lower Egypt.

The Egyptians had also dances with regular figures, forward and back, swing, etc.; these dances were restricted to the lower orders, the upper classes being forbidden to indulge in them.

If we could transport ourselves back to Thebes in its days of grandeur, we should be somewhat astonished at the slight change, in comparison with what is usually supposed, from our own times. Imagine the time of a great religious festival. The Nile is crowded with boats, loaded to their utmost capacity, with passengers, offerings, etc. Sometimes hundreds of thousands came to Thebes or Memphis, and especially to Bubastis, on such occasions. From each boat is heard playing and singing. Within the city all the streets are full; here march by a troop of Pharaoh's soldiers, all the privates uniformed alike, their marching regular, and their drill well attended to; at their head is a military band, (picture found at Thebes) of trumpeters, drummers beating the drum with their *hands*, and other performers; along that mighty avenue of Sphinxes is marching a procession to one of the temples: here also musical instruments, particularly flutes, head the column, and a processional hymn is being sung, to which the white-robed priests keep time while marching, as they carry the sacred golden barge of the God, full of treasure of various kinds.

Here is passing along, a deputation from some far off tributary prince in the heart of Æthiopia, carrying presents for the king, and all around is life, bustle, and enjoyment. In some of the temples music is sounding, (the temple of Osiris, at Abydos, being the only exception,) and the clang of the sistrum is often heard. Truly the life of ancient Egypt was as joyous and varied as that of more modern times.

The sistrum was, until the Napoleonic expedition to Egypt, which gave to the world the wonders of this store house of antiquity, considered the representative of Egyptian music. It was merely a short, oval hand frame which held three or four metal bars; sometimes bells were hung upon these bars, and by shaking the instrument, as a baby shakes a rattle, which it really in principle resembles, a jingling of the bars or bells was produced.

Latterly it has been thought that the sistrum was not a musical instrument at all; but, like the bell sounded at the elevation of the Host in Catholic churches, was used as a means of riveting and impressing the minds of the worshippers. At all events the sistrum takes no rank among Egyptian musical instruments. The harp was really the instrument on which they lavished the most attention; paintings, and fragments of harps have been found, in the so-called "Harpers' Tomb," which caused Bruce to exclaim that no modern maker could manufacture a more beautiful piece of workmanship.

The ancient Egyptian harps look very modern indeed, except for the fact that they have no front board or "Pole," and it seems strange that they could bear the tension without its support; the pitch could not have been at all high. There was a species of harp, of the compass of about two octaves, with catgut strings, (wire strings the Egyptians had not), found in a tomb hewn in the solid rock at Thebes, so entirely preserved that it was played upon by the discoverer, and gave out its tones *after being buried* 3000 *years.* Of course the strings perished after exposure to the air.

Fetis, to whom musical history owes so much, has here fallen into a singular mistake. He says "it would scarcely be believed that the ancient Egyptians with whom the cat was a sacred animal, should have used *cat-gut* strings on their instruments, but the fact is proved beyond a doubt." This is all very true, but M. Fetis seems not to have known the fact that cat-gut has not its origin in the *cat*, but is almost always, in reality *sheep-gut.*

The list of instruments of ancient Egypt embraces harps of various numbers of strings, Nabla, from which come the Roman *Nablium* and Hebrew *Nebel*, a sort of Guitar; Flutes, single and double, (a flute player often headed the sacred processions, and Isis is said to have invented the flute.) Tambourines and hand drums; sometimes the Egyptians danced to a rhythmic accompaniment of these alone.* The flute was generally played by men, and the tambourines by women. Lyres, of various shapes, often played with the hand, but sometimes also with a plectrum, (a short, black stick, with which the strings were struck,) trumpets, cymbals, and some metal instruments of percussion. There are many paintings in which entire orchestras of these instruments are playing together, but probably all in unison.

There exists an excellent painting from a Theban tomb,† in which we see an Egyptian musical party in a private house. Two principal figures are smelling of small nosegays, while two females offer to them refreshments; three females are dancing and singing for the amusement of the guests, who sit around, apparently having a very enjoyable time; below are seen slaves preparing a banquet, which is to follow the music. The Egyptians often had music before dinner.

Another application of music is pictured in a very ancient painting, given by Rosellini,‡ in his great work; in it is seen a woman nursing an infant, while a harper and singer are furnishing music, possibly to lull the child to sleep; in almost all these paintings the singers are represented with one hand to their ear in order to catch the pitch of the instruments more readily.

---

*Wilkinson, p. 240 † Wilkinson, v. 2, p. 222. ‡ V 3, p. 83.

But the most interesting painting has been copied, in the folios of Lepsius,§ from a tomb of great antiquity; it represents a course of *musical instruction* in the department of the singers and players of King Amenhotep IV. (18th Dynasty). We see several large and small rooms, connecting with each other; furniture, musical instruments and implements are seen all around, especially in the small rooms or closets. In the large rooms are the musicians, engaged in practising and teaching; one teacher is sitting, listening to the singing of a young girl, while another pupil is accompanying her on the harp; another girl stands attentively listening to the teacher's instructions, (*class system* evidently); in another part two girls are practising a dance, while a harper accompanies; other musicians are variously engaged. In one room is a young lady having her hair dressed, and in another, a young miss has leant her harp against the wall, and is sitting down with a companion to lunch. This certainly gives a fair insight into the music life of old, and we leave Egyptian music, of which *as music* we know nothing, with more satisfaction after this glance at the *Royal Egyptian Conservatory of Music.*

§ Abtheilung, 3, page 106.

CHAPTER III.

BIBLICAL AND HEBREW.

The earliest scriptural mention of music is in Genesis, Chapter IV. where Jubal is spoken of as "Father of those who handle the harp and organ." But harp and organ must by no means be confounded with our modern instruments of the same name. The harp was probably an instrument of three strings, while all the very ancient references to an organ, simply mean a "Syrinx" or Pan's pipes. The music of Biblical History is, as is almost all the music of ancient nations, combined to a great extent with the dance; the dances of the ancients were what to-day would be called pantomimes, expressing joy, sorrow, fear, or anger, by the motions and expressions of face and body, rather than by the feet.

The real character of the ancient Hebrew music, as well as of many of the musical instruments, is involved in utter obscurity, and no clues to enlighten the investigator, remain in the modern music of this usually most conservative of peoples; much of their musical system was borrowed, until David's time certainly, from the Egyptians.

The music of the modern Jews is tinged in almost every instance with the character of the music of the people around them; thus the same psalms are sung in a different manner by German, Polish, Spanish, or Portuguese Jews.

One little trace of their primitive music remains; on the occasion of their New Year, a ram's horn is blown, and between the blasts on this excruciating instrument the following phrases are addressed to the performer,—

Tahkee-oo, Schivoorim, Taru-o.

These words, which also have a reverential meaning, may possibly at one time have been addressed to the ancient musicians, to give to them the order of the music. Strong presumptive proof that this blowing of the trumpet is the same as it was in King David's time is found in the fact that it is blown in the same rhythm, by the Jews *all over the world.* It certainly requires no forced interpretation to call the Ram's horn (Schofer) one of their early instruments, as it would be their most natural signal-call both in peace and war.

In all the Jewish theocracy, the music naturally took a theosophical character, and is seldom detached from religious rites; we shall find the same spirit running through other of the ancient civilizations, even barbarians seeming to share in the almost universal impulse to praise the Deity with this art, and this should prove to supercilious critics that however ill-sounding the music of other races may appear to our ears, to *them* it was a highly considered art, and as such, merits our attention.

David may be regarded as the real founder of Hebrew music. He must have possessed great skill even in his youth, as the instance of his being able to soothe Saul's crazed mind with his music, proves. This may be regarded as one of the earliest notices of the effects of music in mental disease. What the nature of his inventions and reforms in music afterwards were, and how far he remodelled the style which had been brought from Egypt, cannot now be known, as Jerusalem has been pillaged nearly twenty times since his reign, and every monument, or inscription which might solve the enigma, has long been destroyed.

There are still marks and inflections in the Hebrew Scriptures which are evidently intended to show the style in which they were to be chanted.

Regarding the instruments spoken of in Scripture as being used in the Temple there is also no certainty. In the Talmud there is mention of an organ which had but ten pipes, yet gave one hundred different tones; this instrument is placed about the beginning of the Christian Era, and is called *Magrepha;* it is said of it, that its tones were so powerful that when it was played, the people in Jerusalem could not hear each other talk. Pfeiffer conjectures that it was probably not an organ, but a very loud drum. There are other authorities who have endeavored to prove that the *Magrepha* was simply a *fire shovel;* they contend that it was used at the sacrifices of the Temple to build up the fire, and was then thrown down, with a loud noise, to inform people outside how far the services had progressed. The reader has liberty to make his own choice, for the authorities are pretty evenly balanced, — *organ, drum,* or *fire shovel.*

We must make some allowance for Oriental exaggeration in musical matters, for when Josephus speaks of a performance by 200,000 singers, 40,000 sistrums, 40,000 harps, and 200,000 trumpets, we must imagine that either Josephus' tale, or the ears of the Hebrews, were tough. All these statements only enlarge a fruitless field, for in it all is conjecture.

The flute was a favorite instrument both for joy and sorrow: the Talmud contains a saying that "flutes are suited either to the bride or to the dead."

The performance of all these instruments seems to have been always in unison, and often in the most *fortissimo* style.

Calmet gives a list of Hebrew instruments including viols, trumpets, drums, bells, Pan's pipes, flutes, cymbals, etc., and it is possible that these have existed among them in a primitive form.

The abbé de la Molette gives the number of the chief Jewish instruments as twelve, and states that they borrowed three newer ones from the Chaldeans, during the Babylonian captivity.

According to records of the Rabbins, given by Forkel, the Jews possessed in David's time, thirty-six instruments.

Some of the instruments named in the Scriptures

are as follows:—*Kinnor*, usually mentioned in the English translation as a harp, so often alluded to in the Psalms, ("Praise the Lord with harp," etc., xxxiii: 2,) was probably a lyre, or a small harp, of triangular shape: that the Hebrews possessed a larger harp is more than probable, for they were in communication with Assyria and Egypt, where the harp, in a highly developed state, was the national instrument, but it is a matter of much dispute, as to which of the musical terms used in the Scriptures was intended to apply to this larger harp.

The *Nebel*, or *Psaltery*, was a species of Dulcimer.

The *Asor;*—When David sang of an "instrument of ten strings," he referred to the asor, which is supposed to have been a species of lyre, with ten strings, and played with a *plectrum*, a short stick of wood, or bone, usually black, with which the strings were struck.

The *Timbrel* or *Taboret*, was a small hand drum, or tambourine, probably of varying shapes and sizes; the hand drum was derived from Egypt, for it was customary for women to dance in that country entirely to the rhythm of drums and tambourines; the military hand drum had the shape of a small keg with parchment over the ends; that is to say, the diameter at the middle was greatest.

The Organ;—as before stated this was simply a set of pandean pipes.

Cymbals;—there seems to be no doubt that the Hebrews possessed various instruments of percussion of divers shapes.

Trumpets;—apart from the ram's horn, and other curved horns which were called trumpets, there also existed a straight trumpet of more artificial construction. "Make thee, two trumpets of silver: of one piece shalt thou make them." Numbers ix: 2.

It is probable that the sistrum, the guitar, and pipes, were also possessed by this nation; about nineteen instruments are mentioned in the scriptures, but some of the meanings are so dubious that they have been translated by the general terms, harp, lute, psaltery, timbrel, etc.

How many different opinions are held, upon Hebrew music may be judged from the fact that the word "*Selah,*" which was probably a musical term, and is found in so many of the psalms, has given rise to the most vehement and fruitless controversy. Hesychius says that it means a change of rhythm, in the chanting; Alberti denies this, as it sometimes occurs at the end of a psalm, where certainly no change is possible: some have suggested that it meant a modulation from one key to another; Forkel, however, thinks that the Hebrews were not so far advanced in the science of music as to understand modulation, but Fetis upsets Forkel by remarking that the modulations, though not harmonic, might have been purely melodic, by the introduction of tones, foreign to the key, as occurs in many eastern melodies.

Herder says also "the Orientals even of our

day, love monotonous chants, which Europeans find doleful, and which at certain passages or phrases, change totally and abruptly their mode and time: the word *Selah* was without doubt an indication of such a change." The last part of this opinion, Fetis sets down as pure hypothesis.

Two ancient Greek versions of the Old Testament give the meaning of the word as " forever," and as " for all ages."

Alberti thinks the word is a recapitulation of the chords of the psalm: Rosenmuller proves that this is impossible in some cases.

Augusti thinks it is an expression of joy similar to " Hallelujah."

David Kimchi thinks it a sign of elevation of the voice; Mattheson and Pfeiffer agree in the opinion that it signifies a *ritornella*, or short symphony between the verses, to be played by the instruments alone.

Eichhorn thinks it means *Da Capo*, but Rosenmüller and Gesenius, (the latter treats the matter with great erudition, and his opinion is entitled to respect,) both think that it signifies a rest in the song part, as we might write *Tacet*.

Gesenius has found almost the only corroborative testimony of the whole controversy in the fact that the grammatical root of the word Selah, is repose, or silence.

La Borde has boldly, not to say audaciously, given a unique interpretation. He says " David invented the art of shading the sounds; the word *Selah* is equivalent to the Italian word *smor-*

tando, extinguished, dying away." And then he gives a highly colored picture of the beauty and grace of the effects produced, though all that he proves is that he has a little stronger imagination than the others. We must also give the curious opinion of Wolff, who thinks that "*Selah*" has no sense whatever, and was only added to fill up the metre of a verse.

Several other eminent writers, including Fetis, who gives a full account of this war of opinions,* decline to hazard an opinion in so dark a matter.

Another conjectural description of the mode of singing among the ancient Hebrews, is the commentary of Herder on the song of Deborah and Barak, Judges v.; he says, "probably verses 1 - 11 were interrupted by the shouts of the populace; verses 12 - 27 were a picture of the battle with a naming of the leaders with praise or blame, and mimicking each one as named; verses 28 - 30 were mockery of the triumph of Sissera, and the last verse was given as chorus by the whole people."

One cannot fail to observe some resemblance between this music and the slave music of some sections of the southern states: in the camp-meetings, and religious services, a tune which is well known to all is chosen, and as the spirit moves, often a whole song appropriate to the occasion is improvised Of some such description must have been Miriam's song, after the downfall of Pharaoh's host; she probably chose a tune which was

* Hist. Gen. de la Mus

familiar to the people, and improvised, while the people kept the rhythm, or sang refrains.

Of course the element of poetry was immeasurably greater among the Israelites than among the Negroes, but the similarity of improvisation and religious fervor is noticeable.

When Miriam sang, there was as yet no distinctive style of Hebrew music; we must remember that she had obtained an Egyptian education, and that up to David's time the music was an imitation of the Egyptian school.

The raptures of some commentators as to the exceeding beauty of the music of David, are quite safe, for it is easy to affirm where no one can bring rebutting evidence, but if it partook of the loudness of most ancient and barbarous music,—"Play skillfully, and with a loud noise," Psalms xxxiii: 2 —our modern music may after all be some compensation for its utter loss and oblivion.

CHAPTER IV

ANCIENT GREEK MUSIC.

The mythology of Greek music is too well known, for us to go into any details upon the subject; with this people every thing relating to music, was ennobled and enriched by an applicable legend, or a finely conceived poem. In fact music (mousiké), meant with the Greeks, all the æsthetics, and culture that were used in education of youth, and the strictly *musical* part of the above training had special names, as *harmonia*, etc., to designate it.

The subject of Greek music has given rise to more commentary and dispute, than any other in the entire realm of musical history.

The mode of notation employed was peculiar; it consisted in placing the letters of the alphabet in various positions, straight, sideways, etc., and sometimes even, fragments of letters were used.

There are in existence but three authentic Greek hymns[*] with music, viz: hymn to Calliope, to Apollo, and to Nemesis; there is also in existence, some music to the first eight verses of the first Pythian of Pindar, which Athanasius Kircher

[*] Doubts have been expressed concerning the genuineness even of these.

claimed to have discovered in a monastery near Messina, but the best authorities reject this as spurious. The copies of the above hymns are not older than the fifteenth century, and have probably been much perverted by the ignorance, or half-knowledge of the transcribers, who seeing a fragment of a letter, would restore the whole letter, or change its position, thereby greatly altering the character of the music.

To this fact is to be attributed the dense fog, which has prevented us from fully understanding the ancient Greek music.

On this slight foundation however, learned writers have built an edifice of erudition which consists of countless volumes of pedantry and ingenuity, mixed with a large amount of abuse for those who did not agree with their solution.

As we intend to deal, in these articles, more with curious musical facts than with musical systems, we will dismiss this branch of the subject entirely by referring the reader to the best representative works of this monument of research, which are Chappell's History of Music, vol. L, Ambros' Geschichte der Musik, vol. I., pp. 218–513, Fetis' Histoire Generale de la Musique, vol. III., pp. 1-418. Kiesewetter, and Drieberg also have written profoundly on the subject. These will give the different opinions held in the matter.

The *scale* of the Greeks, is however, definitely known, and was similar to our minor scale, although it contained no sharp seventh. Play on any pianoforte the notes, A B C. D E F G, and you have played the Greek one octave diatonic scale.

The nomenclature was however different, and some commentators have forgotten to explain the fact, that what the Greeks called the *highest note*, meant the longest string of the instrument, and consequently the *lowest* tone.

Another fact which has given rise to much controversy is the pitch of the lyre or phorminx; it seems that the mode of tuning this instrument varied in Greece at different epochs, and even in different localities at the same epoch.*

The word harmony (harmonikē) has also been misunderstood, as it does not mean harmony in our sense of the word, but the arrangement and rhythm of a melody. Whether the Greeks understood harmony or not, in the modern sense, has been the chief cause of the before-mentioned "Battle of the Books."

The lowest note of the scale was called Proslambanomenos, and had not the importance of the middle note, called Mese, which really became the principal note of the scale.

The Greek music practically, was very like our present minor modes, and the singing of some young Greek of two thousand years ago, would probably have sounded pleasantly to modern ears.

The earliest Greek scale had but four tones, and was probably used to accompany hymns. It might still suffice for many church chants.† People seldom think how much music can be manufactured from three or four notes; Rousseau

---

*Lloyd †Lloyd Age of Pericles, Vol. II., p. 222.

gave a practical illustration of it in the last century, by writing a not very monotonous tune, on three notes. But an instrument founded on so few notes might also have been used to give the pitch to the voice in reciting, or half-singing a poem. We must remember that the poems of Greece were chanted in public; and even in modern days, orators pitch their voices higher than in conversation, when addressing an assembly.

Early Grecian music experienced its first real onward movement, when Egypt was thrown open to foreigners. Up to the reign of Psammetichus I., (664 B. C.) Egypt was closed to aliens, exactly as China has been closed in days not long gone by. Psammetichus first opened his kingdom to the Greeks, and Pythagorus learned enough in Egypt to greatly change the character of Greek music. Though some Greek writers with an excess of zeal, have made the statement that he taught the Egyptians, by bringing to them the seven-stringed lyre. Considering the fact that the Egyptians had as many as twenty-two strings, the claim is rather audacious.

But what placed the Greeks in advance of all other ancient nations, in music, was the fact that they early recognized its rank as a *fine art.*

CHAPTER V.

THE PUBLIC GAMES OF GREECE.

The public games of Greece in which music and musical contests were a feature, gave to the art a decided impetus, for when competition began, musical study must have preceded.

The Olympic games were celebrated at Olympia every fifth year, in July, and lasted five days. They were dedicated to Zeus (Jupiter), and were established (according to some re-established, having existed in Mythical ages) by Iphitos, king of Elis, in the ninth century before the Christian era.

For a long time none but Grecians were allowed to compete in them. If there existed internal war in Greece at the time, an armistice was effected during the games. The contestants were trained for ten months previous to the contest. The prizes awarded to the victors were wreaths of wild olive twigs, cut from a sacred tree which grew in the consecrated grove of Olympia, and the victors were presented to the spectators, while a herald proclaimed the name of each, his father, and his country.

The first day opened with a sacrifice to Zeus, after which a contest of trumpeters took place. This contest was not regularly instituted until 396

B. C., but after that period it was not interrupted. There are still annals left of the most celebrated contestants; Archias of Hybla, gained the prize for three successive Olympiads; and Athenæus says that Herodorus of Megara, a most famous trumpeter, gained the prize *ten times in succession*. Pollux says he gained *seventeen* victories, which is well-nigh incredible, but both agree in saying that this remarkable performer was in one year crowned in the four great sacred games, the Olympian, Pythian, Nemean, and Isthmian. His music was so loud that the audience were sometimes stunned by the concussion. Other ancedotes of this wonderful trumpeter remain. He was of giant stature, and slept upon a bear skin, in imitation of Hercules and the lion skin. He could play upon two trumpets at the same time, and when he did so, the audience had to sit farther away than usual, on account of the immense sound. His performances were of great use in military affairs. Once at the siege of Argos, the troops were giving way when Herodorus began to sound his two trumpets, which so inspired the warriors of Demetrius, that they returned to the fight and won the victory.

The trumpet cannot really be classed among Grecian musical instruments, as it was rather a signal than any thing else. It was blown when heralds made any proclamation, in military movements, etc., and seems to have been appreciated only by the loudness with which it was blown.

It was also frequently played at the Olympic games during the horse-races, to inspirit the animals.*

In fact at the public games the music had a most noisy character, and trumpeters were proud of bursting a blood vessel, or otherwise injuring themselves by excess of zeal.

The contest of trumpeters was the only musical (?) one of these games, though flute-playing took place on the fourth day, when according to Krause,† the *pentathlon* took place. This was a set of five athletic games; leaping, running, throwing spear, throwing *discus*, and wrestling. Here flute-playing also served to animate the contestants. The flutes too, considering the purpose for which they were used, must have been played in a violent manner.

Harmonides, a young flute-player, on his first appearance at the games wishing to *astonish* the audience, began by giving such a tremendous blast on his instrument, that he expired on the spot, probably having burst a blood vessel, and having literally blown himself out with his first note. The audience was probably astonished.

The sacred games next in importance, were the Pythian. These games were at first celebrated by the Delphians, every ninth year, but about 590 B. C., the Amphyctions (another Grecian tribe) obtained the control of them, and instituted them every fifth year. They took place on a plain near Delphi, and were in honor of Apollo, commemorat-

---

*Ambros, Gesch. d. Musik, p. 287   † Olympia, p. 106.

ing his victory over the serpent Python; the good principle defeating the evil principle, as in Egyptian, and most other mythologies. Pindar's odes have celebrated the victories at some of these games. Being dedicated to Apollo, it was but natural that music, (under this head, the Greeks understood most of the accomplishments of the muses,) should play the most important part.

Religious poems were chanted, with an accompaniment upon the lyre or phorminx. The first poet-musicians who gained the prize were Chrysothemis,* Philammon, an earlier poet-musician than Homer, and Thamyris. According to Pausanius, all these singers were probably priests of Apollo. The Amphyctions first established prizes for songs with flute accompaniment, and for flute *solos.* Cephallon obtained a prize for songs accompanied by Kithara, a small lyre, and Echembrotus one for songs with flute, while Sacadas of Argos took the prize three consecutive times for his flute solos. After him came Pythocritus of Sicyon, who won the prize at these games six consecutive times, which covers an interval of *thirty years* of triumphs.

Athletic sports also were introduced later. The prizes were, as at Olympia, wreaths only.

The use of the flute both as solo instrument, and as accompaniment, was however, soon abolished, it being used as funeral music, and for dirge playing among the Amphyctions, and there-

---

*The nome, or hymn for which Chrysothemis, gained the prize, celebrated the victory of Apollo over the serpent Python.

fore having too many melancholy associations to allow of its use in these festive games. Finally *solos* on the small lyre (kithara) were allowed prizes.

It is said that at one of these contests a flute player gained the prize in a singular manner. He was playing the straight flute, when the reed in the mouth-piece became closed by accident, on which he instantly changed the position of his instrument, and played it as an *oblique* flute; his presence of mind was rewarded, by winning the prize.

The Nemean games were commemorative of the slaying of the Nemean lion, by Hercules. There was no musical contest in the games, but flutes were used, to stimulate the athletes, and were probably allowed prizes.

The Isthmian games celebrated upon the Isthmus of Corinth, whence their name, were similar to the Nemean; music not being of any importance in them.

In Chios there has been found a stone on which the names of the victors in the musical contests are inscribed. From it we learn that prizes were given for reading music at sight, rhapsodizing, accompanying the voice with a small harp played with the hand, and accompanying with kithara played partially with the fingers of the left hand, and partially with a *plectrum* held in the right hand.

The lesser games of Greece were also not inconsiderable. The great festival of Athens was the Panathenæa, held in honor of Athene the patron goddess of the city. It was established according to tradition, about 1521 B. C., and was at first intended for the citizens of Athens only. It took place about the middle of July.

At the later Panathenæa, the people of all Attica used to attend. There seem to have been two divisions of this festival, a greater and lesser Panathenæa, the former being celebrated every four years, the latter every year. The lesser Panathenæa consisted of recitations, gymnastics, musical competitions, and a torch race in the evening, the whole concluding with the sacrifice of an ox. The greater, was even more extensive. The Homeric poems were sung, dramatic representations took place, magnificient processions marched to the temple of Athene Polias, and the whole city was full of mirth and gayety. The prizes were jars of oil made from the sacred tree on the Acropolis.

Pericles, (fifth century B. C.,) gave to music a greater prominence than ever before in these games, by erecting a structure especially for musical entertainments and contests, the Odeum, in the street of the Tripod; this edifice was very well adapted in its acoustical properties, for according to Plutarch's description, the roof was dome-shaped, or nearly so, and vast audiences could hear solos distinctly.

In Sparta, in the month of August (Carneios) there were celebrated the great Carneian games, which lasted nine days. In these games musical contests also took place, and dances of men, youths, and maidens, as well as gymnastic exercises. Sparta also had a special building for musical purposes. Theodore of Samos erected the Skias, a building for musical uses, in the market place. Sparta was in fact, the cradle of Grecian music.

In the early days, songs were learned and transmitted down, from mouth to mouth. Homer's poems were preserved in this manner for five hundred years. In Sparta however, they first began to crystallize into form and regularity. Yet strange to say, Sparta gave birth to no musicians of eminence, even though she was so long the arbiter, and director of Grecian musical taste.*

Terpander of Lesbos, one of the founders of Greek music, came early to Sparta. He is reported to have gained the prize at the first musical contest of the Carneian games, B. C. 676, and is said to have studied in Egypt, but he certainly could not have done so before his first advent in Sparta, for Egypt was at that date still closed to foreigners, and had even guards set to prevent the landing of strangers by the sea.†

Terpander gained the Pythian crown four times in succession, and was the most famous poet-musician of his time. His fame spread through all Greece, but it was especially in Sparta that he won renown, for his high, manly and earnest strains awoke a sturdy and manly response in the bosoms of the rugged Spartans. It is probable however that at the first visit to Sparta, his songs were not

---

* Gevaert, Mus. de l'antiquite, p. 45.   † Chappell, Hist. of Mus., p 32

so powerful. At that time, (676 B. C.) he probably sang chiefly the poems of Homer. We say *sang*, but it is not even sure that they had, what we should call a tune, attached to them; they were possibly recited in a musical pitch of voice, which could not be called even a chant.

There was at this time, little music among the Spartans, and that of rather martial, or else of religious character; as for example we learn that the Spartans marched into battle to the sound of many kitharas, as did also the Cretans, and it was supposed to have been in honor of the Gods, that they did so; though Thucydides, more practically, says that it was only that they might move forward regularly and in time. On Terpander's second visit to Sparta, he changed the entire mode of Spartan music, and enlarged it. The return happened in this wise: —

At the beginning of the second Messenian war Sparta was in great perplexity. Messenia by alliances with other tribes threatened destruction from without. Within all was dissension; agriculture prostrate, antagonism between those who had lost their lands through the wars and those who possessed them, a demand for a new distribution of land, and prospective anarchy. At this juncture, the Oracle of Delphi was consulted, and gave reply that "discord would be quelled in Sparta when the sound of Terpander's harp was heard there," and told the Spartans, also to call the counsellor from Athens. So Terpander was sent for, and also the counsellor Tyrtaeus from Athens.

The effect of Terpander's songs upon the populace on this occasion is described as something remarkable; men burst into tears, enemies embraced each other, and all internal dissension was at an end.*

It is recorded therefore, that Terpander with his harp had quelled all dissension in Sparta, but by this anecdote we may see that in what the ancient Greeks called music, the words really played the most important part. To show this yet more clearly, we will here give an instance from later Athenian history where the same power was exerted for a similar purpose. A war between Athens and Megara, for the possession of the island of Salamis, had resulted in such continued disaster to Athens, that the Athenians had left the island to its fate, and it was forbidden upon penalty of death to broach the subject to the public again. Solon however, attired himself as a messenger from the island to the Athenians, and in this character sang a song which roused such a martial spirit, that on the instant a large body of volunteers was formed, who, under Solon, effected its reconquest.

Terpander and Tyrtæus composed most of their songs in march rhythm, and after this the Spartans sang hymns, while marching into battle to the sound of many kitharas, which were afterwards displaced by the more penetrating flute.

Terpander also composed love songs, and banquet songs as well as nomes or hymns, and his

* Diodorus.

choruses were sung at all Spartan festivals and sacrifices, they were taught to Spartan youths and maidens, and all seemed to vie in doing him honor. He had really helped the music of Greece to a higher plane, for it is said that he enlarged the lyre or phorminx from four strings, to seven, and also made improvements in the scale.

Contemporary with this poet-musician was Olympus, who must not however be confounded with an Olympus who lived six hundred years previously, that is, about 1250 B. C. Plato says that the music of Olympus was especially adapted to animate the hearers. Plutarch says that it surpassed in simplicity and effect, all other music. He is said to have composed the air which caused Alexander to seize his arms, when it was sung to him; according to Aristotle his music filled all hearers with enthusiasm. Much relating to Olympus must however be relegated to the land of myths. It has even been doubted whether he ever really existed, though that is carrying scepticism too far.

Among the other characters which existed on the borderland of Greek musical history, may be mentioned Polynestos, and Alcman who brought to Sparta in its full glow, the love song, (Lydian measure) Alcman seems to have been easily aroused to sing of female beauty, and composed some choruses especially for the

"Honey-voiced, lovely singing maidens,"

which were sung by female voices only.

The fragments which remain of Alcman's verses do not justify the immense fame which he seems to have enjoyed in Greece. Alcman was preceded by Thaletas of Crete, who was sent for by the Spartans 620 B. C. to sing to the Gods, in order that Sparta might be freed from a severe plague, which was then ravaging the state. The plague ceased, and Thaletas for a time stood at the head of all Spartan music. That country as above mentioned, either would not, or could not encourage home talent.

Sacadas of Argos came soon after with a yet more luxurious style, and introduced the flute as an accompaniment to chorus music.

To this foggy period of history, also belongs Tisias of Himera, who made an indelible impression on Greek music. He was the first who regulated the motions of the chorus, and who reduced chorus singing to a settled system; from the fact that at one period of the song, (the *epode*, or *finale*) he made the chorus stand quiet, instead of dancing he received the nickname of "Stesichorus." In some of the works of Stesichorus, one can easily see the germ of the choruses of Aeschylus or Sophocles.[*]

If in the ancient Grecian music, the composer, poet, and performer seem to be spoken of in common, the reader must recollect that in those days, *all three* branches of the art were united in one individual. It will also aid some readers, if we define here what the functions of the Greek

[*] Ambros Ges. d musik, p. 265, v. 1.

chorus were. In the earliest days, the whole chorus simply sang refrains after the solo of some cultivated singer; gradually whole compositions were entrusted to their charge. Pantomimic action probably always existed in connection with their songs, as with almost all ancient singing. Stesichorus first gave them different historical or mythological subjects to act, in a dramatic manner. At a later epoch the chorus entered in a peculiar manner into the action of the drama. They stood upon the stage as interested spectators of the various events; they advised the Protagonist or only individual character* as to his course of action, and when some startling incident, a murder for example, had taken place, they would strongly express their feelings, horror, dismay or fear, and thereby intensify the effect upon the audience.

An imitation of the Greek chorus may be found in Schiller's "Bride of Messina."

Stesichorus was deservedly honored as the founder of Greek chorus music, and a statue was erected to his memory. Among those next following his era we find Ibycus, a poet-musician attached to the court of Polycrates, tyrant of Samos. This mighty sea king and despot had a considerable liking for music; for we learn also that he kept a choir of beautiful boys, whose duty it was to sing sweet Lydian melodies during his meals. About 580-70 B. C. Alcæus and Sappho

---

*Later there were more characters added, but at first, the whole action consisted of dialogues between a solitary actor and the chorus.

became leaders in Grecian musical culture, or poetry, for the two are inseparable. The two poets seem to have formed a mutual friendship. Of Sappho we have remaining an ode to Aphrodite which makes it a matter of regret that the remains of her poetry are so fragmentary.* At Mytilene she seems to have gathered around her a large and elegant circle, composed entirely of females to whom she taught poetry and music; in fact her house must have been a musical university for her list of scholars embraces names from all parts of Greece. Ottfried Müller† compares her life, surrounded by all these fair followers, with that of Socrates surrounded by the flower of Athenian youth.

Sappho's career is the more wonderful from the fact, that among the ancient Greeks, the entire mission of woman was supposed to consist in rearing her family, attending to the first education of her sons, who at an early age passed into the hands of their teachers, teaching housewife's duties to her daughters, and attending to them herself; according to Pericles, that woman was most to be prized of whom no one spoke, either in praise or blame.

Sappho's poetry had great effect even on the rough character of Solon, the law giver; hearing for the first time one of her songs, which his nephew sang to him, he vehemently expressed the

---

*Jullien however, thinks Sappho in common with many other ancient poets much overrated. Theses Supplementaires, p. 439

† Geschichte der Griech. Lit

wish that he might not die before he had committed to memory so beautiful a song.

Sappho's name is almost the only female one in the whole realm of ancient Greek music, which was pure, noble, and uncontaminated. Latterly, even her character has been assailed, but the accusation has been refuted by Herr Welcker, of Bonn, (in the *Rheinisches Museum*,) Ottfried Müller and other learned writers. After her, music as practiced by the female sex, was handed over to the most degraded, (the *Hetarae*) and seems to have borrowed from Egypt many lowering qualities,* including dancing girls and ribald songs.

Anacreon of Teos, introduced into Greece the light, airy songs, in praise of woman, wine, etc., "It is no great stretch of fancy," says a thoughtful writer,† " to imagine his songs as expressing our modern *Allegretto Grazioso, Andante Scherzoso*, etc."

From precisely this point however (the lack of signs of expression in all Greek music) another writer‡ deduces the opinion that Greek music must always have been in a crude state, and by no means of the beauty which some enthusiasts ascribe to it.

* Lucian. Lapithæ
† Ambros. Gesch. d. musik, v. 1, p. 260.
‡ Jullien, Theses Supplementaires, p. 130.

CHAPTER VI.

THE PHILOSOPHERS, AND GREEK SOCIAL MUSIC.

From the sixth century B. C., music may date its entrance into the positive sciences, for Pythagoras, born about 570 B. C., first began to analyze music from a scientific point of view, and to ascertain how far it rested upon natural laws. Pythagoras is said to have been the son of a wealthy merchant. He was as before mentioned, one of the earliest Greeks in Egypt, and after having been instructed for some time by the priests, had at last the honor of being admitted into the Egyptian college of priesthood.

After remaining in Egypt twenty-two years, he spent some time among the Chaldeans, and at last returned, full of wisdom, to his native Samos. But here the sensuality of the court of Polycrates was so little to his taste, that he departed to the city of Croton in southern Italy, where he founded the order of Pythagoreans.

With the order itself, we have little to do, but when we consider that its founder was the pioneer of scientific musical research, its proceedings become in some degree interesting.

"All is number and harmony" was the fundamental maxim of this philosopher,* and he sought for the laws in music, therefore, in nature. This led to some mistakes of course, for the laws of nature had not been made clear enough for thorough guidance in that era. It is said that Pythagoras one day, passing by a blacksmith's shop heard the blows of different hammers sound the fundamental, fourth, fifth, and octave, and entering, he weighed the different hammers, thereby obtaining the proportion of these intervals to each other.

This story has been proved to be a silly myth, for the proportions given are wrong. He should have weighed the anvils not the hammers, and anvils of such difference in size as would be requisite to produce these intervals would not be seen in blacksmiths' shops.

Pythagoras taught that not the ear, but mathematics, should be the guide in music. He held that the universe was constructed on a musical plan, and was probably the first to introduce among the Greeks the theory of the music of the spheres. The fact that man could not hear this music,† was explained by the statement that the sounds were either too deep or too high for our ears. The reasoning was plausible enough, and has been confirmed by science, for sounds

---

* The very title "philosopher" was of his own coining, for previous sages called themselves Sophos (wise), but he preferred the better name of Philosopher (lover of wisdom).

† Some of the pupils of Pythagoras, maintained that he only of all men had heard the harmony of the spheres.

of less than sixteen vibrations in a second are inaudible on account of their depth, and those exceeding 38,100 vibrations in a second are too high for the human ear to perceive.* Starting from this premise Pythagoras formed a scale founded on the seven planets, as known to the astronomers of that time. This was its form:

Moon.	Mercury.	Venus.	Sun.	Mars.	Jupiter.	Saturn.
E	F	G	A	B	C	D

The sun was Mese, the controlling middle note, around which all the others circled.

The order of Pythagoreans were held together by the firmest ties, and Pythagoras has been, not inaptly, compared in this capacity with Ignatius Loyola. His adherents, who numbered about three hundred were, in most cases, wealthy and noble, and the power of the society was always upon the side of aristocracy.

Pythagoras was very select in the admission of members, exercising great vigilance lest improper or undesirable persons should be allowed to enter; in this he was guided not a little by his skill in Physiognomy. The initiates had, it is said, to pass through a most rigorous and lengthy period of probation, they were obliged to maintain silence for five years,† and in other ways had their powers

---

* The sense of sound differs in different ears. In Chappell's Histy. of Music, page 251, an account is given of a wire of sixty-four feet in length, arranged by Sir F. A. Gore Ouseley, to sound the C, four octaves below C in the bass clef. The note was inaudible, but when taken at half length some of the listeners heard it, while at quarter length it was audible to all.

† See Lucian Auction of Philosophers. Some say two years.

of endurance, severely tested. After entering the brotherhood,* the mode of life was entirely dictated by Pythagoras. The members were clothed in pure white. They were forbidden all animal food, and beans. They had different grades of advancement among themselves, the highest being undoubtedly instructed in a purer religion than that which obtained around them, though outwardly they conformed with the religion of the populace. Mathematics, music, and astronomy were studied, and gymnastics regularly practised.

Playing upon the lyre was obligatory, and none of the order went to sleep at night, without having previously purified his soul, and set it in harmony through music; and at rising in the morning, the strength for the day's labors and duties, was sought for in the same manner. Pythagoras wrote many songs as correctives to undue excitement and passion; he is said once to have brought to reason a young man beside himself with jealousy and wine, by the power of a song.

Clinias, a Pythagorean, took up his harp and played whenever any passion arose in his breast; to a person who asked him the reason of the action, he replied, " I play to compose myself."

While the music of Terpander, Olympus, etc., was intended for high state and religious purposes, that of Pythagoras was intended to bring the art into domestic and inner life. Choruses

---

* Women were also admitted, but probably only to attendance on lectures, not to membership.

were, however, also chanted by his followers, and were adapted to various occasions, as for example, at the opening of Spring, the scholars would gather in a circle around the harper, who played the accompaniment, and sing pæans of welcome to the opening season. Other philsophers also allowed music to enter into their teachings, though not to so great a degree, but almost all of them understood enough of music to form an opinion.

Plato seemed decidedly to object to instrumental music, for he says " the using of instruments without the voice is barbarism and charlatanry."*

Aristotle was disposed to allow more freedom, for he spoke of music as a delicious pleasure, either alone (instrumental) or accompanied with voice; but in instrumental solos he admitted the lyre and kithara only, and rejected the flute, which he thought not to be a moral instrument, and only capable of inflaming the passions.

The philosophers as a class were really not very advantageous to musical progress, for they fought tooth and nail for the old school of music.

They sought only moral effects by the means of great simplicity, and any intricate innovations displeased them; but in spite of their resistance the art began to improve.

The Skolion, or banquet song had a great influence on the music of Athens. At the banquet, or symposium, the harp was passed from hand to hand, and each person who made any pretence to education or good breeding was

* Legum II.

expected to be able to improvise or at least to sing a good *skolion*.

There was certainly in the time of Pericles, music enough to choose from, for there is much evidence that the Athenians of that day possessed an extensive library of music;* and it was in this era, the early part of the fifth century B. C., that the social music reached its height.

Themistocles once being present at a banquet had the harp (kithara) presented to him, and was desired to sing his *skolion;* full of confusion and shame he was obliged to acknowledge his ignorance of music, and we can judge of the value in which the art was held, by the sneers and jests which were pointed at him. At last stung to the quick by the sharp witticisms, he retorted, " it is true I do not know how to play the kithara, but I know how to raise an insignificant city to a position of glory."

The *skolion* was a really poetical and worthy song, and must not be confounded with those lower and vulgar songs which were sung to the guests by hired jesters and buffoons.†

The subjects of the *skolion* were sometimes of rather a lofty style; praise of heroes,‡ calls to the gods, rules of life, often joyous, sometimes sedate; but in all of them a less exact rhythm and style were allowed than in other compositions. A few have been preserved to our day; **one**

* Lloyd. Ages of Pericles, Vol. 2, p. 239.
† See Lucian. Lapithæ.
‡ Ottfried Muller, V. I, p. 343.

begins, "my kingdom is my spear and sword," another composed by Chilon contains the following beautiful thought; " Gold is rubbed upon the touchstone, and thus is tested, but the soul of man is tested by the gold, if it be good or evil." But the kithara, although used in the skolion, was not the only instrument of the fashionable young men of ancient Athens, for the flute found great favor among them; in fact flute playing grew to be quite a mania for a time. It was part of the musical education of youth. Most of the teachers of the instrument came from Bœotia.

Flute players of ability were held in high honor; the art of flute playing received such an impetus that different flute schools were established in Athens; even rival methods of playing and teaching existed.*

Flutes were played in almost every place where music was required, to accompany hymns, at worship, and even sometimes the Greeks represented the combat of Apollo and the Python on this instrument, with kithara accompaniment; this may be considered as the earliest "song without words" in existence.

The ancients had some other attempts at tone pictures. Once an Athenian kitharist played to Dorian, a representation of a storm at sea; on being asked how he liked it, that ancient wit answered, " I have seen a better storm in a pot of

---

*Socrates intimates that the hiring of a large retinue of servants, and the purchase of an expensive flute, went very far towards establishing a reputation as a skillful flutist.

boiling water." This would make the origin of the phrase "a tempest in a teapot," over two-thousand years old.

Sometimes all Athens was divided into cliques for this or that flute player; and the price paid for flutes were appalling, some being sold as high as three thousand dollars, many flute-makers becoming immensely wealthy.

It received a slight check however, when Alcibiades, about 409 B. C., declined to play it, alleging as a reason, that it spoilt the shape of the mouth. Alcibiades stood at the head of the fashion as well as of the state, and after such a *dictum* the *beau monde* of Athens laid aside the flute; but some ingenious flute maker took alarm, and invented a mouth-piece which obviated the difficulty, and which Alcibiades found more to his taste, on which it resumed its place in popular favor.

In Sparta it led the chorus, and was the military instrument, but the Spartans disdained to make it a study, and only felt bound, at this era, to discriminate between good and bad music.

In some Ionian cities, the human victims were led to the sacrifice, or to their execution to the sound of flutes; and this dead march (called the Nome of Kradias) was said to be peculiarly depressing.

Plutarch makes a warm defence of the flute, against the criticisms of Plato and Aristotle. "The flute" he says "cannot be spared from the banquet, leads the hymns to the gods, and with its rich and full tones spreads peace and tranquillity throughout the soul;" but we must remember that this was written at a much later epoch, when flute playing became more universal than in the days of Pericles, and when the instrument had probably been altered and improved.

Flute players sometimes made large fortunes. Nicomachus was known for his wealth in jewels acquired by his skill on the instrument.

Lamia was one of the most famous of Athenian flutists. This female was celebrated through Greece and Egypt for her skill, as well as for her wit and beauty. The latter was not overrated, for a portrait of her has been discovered in a signet, which amply confirms the accounts of her charms. Although born in Athens, she went early to Alexandria, in Egypt, to study her art; somewhat as our modern musicians go to Italy or Germany. She was received with open arms at the Egyptian court, and was detained for a long time. Captured by Demetrius Polyorcetes, she soon succeeded in conquering her conqueror, and on her return to Athens, a temple was built to her, and she was worshipped under the name of *Venus Lamia*. Her powerful "friend" Demetrius, may have had something to do with this deification, but at all events, there were still left some Greeks (Lysimachus for example) who had the manliness to protest against the desecration, for the character of Lamia was far different from that of Sappho.

It was not flute players only who earned immense salaries, for we learn that Amabœus the kitharist, received nearly one thousand dollars for each performance, and all flute-players, and kitharists, were welcomed and honored at the courts of Greece, Egypt and Asia.

Ptolemy Philadelphus gave a large musical festival in Alexandria, Egypt, about 280 B. C., at which six hundred skilled singers, kitharists and flutists assisted; there have been larger festivals in point of numbers in ancient times, but few, where so much educated talent assisted. Ptolemy Physcon*, an amiable Egyptian ruler, 146 B. C., who married his brother's wife, killed his baby nephew, or step-son on the wedding day and afterwards married his niece, or step-daughter (for he made the relationship very mixed) winding up by killing all the progeny as *finale*, seems to have patronized and enjoyed music, in spite of his family troubles.

Ptolemy Auletes, 80 B. C., was known as the "flute lover," and though king of Egypt was yet a very skilful virtuoso on this instrument.

We must not omit here to mention a species of Greek music which was an outgrowth of the sacred games.

We have already stated how great the honor of achieving a victory at these games was considered; and it was very natural that when a whole city celebrated with joy the triumph of one of its sons, the poets would also sing in high strains, the praises of the successful hero. These poems soon became a necessary adjunct to the festivities, and may be said to form a school of their own.

* Physcon was a nickname signifying thick belly.

They were chanted by a chorus under the direction of the composer; and although at first they may have been spontaneous, yet afterwards they became entirely a matter of purchase.

When a young man had carried off the victor's wreath, he would frequently send word at once to some famous poet-musician, to write a chorus in his honor. Sometimes the city itself would order the poem, and in Athens about 540 B. C., statues began to be erected to the victors who were natives of that city.* Simonides, born about 556 B. C., may be regarded as the founder of this style of composition, and he certainly was the founder of the custom of receiving pay for laudatory verses.

His contemporaries sneered greatly at him for this, and Pindar proves him to have been very avaricious, but it really seems to have been no more than just that the poet should have been compensated for his exertions, as he not only had to write the poetry and music for the occasion, but also to drill the chorus and lead the singing.

The ceremony of praise to the victor was either celebrated at the conclusion of the games, upon the spot, or upon his return home; sometimes also in after years, to keep alive the remembrance of past triumphs.

The festivities were both religious and social. They began with a procession to the temple, after which sacrifices were offered, either in the temple, or in the victor's house; this was followed by a banquet, to which came the poet with his chorus.

*Mullers Gesch d. Griech Lit. v. 1, p. 380.

and intoned the triumphal ode, the latter being considered the greatest event of the occasion.*

Simonides seems to have been in the market for all kinds of Epinikia, or triumphal odes. Leophron of Rhegion, having won a race with mules at one of these games, ordered a chorus on the subject from the poet; Simonides felt a little indignant at the proposal and replied, curtly "I don't sing about mules," but Leophron being very anxious in the matter, offered a large price, upon which Simonides reconsidered his determination, and wrote the ode. It began by saluting the mules in an ingenious manner, only noticing one side of their ancestry,—"Haili oh ye daughters of the stormy footed horse."

Simonides was not wholly, however, in this lower line of poetry; he often competed in public musical, or poetical contests, and won fifty-six oxen and tripods by such means. Even at eighty years of age he added another to his lengthy list of victories. He was also considered as very learned, and was sometimes reckoned among the philosophers.

One of his chief competitors at Athens, was Lasus of Hermione, who was a practical and theoretical musician of some eminence.

Among the works of Lasus, there are some which are curiously constructed. In his hymn to Diana, and in the Centaurs, the letter S (sigma) is entirely avoided. The flute-players who accompanied the choruses greatly disliked the

---

*Muller Gesch. v. 1, p. 399.

hissing sound of S. as it did not blend easily with their playing, and it was this fact which probably led Lasus to so curious a style of poetry.

Among the scholars of Lasus was Pindar, (born in the spring of 522 B. C.,) who came from a noble Theban family. Pindar's parents were musical, and there were several flute-players in his family, but he soon became far more than a mere flute-player. He came to Athens, to study music, at a very early age, for after his return to Thebes he began a further course of studies under Corinna and Myrtis, two famous poetesses, then in Bœotia, all of which was done before his twentieth year.

He strove in public contests with the two latter, but always unsuccessfully; Corinna defeated him five times, which result, Pausanius thinks, may have been partly due to her personal charms.

Corinna once offered to beautify Pindar's early efforts with mythological allusions, but on his bringing her a poem, the first six verses of which touched on every part of Theban Mythology, she smiled and said: "One must sow seed by handsfull, not by bagsfull."

Pindar's poetic career began very early, for at twenty years old he wrote his first Epinikion (triumphal ode), in honor of a youth of the tribe of Aleuads.* His services were soon sought for throughout all Hellas; for although he imitated Simonides in writing for hire, yet his muse was unquestionably a nobler one, and his *Epinikia* bear an air of heartiness which seems to be

* Muller Ges. v. 1, p. 394.

unfeigned. His songs were bolder and truer, and not altogether composed of flattery, and he seems to have been an eye-witness of many of the triumphs which he describes.

He also was engaged as poet to Hiero, of Syracuse, Alexander, (son of Amyntas of Macedonia,) Theron of Agrigentum, Arcesilaus, King of Cyrene, and for several free states; with the two former he was an especial favorite, and yet his position never seemed that of a parasite, or a courtier, for he told them the truth bluntly when occasion demanded. His life was chiefly spent in the courts of his various royal friends. He once resided at the court of Hiero, at Syracuse, for the space of four years.

He died at the advanced age of eighty years.

The names of Simonides and Pindar may be considered as the greatest in this branch of Greek music and poetry; and although the subjects were of local interest only, yet Pindar has invested them with such beautiful imagery that he has shown us (to alter the phrase of an ancient,) that it is better to be a great man in a small **art, than a small** man in **a great one.**

CHAPTER VII.

GREEK THEATRE AND CHORUS.

Among the many institutions which contributed to that polished civilization which was the glory of ancient Greece, none were higher in aspirations, or more prolific in results, than the Tragedies and Comedies which were at certain intervals presented in the Theatre at Athens. The Athenians were by this agency, brought to a cultivated discrimination in music and poetry, and as we shall see later, the choruses being chosen from the body of the people, and demanding an amount of musical ability in the members, caused the study of music to become almost a necessity to all.*

In its early days the Drama, (if it be worthy of the name,) must have been a mere masquerading on any raised platform. It had its origin in the festivities of Dionysius (Bacchus), for at the earliest Dionysian festivals, the populace smeared their faces in wine lees, and thus disguised, sang choruses in honor of this god of mirth.

In later times, linen masks were substituted, but only in the days of Thespis, did the art assume some regular shape.

*At seven years old the study was usually commenced

Comedy may be said to have arisen about 562 B. C., when Susarion and Dolon travelled around, caricaturing the vices and follies of their time, from a rude scaffold.

The first Tragedy was acted in Athens, by Thespis, from a wagon, in the year 535 B. C. In the same year Thespis received a goat as reward for playing "Alcestis" at Athens. Goats were frequently given as rewards for this kind of composition, and the word Tragedy is derived by some, from the words Tragos, a goat, Odé, a song, literally a "goat-song."

The earliest attempt at dramatic action, with a plot, or incident to give it connection, was the representation of the gift of the grape to mankind, by Dionysius; this required three *dramatis personae*, therefore Thespis changed his linen mask three times.

Solon was not well pleased with the new art; striking his stick upon the ground he said: "If this sort of thing were allowed and praised, it would soon be found in the market-place;" and to Thespis who was singing a recitation in the character which he was acting, he said: "Are you not ashamed to lie so?"

Solon had probably forgotten that when he aroused the Athenians to the reconquest of Salamis, he had assumed the character of a herald from the island. Solon had predicted right however, the drama became the most cherished institution of Greece; even in its earliest stages, the state fostered it, and it always attracted the people, for it was both a religious, and popular enjoyment.

The sons of Pisistratus did much in these days to encourage and stimulate it. They arranged contests, rewards, etc., with profusion.

The tragedies of Thespis which he both wrote and acted himself, had but one performer, who, rapidly changing his mask, assumed various different characters in the play. The monotony was soon felt, and in order that dialogues might be used, a chorus was introduced, and then much of the action consisted of duets between the solitary performer, or *protagonist*, and the chorus.

Phrynicus, a few years later, allowed this single actor to take both male and female characters; but the first thorough representation of tragedy, with its properties carefully attended to, is due to the great tragic poet Aeschylus, who instructed the actor and the chorus carefully, and gave attention to thoroughness in its every department so far as then known.

The platform and auditorium were still uncouth wooden structures, until a poetical contest took place between Phrynicus and others, when the benches were so crowded that the whole structure gave way and many were injured; after this the theatres were built of stone.

The performances were still regarded as belonging to religious rites; the seats were at first built in a semi-circle around the altar of Dionysius, and the theatre never became, as with us, an every-day matter, but was only used at certain Dionysian festivals, which occurred about three times each year. Aeschylus aimed very much at the terrible in his tragedies, and the poets of this era never sought to "hold the mirror up to nature," but rather to represent something awe-inspiring and supernatural; therefore the actors had to prepare themselves in many peculiar ways for the stage.

The characters of tragedy were represented as much larger than human beings; to effect this the tragedian wore a kind of stilt-shoes with very high heels, called *cothurne*, padded out his body in proportion to his height, lengthened his arms by adding an artifical hand, and wore a mask of large size, over his face. The stage upon which he appeared, was also elevated above that on which the chorus stood, and the latter not being artificially enlarged, must have appeared as pigmies, beside these gigantic heroes.

The voice was pitched in a style corresponding to the magnitude of the body; it has been suggested* that the large tragic mask may have concealed some contrivance for strengthening the voice; however this may be, it is certain that the voice of the tragedian needed to be metallic, solemn and majestic, and that this, though partly a natural gift, had to be strengthened by long and severe practice, and a vast amount of physical strength was also required to move about naturally when so extremely bundled up.

Lucian in his "*De saltatione*," ridicules the tragic actor's equipment. He says: "What a ridiculous thing it is, to see a fellow stalking

---

* See O. Muller, Gesch v. 2, p. 44

around upon a pair of high heeled boots, with a terrible mask on, and a wide gaping mouth, as if he intended to swallow the audience,* not to mention the unseemly thickness of breast and body, all of which is done to hide the disproportion between his extravagant height, and his meagre body. Bawling aloud, and writhing his body in a thousand odd gestures;" and then he alludes to the better singing and acting of previous time, "but all sense of fitness is lost," he concludes, "when Hercules enters singing a mournful ditty, without either lion's skin or club."

With regard to the immovable mask, Ottfried Muller supposes that the picture is overdrawn, for facial expression had far less to do with the action of the drama of that day than we imagine; the character had not so many changing emotions to depict, as in modern plays; he says† "we can imagine an Orestes, or a Medea, with a set countenance, but never a Hamlet or Tasso."

We must also remember that the vast extent of the Athenian Theatre, made it next to impossible to distinguish much play of feature, and that the same masks were not worn throughout the play, but changed at any great change of emotion. Oedipus in the tragedy by Sophocles, after misfortunes came upon him, wore a different mask from the one worn in his days of prosperity.

The first plays represented were relative to the history of the gods, and demigods, but Phrynicus

---

* The lips of the tragic mask were usually half open.
† Geschichte d. Griech. Lit p. 44

made a bold innovation by representing contemporaucous events upon the stage. He once ventured to represent the conquest of Miletus, from the Athenians; the effect, according to Herodotus, was startling, the whole audience burst into tears, and the Athenian government forbade any further plays on that subject, prohibited the piece from ever being represented again, and fined the poet heavily.

The contests between rival writers, by simultaneous production of their pieces was a fruitful source of jealousy. Aeschylus upon being vanquished in one of these by Sophocles, took his defeat so much to heart, that he left Athens for some years, and took up his residence in Sicily.

In the plays of Thespis and Phrynicus, one actor only was employed; Aeschylus enriched his works by adding a second performer, called the *Deuteragonist*. Sophocles went beyond by adding the third, or *Tritagonist*, and desired even more, for in his Oedipus in Colonus, he found that four players were a necessity, and wrote the tragedy for that number, but dared not publicly make the innovation, and therefore this great work remained unperformed until after his death.

The above mentioned three performers, had their distinct lines of duty, as we to-day have upon the stage, actors for each kind of character, but the distinction was carried to great height on the ancient stage, for the first actor always came on the stage from the right entrance, the second from the left, and the third from the centre.

The stage of the Athenian theatre was very wide but not deep, and the scenery was very simple; sometimes the house of the chief character was represented, sometimes the tent of a hero, but oftenest the entrance of a palace, before which the entire action of some dramas could take place. They were always exterior views, and no scenes of the interior parts of a dwelling were ever used. The whole active life of the Greek was passed in the open air, so that it seemed more natural to him to represent his characters as living similarly. The female characters were often personated by boys.

There were many expedients to make the following of the action of the play easier to the spectators, in such a vast space; programmes they had not, opera glasses did not exist, so certain formulae took the place of both; when standing on the stage of the Athenian theatre, and facing the audience, the harbor and city of Athens were on the left hand, and Attica on the right; a person entering from the right hand, was therefore presumed to be a stranger who had come over land; and from the left as coming from the city.

The stage also possessed some mechanical effects, such as chariots descending from the skies, birds or even immense beetles soaring aloft carrying persons with them, forms arising from the deep, thunder, lightning, etc. The chorus was an immense help to the audience in following the events of the piece, and we must now describe this characteristic part of Greek tragedy

The dramatic chorus probably appeared first as Satyrs, the natural attendants of the jolly god Dionysius, in the plays of Thespis, and were then numerous and ill disciplined.

Aeschylus lessened the part of the chorus in his tragedies, and they no longer sang an unceasing duet with the Protagonist, for the addition of a second actor, made dialogues possible without their assistance.

The number of *Choryeutes* (chorus players) in Aeschylus's tragedies was twelve; Sophocles, and Euripides had usually fifteen.

In the tragedy of the "Eumenides" there was a special chorus of fifty members; these were apparelled as the hideous furies of that name, all in black, with angry countenances, snakes twining in their hair, and blood dripping from their eyes; and suddenly these frightful apparitions appeared on the stage: the effect was terrible, women shrieked, and fell in convulsions, and several children died of fright This event proves that the stage effects were rather realistic in those days.

The chorus was felt as an inconvenience by Euripides, who yet could not break the shackles of custom sufficiently to do away with it.

The arrangement of the chorus was changed when it was transplanted from lyric to dramatic use. The dithyrambic chorus stood around an altar singing hymns, and was wholly occupied with its music: the dramatic chorus stood in the shape of a square, the director taking good care to place the best dressed and handsomest choryeutes in front.

The songs were accompanied with well regulated movements, usually of a stately and dignified character, such as befitted the characters which they were representing, the parts which they performed usually being those of Matrons or Patriarchs, who were best suited to give counsel, comfort, or admonition to the acting characters of the drama.

The formation of choruses, was a matter of legislation. The archon of the city, gave the task of forming the choruses, to some of the wealthy citizens, who had the title of *Choregus.* This person was not the chorus leader, but the founder of it. He had authority from the archon to receive and select able singers; when he had the organization formed, he engaged a *choryphaeus* or director, to instruct the members in singing and dancing; he engaged flute-players* to accompany them, and paid a regular salary to them all, that of the flute-players being higher than that of the singers. He had to board and lodge them; to supply them with good beverages during rehearsals; to see that they received nutritious food, and such as was good for their voices; to supply them with masks, and costumes for their parts, and other duties all tending to the well being of the chorus. The choregus received no pay for this, but if in a dramatic contest his chorus was

---

* Some Dithyrambic poets kept a band of flute-players to accompany their choruses.

adjudged to be the best, he received a wreath as a reward.

Expensive as this honor was, yet it was sought after by all the richer class of Athens, as it was an ostentatious manner of showing their munificence, for the tragic choruses vied with each other in the splendor of their attire, their costumes being superb mantles of gold, and purple. So costly was it that the saying became a well known jest, that the way to ruin a man, was to get him appointed choregus.

The costume of the actors was also rich, without much reference to the part they were playing. Hercules came on the stage in purple and gold instead of with a lion's skin.

The poet who had just completed a tragedy, and succeeded in obtaining a hearing for it, applied to the Archon for a chorus; that functionary, if he had confidence in the applicant, would assign him one of the choruses which had already been formed and on receiving the permission from the *choregus*, the composer would set to work, drilling them in their various songs, attitudes, and movements. The director did not use a stick for this purpose, as in modern days, but beat the time with a heavy pair of iron shoes which he put on for the purpose.* The chorus of comedy was a less expensive and smaller affair. The music which it sang was also less difficult and grand.

*There was, and possibly is still, in some parts of Italy, a custom analogous to this, when the director of the orchestra marked time by rapping his baton regularly on his music stand instead of simply waving it

The comedy chorus consisted of twenty-four members, who came on the stage in detachments of six each.

The comedy costumes of both actors and chorus were something like what we are accustomed to see in farce or pantomime; there was something comical and exaggerated about them, which occasioned mirth of itself. The masks were decidedly comic, and usually caricatured the countenance of some public person well known to the audience. The comedy, especially in the older days that of Aristophanes sought to teach the people by holding up to ridicule, all such persons or measures as seemed to the poet worthy of censure; therefore it dealt almost exclusively with the events of the day, and such characters as Alcibiades, Socrates, Cleon, etc., are constantly appearing, and in the most mirth-provoking manner.

It is a matter of regret, however, that Aristophanes wielded so much influence, for he brought it to bear against Socrates, whom he was narrow-minded enough to take as the representative of Sophistry, and raised a popular feeling against him by his comedy of "The Clouds," in which he attributed the most interested motives to that grand philosopher.

It is unfortunate for Cleon that the caricature of Aristophanes was accepted as a portrait, and he has come down to us only as the noisy impudent demagogue, as portrayed in "The Knights;" yet Cleon must have been a rough and sturdy leader of the populace, to have attained so much power.*

Aristophanes was aristocratic in his tendencies, and could not forgive the tanner, for having risen from his humble sphere.

It required much courage however to attack the leader of the democracy, with such boldness. Even the mask makers refused to make the comic mask of Cleon; and when the mask was obtained no actor dared to play the character, so that Aristophanes was obliged to act it himself. Cleon embroiled Aristophanes in three lawsuits in consequence of his audacity.

The choruses of these comedies had sometimes to assume very odd parts, as in the two comedies of the "Birds," and the "Wasps," where they represented those creatures. The masks were made to correspond to the character assumed, and in "The Wasps" each man had a short spear or sting, which they sometimes thrust out, or drew in, and the whole chorus would sometimes move about quickly with a buzzing noise. The wasps were a satire upon the swarm of Athenian magistrates.†

One is forcibly reminded in these plays of the recent inventions of the French *Opera Bouffe*.

In the later comedies, private intrigues began to form the plot, and there was no great difference between these and the plays of modern times.

---

*Thucydides also gives an unfavorable picture of Cleon. Grote in his History of Greece, defends Cleon's character.

† Muller, p. 207, v. 2.

CHAPTER VII.

THE DANCES OF ANCIENT GREECE.

The dances of Greece were of considerable variety, and seem to have been both refined and coarse in their character. The earliest were probable merely military manœuvres, which were performed to songs, or to accompaniment of flute or kithara: or festival dances at the Bacchanalian or Dionysian revels. The chief dances may be classed as the Pyrrhic, the Cordax, and the Emmeleia.

The chorus itself, in very early times, was, in some parts of Greece only used to heighten the effect of a solo song, by its pantomimic dancing.

In Crete, youths and maidens joined hands and danced in a circle; in the centre of such a circle sat the musician, who sang to the accompaniment of a kithara, while the chorus expressed by their actions, *not by singing*, the various emotions which he chanted.

The Pyrrhic, or war dance, was the pride of all Greece, and all young men studied it.

In Sparta there was a law that all parents should send their sons, above the age of five years, to the public place, to have them instructed in the armed dance; on these occasions they were led by the teachers who made them sing hymns, etc., as they danced. The Pyrrhic was in fact, a mock battle, in four parts, representing the pursuit, overtaking, combat, and capture of the enemy, and was used as drill, to make young men proficient in the use of their weapons; it was accompanied by flute, which instrument was the one which the Greeks thought aroused the energies most.

The origin of the Pyrrhic is given as follows,— When Zeus, (Jupiter) was born, his father Kronos, (Saturn) knowing that he should be dethroned by him sought his life; he was hidden by the Corybantes, who on Kronos' coming near, fearing that the child would be discovered by its crying, began to dance about, and clashed their swords and shields, thus drowning its voice and saving its life.

Dancing was equal, and often combined, with singing, and was held in the highest estimation by the upper classes, and even the philosophers of ancient Greece; though of course only in its higher branches, the lower being usually abandoned to paid performers, as we to-day draw a wide distinction between a fashionable ball-room dance, and a ballet, though both are called dancing.

Skill in dancing, was a most envied accomplishment, for it meant both grace, and the talent of expressing all emotions without words.

Lucian* says the real art of the dance is to express an action, and gives a long list of mytho-

---

* De Saltatione

logical and historical deeds which were suited to representation. "The dancer" he says "must understand history, mythology, rhetoric," etc.

One person performed the whole dance, no matter how many characters were included in the action, and therefore he had to change his dress sometimes with much rapidity. The Proteus of the fables, is imagined to have been only a dancer skilled in sudden changes.

The philosophers not only praised, but practised the art. Plato led a chorus of dancing boys; and considered those to be rough, uncouth churls who disliked so pleasant a gift of the gods.*

Alcibiades danced in public, arrayed in great splendor. Sophocles was a celebrated dancer, and leader of dancing; while yet a boy, after the Greek victory at Salamis, he is said to have danced (according to some, naked) before the trophies.

Socrates often entertained his guests with dancing, and studied it himself at an advanced age.†

Exact information respecting the dance is lacking, some commentators deeming it to have been very like our modern ballet, others maintaining that there was a vast difference; Czerwinski and Wieland hold the former opinion, and to all appearance justly. Some erudite writers have endeavored to give the most circumstantial accounts of the ancient manner of dancing.

Meibomius, one of the earliest writers on this

* Czerwinski Geschichte d. tanz kunst, p. 19.
† Lucian, de Saltatione

subject, endeavored to dance an ancient Greek dance to an ancient Greek tune, before the court of Sweden, and Scaliger in the sixteenth century danced the Pyrrhic dance fully armed, before the Emperor Maximilian;* both assumed far too much knowledge in the matter.

There were undoubtedly numerous dancing schools, and possibly also some set figures prescribed in certain dances, but these figures had no names attached to them, and cannot be determined with certainty. The time was marked as in chorus, by a leader, tapping on the floor with heavy iron shoes. There are indications that a dance similiar to the Virginia reel, and other contra dances were known to them; also a dance which resembled the game of "follow-my-leader," where all imitated the postures and gestures of a leader.

Many variations were allowed; Cleisthenes having promised the hand of his daughter to the most successful dancer among her lovers, Hippoclides, of Athens, tried an innovation on the usual style; having danced the Emmeleia, or tragic dance successfully, he ordered the attendants to bring him a table, upon which he sprang, and standing on his head gesticulated with *his legs*. Cleisthenes indignant at this new departure, exclaimed " Oh son of Tisander you have undanced your marriage;" Cleisthenes caring more for his skill than for his marriage, replied "that is perfectly immaterial to me."

* Czerwinski, Gesch. d. Tanzk.

The Emmeleia, was the stately dance belonging to tragedy, and was the one most practised by the poets of that time, as they were often obliged to teach it to the chorus, thus adding the business of dancing master, to their already numerous duties.

The Sicinis was a dance of demigods, and was suited to the immense figure of the heroes of tragedy, already described. There was also a dance representing Theseus wandering about in the labyrinth, the figures of which must have been very twisted and irregular.

There was a species of dancing at banquets and revels, by paid female performers, at which the shape and form of the dancer were as lavishly displayed as in the modern ballet.*

The Cordax, or comic dance was throughout vulgar and unseemly, and no Athenian could dance it unmasked, without bringing down upon himself the reproach of the greatest impudence and immodesty. It was so outrageous that the comic poets often tried to do without it. Aristophanes, in "The Clouds" prides himself that he does not use it in that comedy. The *cordax* was a dance wherein the utmost vulgarity was not only allowed but *demanded*.†

Lucian in his treatise "de Saltatione" intimates the existence of various other dances which in his day had fallen into desuetude, as the dance of the *Cranes;* also the Phrygian dance, which was only

* Phillina, in dialogues of the Hetaræ.
† O. Muller Gesch. Griech Lit. v. 2, p. 210.

to be danced when the performers were drunk, and jumped about, with uncouth irregular leaps to the music of the flute.

Lucian also gives a specimen of the raillery of the people, when the dancer was not suited to the part; when a small person undertook to act Hector, they would call out, "we want Hector, not Astyanax." To a fat dancer, on making a leap they called "be careful, you'll break the stage;" and to a lean, sickly looking dancer they cried "go home, and nurse yourself, never mind dancing." Such little remarks are not unsuited to the *gamins* of the New York or London theatres.

We have dwelt rather long upon Greek Music, Theatre Chorus, and Dancing, but the subject has more than usual interest, as in the Greek art, of all descriptions, we find the seeds from whence has sprung our own.

CHAPTER VIII.

ANCIENT ROMAN MUSIC.

Art-love was not a distinguishing characteristic of the ancient Romans, and we are not astonished therefore, to find them borrowing music from Etruria, Greece, and Egypt; originating nothing, and (although the study was pursued by the Emperors) never finding anything higher in its practice than a sensuous gratification.

In the earliest days of Rome, the inhabitants were exclusively farmers, or warriors, and their first temples were raised to Ceres, or to Mars.

The priests of Ceres came originally from Asia Minor, and were called the Arval Brotherhood; flute-playing was a prominent feature in their rites, and they were all proficient upon that instrument. Their number was limited to twelve.

The worship of Mars was conducted by the Salian priests, whom Numa summoned to Rome, from Etruria. These also used the flute as an accessory to their sacrificial rites. In these primitive days of Rome, much was borrowed from the Etruscans, in style and instruments of music.

The earliest songs of Rome were in praise of Romulus, and told the story of the twin brothers, and the divine origin of the city. They were sung by choruses of boys. Similiar songs were sung during meals by the elders, with an accompaniment of flutes; these latter songs being especially directed to the young men and inciting them to be worthy of the deeds of their ancestors.*

Under the rule of the Emperors, all these worthy compositions went to decay, and were replaced by a much more degrading school of music. At no time, however, was music considered a necessary part of the education of Roman youth.

There existed in the later days of ancient Rome, some music schools, but the study was far less universally pursued, than in Greece, at the same epoch. The musical course, has been given by Quintilian, as follows,—

Theoretical. 1st. { Arithmetic / Physics.
2nd. { Harmony, / Rhythm, / Metrics.
Practical.—Composition. { Rhythm, / Melody, / Poetry.
Execution. { Playing Instruments, / Singing, / Dramatic Action.

Which makes a rather formidable array, even to modern eyes.

Among the Roman musical instruments, the flute was the most popular, and essentially national. We have already stated, that it was used in the

* Valerius Maximus, Book 2, x.

worship of their two chief deities; it was in secular use to a yet greater extent.

This flute (Tibia) was hooped with brass bands, and had an immense resonance. It was used by both sexes, but in public, and on most religious occasions, was played by men.

The frequency with which it was used, made the art of playing it, a most remunerative one, and the flute-players soon formed themselves into a guild, or protective society. This guild had many privileges accorded to it, and existed for a period of some centuries. The "Guild of Dionysian Artists" was a society of later date, and was a Musical Conservatory, Academy, and Agency all in one. It flourished greatly under the patronage of various Roman Emperors, and for a long time supplied singers and actors to the Roman world.

Valerius Maximus* has given an anecdote which shows how powerful, and exacting the Guild of flute-players could afford to be.

They were one day excluded from the Temple of Jupiter, where they had been allowed, by ancient custom, to take their meals; upon which the entire Guild left Rome, and went to the village of Tibur near by. This caused great embarrassment, no religious services could be held, and scarce any state ceremony properly conducted. The senate thereupon sent an embassy to induce them to return; in vain, the angry musicians were inflexible. The wily embassadors then called the

Book 2. s. iv

inhabitants of Tibur to their aid, and these pretended to give a great feast, to welcome the flute-players. At this feast, the musicians were all made very drunk, and while asleep from the effects of their liquor, they were bundled into chariots and driven back to Rome, where all their old privileges were restored. and newer, and greater ones added.

They received the right to give public representations, and spectacles, in Rome; but at these they were always masked, the reason given, being their shame at the manner of their inglorious return to the city.

Flutes were used at funerals. and it appears that at one time the luxury and pomp of Roman obsequies grew so excessive that a law was passed limiting the number of flute-players on such occasions to ten.

Only at one time did the flute disappear from any public worship, and that was when the worship of Bacchus was introduced into Rome. To this rite the kithara was used; but this worship which was somewhat refined, though jovial, among the Greeks, became among the Romans so debauched and uxorious, that it was soon prohibited by law.

The flute was used in combination with other instruments at times. Apuleius speaks of a concert of flutes, kitharas and chorus, and mentioned its deliciously sweet effect. It was also used as a pitch pipe, to give orators a guide in modulating their voices when addressing an assembly; thus Caius Gracchus always on such occasions, had a slave behind him, whose duty it was to aid him to commence his orations in a proper pitch, and when his voice sank too low, or became too shrill, to call him to better intonation by the sounds of the flute.

Although the flute was the favorite Roman instrument, it was by no means the only one. Trumpets were used to a great extent. A one-toned trumpet of very loud voice, was used for battle signals. These were of very large size, usually of brass, and their sound is described as "terrible." There was also a smaller, shepherd's trumpet of mellower tone.

Another much used instrument, of peculiar character, was the *sumphonium* which did not differ materially from the modern bag-pipe.*

Instruments of percussion, were few, and not indigenous to the Romans; such as were used came from the East, and were chiefly used in the worship of Eastern deities, at Rome. When the worship of Bacchus was prohibited, they passed away, with that licentious rite. The most complicated instrument of the ancient world, appeared in Rome during the first century of our era It was an *Organ*, not as in the scriptural days a mere syrinx, or Pans-pipes, but an undoubted organ somewhat similar in its effect to our modern instrument.

The instrument is said to have been invented by Ctesebius of Alexandria, in Egypt, who lived

---

* These are still used in Italy, and their performers are called Zampognari. The derivation is obvious.

about 250 B. C. They did not appear extensively in Rome however, until nearly 300 years later. This organ has given rise to much fruitless discussion. In the field of musical history especially, "a little knowledge" has proved "a dangerous thing," for where slight descriptions exist of instruments or music, latitude is left for every writer to form his own theory, to fight for it, and denunciate those who differ from it.

We have seen what a battle was fought over the three little manuscripts of Greek music, what a host of differing opinions were held about the Scriptural word "Selah," and now about this hydraulic organ, each writer mounts his hobby horse, and careers over the field of conjecture. Vitruvius, has given a full description of the instrument from personal inspection, but as his technical terms have lost all significance to modern readers, and have been translated in various ways, and as his work contained no diagrams, or illustrations of the various parts, it is useless.

Some writers* imagine the organ to have had seven or eight stops, that is, so many different *kinds* of tones, which would place them nearly on a par with our own. Others† think that they possessed seven or eight *keys*, that is so many *tones* only. It has been a point of dispute as to what function the water performed in working it. Vitruvius is rather hazy on this point, saying only that it is

* Chappell, in his History of Music, is the most lucid of these.
† See Fetis' Hist. Gen. de la Musique

"suspended" in the instrument. The water, when the organ was played was in a state of agitation, as if boiling.

There are medals still in existence, which were awarded to victors in organ contests, on which this instrument is represented, with two boys blowing or pumping, but the representation is too small to clear up any doubtful points.

So much is certain, the organs were very powerful in tone, being therefore the instruments best adapted to the large amphitheatres of Rome, and were extremely popular, for it was complained that young men forsook their other studies to learn to play them. The only possibility yet remaining that their construction may be known to us, is in the chance of discovering one in Pompeii.*

The functions of music in Rome were similar, though in a less degree, to its uses in Greece. At the sacrifice, the banquet, the contest, and the theatre, music was always an important adjunct, Prophets sometimes inspired themselves by it, as in the east.

There were various games, public and private, at which competition in music took place. But it was not, as in Greece, an art of simplicity and feeling; the love of the extraordinary, the colossal and *outre*, the desire for the most vulgar modes and excess of obscenity, soon degraded the art from the rude simplicity it possessed in the days of the republic.†

* Fetis Hist. v. 3
† Gevaert Hist. de la Mus. de l'ant. p 56.

This desire for colossal effects was apparent in the Roman games. Seneca says that in Nero's time, the chorus was more numerous than formerly the whole audience. Hosts of trumpeters, flute-players, etc., crowded the stage. It is also well illustrated in the splendor of the Triumph.

Triumphs were of two kinds, the lesser of which was called *Ovatio*, and was decreed for unimportant or easily-gained victories.

The grand Triumph (for important victories) was the highest military honor that could be bestowed.

When it had been decreed by the Senate, the victorious General entered Rome by the triumphal gate, where he was met by a procession of the entire Senate; here he gave an oration in praise of the valor of his army, and entering his triumphal chariot, the procession began. The order was as follows: —

Musicians, singing and playing. These were chiefly trumpeters, and the singers chanted triumphal songs.

The Senate and Magistrates.

The animals for the sacrifice, usually oxen, with their horns gilt, and decked with garlands, accompanied by the priests.

Music, flute players, to assist at the sacrificial rites.

Wagons, filled with statues, plate, armor, ensigns, etc., the spoil captured from the enemy.

The tribute from various countries, usually golden crowns, or ornaments sent to grace the occasion.

The captive leaders, kings, or generals, with their wives, in chains.

Lictors with the fasces twined with laurel.

Musicians and dancers dressed as Satyrs, crowned with gold. In the midst of these was a mimic, dressed as a female, who by his performance and gestures, insulted and burlesqued the captives.

Persons sprinkling perfumes.

The victorious general, dressed in purple and gold, crowned with laurel; he was seated in a circular chariot, drawn by four white horses. In his right hand he held a branch of laurel, in his left an ivory sceptre, surmounted by an eagle. His face was painted of a vermilion color, and a golden *bulla* hung from his neck.

Sometimes the chariot was drawn by elephants.

The children of the victor were allowed to ride with him, and he was attended by many relatives and citizens dressed in white. Behind him stood a slave carrying a richly gemmed crown, whose duty it was to admonish him constantly during the triumph, by whispering in his ear, " Remember that thou art a man."

The Military Tribunes followed, and the procession closed with,—

The whole army, horse and foot, crowned with laurel, and carrying various ornaments which they had won in the war.

They sang as they marched, the praises of their general, and of their own bravery; but sometimes (for it was a day of license and carnival) they sang the coarsest ribaldry and jokes concerning their leader; thus the army of Julius Cæsar, sang some very personal and vulgar verses about him, at his triumph.

The procession moved from the *Porta Triumphalis*, along the *Via Sacra* to the capitol.

All the shops were closed, the temples all open. The buildings along the route were decorated. Stands and scaffoldings were erected for the convenience of spectators. Banquets were spread before every house, to which all comers were welcome. It was in short a perfect carnival, but far exceeding in its proportions that of modern Rome.

When the procession arrived at the Temple of Jupiter at the Capitol, several of the captive leaders were taken from the ranks, and put to death, for ancient Rome was cruel even in her rejoicings; the oxen were also sacrificed, and the wreaths, with which their horns were decorated, were thrown into the lap of Jupiter's statue.

In the evening there was a grand banquet to the victorious General (Imperator), after which he was escorted to his home with music and song.

Nothing better illustrates the cruel, coarse, and sensual character of Roman music than that employed at such a triumph. Loud trumpet tones, a vile and ungenerous musical pantomime, the sacrificial music, and rude impromptu songs of the soldiery were the chief musical accessories of the greatest popular festival.

CHAPTER IX.

MUSIC OF THE ROMAN THEATRE.

In Rome as in ancient Greece there was a school of music, which was devoted to the stage; but it was not held in such high esteem, nor was it the work of the poet to supply it.

In the French *operas bouffes* of our day we find the libretto and music to be the work of different persons, and in this respect the Roman comedies resembled them, save that while we rank the music above the text, the Romans valued the words far more than the music; but in other respects there was also much resemblance between the Roman tragedies and modern *Opera Seria*. They divided the music into parts, such as dialognes or duets, solos, and choruses.

Cicero says that a connoisseur could instantly determine by the style of the music alone, what tragedy was being performed; this would indicate an amount of tone-painting, which justifies our comparison of the Roman with the modern stage.

The theatres were, as usual, of immense size. The Emperor Trajan built an Odeum, or music hall, of which Apollodorus was the architect, which was capable of seating twelve thousand spectators. These structures were usually built of stone, and in the most thorough manner; there is however one notable exception to the rule. In the reign of Tiberius an amphitheatre erected by Atilius at Fidenæ, fell in during a gladiatorial contest, and twenty thousand persons lost their lives.*

The music of the stage, tended rather to virtuosity than to real beauty, the natural result being, that while Rome possessed many skillful performers, she had no musical composers of eminence.† The names of the composers of music to the comedies of Terence and Plautus are still extant, but they seem to have enjoyed no special renown.

Quintilian speaks of the weak and womanish music of the stage, and Martial in satirizing the Gaditanian female singers which were so much sought for in the later days of ancient Rome, says, that it was the surest sign of a fashionable dandy, to hear a young man trilling out the latest Gaditanian ditties.

Many of the theatrical performers and singers were slaves, who were bought for the purpose, and the most stringent and cruel measures were taken to prevent them from ruining their voices by any kind of debauchery. Theatrical factions also existed for this or that singer, in which at times many lives were lost.‡ Laws were afterwards enacted, to guard against such riots.

---

* Tacitus Bk. IV.
† Gevaert. Mus. de l'ant. p. 58.
‡ Tacitus Bk 1.

Another and less tolerable branch of Roman public musical diversion was the dance, which although most skillfully performed by talented pantomimists, was so indecent in its general character, and choice of subjects, that it received strong condemnation from many writers of that day.

Many anecdotes remain, showing how well acted this art must have been.

Demetrius, the cynic (in the reign of Nero) having reproached a dancer, that his art was but an adjunct to music, the performer caused the musical accompanists to cease playing, and enacted the subject of Mars and Venus without music, and in such a manner that Demetrius was obliged to retract, and said, "Even your hands seem to speak."*

The professional dancers, or musical pantomimists, were most appreciated under the luxurious reign of the Cæsars. A prince of Pontus once came to the court of Nero, where he was royally entertained; as he did not understand the Latin language, he could not appreciate theatrical representations, but a celebrated dancer appearing. he was able to understand his actions from beginning to end. On his departure, when Nero had given him presents, he said. "If instead, you would give me this dancer, it would be the greatest favor of all;" on being asked the reason, he replied that he had many barbarian neighbors, whose language he did not understand, and that

*Lucian *de Saltxione*.

such an unfailing interpreter would be of incalculable value to him.*

We can learn how much these performers entered into their acting by the following anecdote. A dancer once acting the part of Ajax, in a double character dance, became so frenzied, that he tore the clothes off from the time-beater, (or conductor of music) seized the flute of the accompanist and broke it over the head of Ulysses. The better class of spectators condemned such a novel exhibition, but the lower orders applauded vociferously. The performer afterwards became calm again, but, on being desired to repeat the performance, he replied that it was sufficient for a man to make a fool of himself once.†

The dance in Rome was esteemed only as an amusement and sensual enjoyment, and was not studied by the respectable classes, save sometimes in connection with singing, in which case it was not driven to such excess as the pantomime dance described above; but neither song, instruments, or dance were studied to any large extent among the masses of the Roman people.

* Lucian de Saltatione.
† Lucian ibid.

CHAPTER X.

MUSIC OF THE ROMAN EMPIRE.

Under the luxurious reign of the Cæsars, music attained unusual prominence in Rome, but it was still the music of virtuosity, rather than true art. Skillful performers multiplied, while talented composers did not exist. The choruses were augmented to the utmost, their numbers exceeding all previous extent.* New instruments began also to appear, the sumphonia, the hydraulic organ, and others. The study of music began to be fashionable (in some at least of its branches) and the emperors themselves did not disdain to practise the art. It is a singular fact, however, that exactly those emperors who were the greatest rascals, took the greatest interest in music. Domitian founded games in honor of Jupiter, in which he introduced Kithara playing and other musical contests to amuse the populace. Heliogabalus sang, danced, played the flute, organ, and pandura, and was proficient in giving musical recitations with flute accompaniment. Caligula studied singing and dancing, and was so fond of the former, that when at the theatre, he could scarcely ever refrain from following the melodies

*Seneca.

which the tragedians sang, by humming along with them. It is related of him,* that during the height of his power and tyranny, he sent, one night, a summons to three men of consular rank, to attend him at once at his palace; in fear and terror, the three hastened to obey, scarcely doubting that the night was to be their last on earth; on arriving, they were most agreeably surprised to hear the sound of flutes, and the emperor himself suddenly burst out before them, arrayed in full theatrical costume, and sang them a song, after which he bowed and retired, upon which they were dismissed, and returned to their anxious families; we can imagine that, under the circumstances, Caligula received very hearty applause that night.

Vespasian established musical games, and gave large sums to actors and singers.†

Titus was a good singer and player.

In the later days of paganism, when the music of the Christian church had already manifested its power and superiority, the Emperor Julian endeavored to bolster up the religion of the ancestors, and fight the church with one of its own weapons. He therefore sought to make an extensive reform in the religious and sacrificial music. He endeavored to form music schools at Alexandria, in Egypt, where a new school of singing and composition might be inculcated, and whence Rome might draw the material for a

* Suetonius Calig. LIV.
† Suetonious Vesp. XIX.

better religious music than had formerly obtained. In one of his letters, he says: "I deem no study more worthy of attention than good music. I desire that you select from among the population of Alexandria certain well born lads, who shall be supplied each with two Egyptian artabai per month, besides rations of corn, wine and oil, and be provided also with clothes by the comptroller of the treasury. The boys are to be chosen for a definite time according to their voice. Should any give promise of further abilities to reach a high degree in the science of music, let them be informed that we propose to offer to such, very substantial rewards. That the minds of these lads will, independently of our encouragement, be benefited by that cleansing power which perfect music exerts, we may rest assured on the authority of those who in past times have laid down excellent regulations on the subject. So much for the new choristers. As for those now under the instruction of the music master Dioscurus, make them act here all the more diligently to their practice. Since we are prepared to assist them in whatever way they may choose."*

This beautiful scheme was frustrated by the death of its great originator, about two years afterward.

But among all the Roman Emperors, none was a more passionate virtuoso, and devotee of skillful music than that incomprehensible monster, Nero We shall enter into considerable detail regarding

† Letters of Julian, No. 56.

this curious emperor, as he may stand as a type (although an exaggerated one) of the soulless and sensual musical *virtuosi* of his era. In giving his history (so far as it relates to music) we follow mainly the version of Suetonius.

He studied music in his early youth, and first appeared publicly in the games of the Roman youth, entitled the *Juvenalia;** here he seems to have made no remarkable impression, either by his voice or dramatic action. Immediately on his accession to the throne, he sent for the famous harper Terpnus, and took the greatest pleasure in his performances; it was his habit to sit with him after supper till late into the night. At last he began to practice upon the instrument himself; and at the same time he began to apply himself assiduously to the cultivation of his voice, although it is the testimony of all his historians, that his voice was rather thin and husky.

The care he lavished upon the preservation of his voice, far out-does that of any modern *prima donna;* he would lie on his back during part of each day, with a sheet of lead on his stomach, or chest; he used emetics and clysters copiously when it seemed at all out of order; his food was always regulated with reference to its effect upon his voice, and he forbore from eating many fruits and pickles, because they were prejudicial to it.

He never delivered any addresses to his army because he feared that he might thereby strain it; all his speeches to the soldiers were delivered by

---

* Tacitus. Bk. XX.

proxy, even though he were present. On all occasions, he had his voice-master by him, to caution him whenever he should be in danger of over-straining, and this instructor was ordered, if the warning should by any cause be unheeded, to clap a napkin upon his mouth by way of enforcing his advice. Through the whole reign of this emperor however, there was never less misery than while he was applying himself to his musical education, or was upon his musical tours.

Encouraged by the improvement (real or imagined) in his voice, he became desirous of appearing upon the public stage. The unjust valuation which he placed upon the art, being apparent by his remark that "music unheard, was valueless and unregarded."

His first public appearance took place at Naples, A. D. 63; while singing, the theatre was shaken by an earthquake, but Nero was not to be checked, even by the elements, and sang to the end of his song.* After the theatre had been vacated, it fell in; and Nero composed lengthy hymns to the gods for his escape.†

On his return to Rome he was desirous of showing his skill in that metropolis; at first he only sang to select audiences of friends at his own palace, but infatuated with the applause of this flattering circle, he was only too glad to follow their suggestion that such a fine voice should not be hidden.

* Suetonius, XX.
† Tacitus, XV.

He instituted games in his own honor, entitled the *Neronia,* which were celebrated in imitation of the Greek sacred games, every fifth year; at these games he had introduced contests of flute and organ-players; he was too impatient to wait until the allotted interval should have expired, but ordered that the games should be celebrated in advance of their accustomed time, and placed his name on the list of musical competitors;* the Senate sought to avert such a disgrace, by offering to decree the victory to him, without requiring him to compete, but Nero answered, that he stood in no need of favor or protection; that he depended entirely upon himself and upon his own merits; that he would fairly enter the lists, and that the decision should come from the judges.† When his name was called, he came on in his regular turn, attended by a suite of high military officials, one of whom bore his harp. After taking his place he announced that he would sing the story of Niobe; this he did, and kept it up for hours, but at the conclusion he (suddenly changing from singer to emperor) deferred the awards of the judges for one year, as this afforded him an opportunity to appear again in that time.

The people gave on this occasion immense applause, but whether they were most pleased by the music, or by the novelty of the whole affair, is doubtful.

* Suet. Nero, XXI.
† Tacitus, Bk. XXI.

But Nero could not wait even the exceptionally short time which he had set, and appeared at numerous private shows, which were given from time to time by private individuals of wealth and station. For these performances he was glad to be offered compensation, not from any avaricious motive, but because it stamped him as a thorough and professional artist; of course many courtiers took advantage of this foible and were very glad to pay him a princely *honorarium*. He was offered on one occasion 1,000,000 sesterces for one appearance; this sum being equivalent to $37,500 puts the enormous salaries of the modern prima donna to the blush.

He sometimes sang for two or three days in the same place, only pausing occasionally to take refreshments and recuperate, and seldom was any song of his less than a day in length.

This in itself might have been an easily-avoided bore under ordinary circumstances, but he prevented the possibility of a decreasing audience, by posting sentinels at the doors, and forbidding all egress. We can judge of the terrible dulness of these occasions by the fact that some spectators, at times, jumped from the windows, at the risk of their limbs, while others feigned death and were carried out for burial.[*]

There were spies scattered through the audience, and any inattention to the emperor's singing was dangerous. The soldiers chastised every one who did not applaud properly. If any

---

[*] Suetonius Nero. XXIII.

of the lower classes presumed to give adverse criticism, they were summarily dealt with, while those of the upper rank who showed their weariness, were marked out for future vengeance. The emperor had in reality the life of any subject in his power, while seemingly only exerting legal authority; for he had hundreds of informers, spies and perjurers about his court who could fasten any charge on any person however high in station, and the awe-struck senate was always ready to condemn. Many when charged with any crime by the emperor's minions, at once committed suicide as the shortest way out of the scrape.

Among those who fell under Nero's displeasure for not appreciating his music, was the future emperor Vespasian, who during one of the songs, fell fast asleep. Nero was with difficulty persuaded to spare his life, but finally contented himself with banishing him from the court. The scene must have been to some extent, ludicrous, when these poor, bored victims of the emperor-musician, applauding vehemently, cried out for more. Yet the applause did not always fall in the right place, and to obviate this difficulty, the emperor formed a corps of *claquers* or professional applauders, whose duty it was to lead, and direct the applause at the proper moments. This army of *claquers* consisted of many fashionable young men, and five thousand commoners. They could easily be distinguished by their elegant attire and curled locks.

The system pursued was similar to that at

present used in some of the Parisian theatres; there was one chief, or leader, and several deputy commanders; the force was divided into small parties, and mingled among the *bona fide* audience, and at a signal from their chief, there would be applause of the required kind.

Nero lavished large sums on this *corps*, and was ever susceptible of flattery to his musical talents: on some Alexandrians singing some verses in his praise, he was so elated that he sent to Alexandria for more singers and conferred many benefits upon them.

Once while singing in the Roman theatre, in the character of Orestes, the murderer of his mother (which he certainly ought to have acted well, for Nero killed his own mother) he came on the stage loaded with chains, on which a young soldier rushed on the stage to deliver him; this compliment to the reality of his acting was specially grateful to Nero.

The passion for acting and singing were with him almost monomania; during the immense conflagration of Rome, which he himself had kindled, (and which burned for six days and seven nights) he stood upon the tower of Mecaenas, and was so impressed with the spectacle, that he hastened to his theatre, put on the appropriate costume, and sang " The Destruction of Troy: " hence the proverb " Nero fiddled while Rome was burning," which might run more appropriately " Nero sang because Rome was burning," for it was not callousness, as has been implied, but rather the reverse of it; a venting of the emotions caused by the grandeur of the spectacle.

That he had implicit belief in his musical powers, there can be no manner of doubt, for he had thoughts of possibly using it as a profession; it had been foretold that the time should come when he would be forsaken by all; on which he replied to the soothsayer "an artist can gain his livelihood in any country."

In Greece at the public games, the musical contests were still an important feature,* and the cities where they were celebrated, hearing of Nero's vanity in music, sent envoys to him with several golden crowns, as tribute to his abilities in the art; Nero was gratified beyond measure, and said that the Greeks had the only proper appreciation of music. He gave a sumptuous supper to the envoys, after which they begged that they might be permitted to hear that divine voice; Nero, nothing loth, consented, and as might be expected the Greeks went into ecstasies of applause. This determined Nero to make a musical tour through Greece, and attend the sacred games there.

He started on his journey with a vast retinue, among which were the entire force of claquers. Arriving in Greece he ordered the games which did not fall in that year, to be celebrated out of course, and also, contrary to all precedent, established musical contests at the Olympic games,

---

*See chapter on Games of Greece.

that he might have the honor of appearing in them.*

At these games, he appeared with all his enforced boredom, none being allowed to leave the theatre, during his performances. The anxiety and earnestness he displayed in these contests are almost incredible. He bribed better artists to allow him to win, and he would address the judges, telling them that he had made all study and preparation, and taken all the care necessary for so important a contest, but the issue was in their hands, he hoped therefore they would not regard any purely accidental mishaps. The judges would thereupon mildly encourage the timid contestant.

He always adhered strictly to the rules imposed upon the contestants; he would never spit, or wipe the perspiration from his forehead; once on dropping his staff, he was greatly alarmed lest the accident should lose him the prize, but was reassured by one of the contestants who told him that he was sure that the judges had not perceived the occurrence; after the conclusion of his song, he fell on his knees, stretching out his hands in humble supplication for the verdict of the judges. But when the victory was awarded to him, (as it was always sure to be) his humility was thrown to the winds; he then caused his own heralds to proclaim him as the victor, and soon set up statues of himself in the various cities, with laudatory

* Nero however sometimes took part in other contests, he was as poor and persistent a charioteer as musician.

inscriptions, according to the custom of Greece. Not content however, with this, he also caused the statues of all previous victors to be pulled down and thrown in the sewers.

He took the prize (of course) in every Greek contest in which he participated. Competition was freely invited, though not as freely tolerated.

In one of the Grecian contests a musician entered the lists against him, who was very proud of his skill, and could not be bought; he contested the prize so obstinately and skilfully, that Nero's soldiers also entered the contest by driving him to the wall, and killing him in sight of the audience;* the prize was awarded to Nero.

His return from the tour was made with grand pomp; on reaching Naples, he had a breach made in the walls (according to Greek custom) and made his triumphal entry into the city, through it. In the same manner he entered Rome and Antium. In Rome he arrogated to himself a full triumph, and entered in state; all his prizes to the number of eighteen hundred were placed in chariots, and appeared in the procession, each one bearing an inscription as to where and when it was won. Statues were set up, and medals struck in honor of his unprecedented musical success. From this time forward, until his death he did not abate in his musical studies or ardor.

Towards the close of his reign, he took much interest in the water organ, of which we have previously given a description.

* Tacitus, Book XVI.

When his affairs were at a crisis, soon to be followed by his death, he still gave most of his time to his favorite study. One day when messengers first brought to him the tidings of a new rebellion, it is related that he spent a few moments in consultation about these momentous state affairs, and the rest of the day in showing to his courtiers some new organs which he said he intended shortly to introduce into the theatre.

When apprised of the fact that the legions of Julius Vindex had mutinied, and that that able general had also declared against him, he was sufficiently aroused to march against him, but, ever a maniac on the subject of music, he declared that he intended to do nothing but appear in the camp of the rebellious legions, and weep and sing to them pathetic songs, which should so affect them that they would at once return to their allegiance; the next day after the bloodless victory he promised to appear and sing songs of triumph in the theatre; and he thought it well that composers should begin to write the triumphal odes at once.

In preparing for the expedition, his chief care was not for instruments of war, but to provide safe carriage for his musical instruments; many wagons were filled with these, as he took along several water organs. But the expedition never took place, and he never had the chance of testing the effects of pathetic music upon the Roman legions, for all the army declared against him and he suddenly found himself deserted by his court.

and proscribed by the senate. In his downfall nothing hurt him more than that his enemies spoke of him as "that pitiful harper," and he constantly appealed to his attendants if any could excel him in the art.

He at this crisis made a vow that, if his reign continued peaceably, he would appear in the games he intended to give in honor of his success against the insurgents, and play the water organ, flute and sumphonia, as well as enact a play, and dance; but these inflictions the Roman people were spared.

In one night his seemingly strong power vanished, and he was compelled to fly for his life, attended only by three or four persons. Having made his way to the suburban residence of Phaon, one of his freedmen, it was soon apparent that he could not escape, and that he must die, either by the hands of the infuriated Romans, or by his own. Weeping and sobbing, while his attendants prepared his grave, almost his last words before his suicide were "Alas! what an artist the world is now to lose," thus in his latest moments, keeping up that egotism and infatuation for music which had been one of his ruling characteristics through life.

The musical side of Nero's character is certainly to some extent ludicrous, but there were other and far darker sides to his hideous character. These of course are not within our province to dwell upon, but we have chosen to give a full description of his musical life that the reader may clearly see how little of true art, or love of art could have existed in so oppressive an atmosphere.

CHAPTER XI.

HISTORY OF CHINESE MUSIC.*

In Brande's dictionary of arts and sciences, under the head of "Chinese music," the whole fabric of Chinese music is swept away in one short sentence, at the close of which, the compiler curtly says, — "We ought, perhaps to apologize for saying *so much* of it."

No right minded and just reader will echo so flippant an opinion; a nation which more than four thousand years ago, had studied music as an abstract science and which understood the laws of musical proportion centuries before Pythagoras was born, certainly deserves more than a passing notice from the musical historian, no matter how barbarous its present music may seem.

The Chinese life and character, while apparently full of fancy, is in reality quite emptily rational and pragmatic. In all the scientific facts relating to music, the Chinese made early and thorough investigations, but in that inventive inspiration which is the soul of art, they seem to have been deficient. They possess a very full account of their music both of modern and ancient days.

* In the early historical part of this article, we have mainly followed the dates used by La Fage.

Their musical history teems with facts, and anecdotes, dating back far beyond every other nation except the Egyptian. Their literature contains a vast number of treatises and comments on the musical art, many of which are, however, couched in very mystical and ambiguous language. In the Imperial library at Pekin, there are four hundred and eighty-two books on this subject exclusively.*

The invention of music, is ascribed by the Chinese to supernatural beings.

The emperor Chi-hoang-che, who reigned in the time of the spirits, is said to have invented the rules of pronunciation, the written characters of the Chinese language, and finally music.† A mythological character named Tong-how composed the earliest songs.

Kai-tien-chi, the ninth emperor of this spiritual dynasty, is credited with many of the earliest songs. He also invented eight kinds of instruments (which will be described later) the names of which are certainly poetical enough,—

1. Love the people. 2. The black bird 3. Don't cut the trees. 4. Cultivate the eight different grains. 5. Chant the celestial doctrines. 6. Celebrate the merits of the sovereign. 7. Imitate the virtues of the earth. 8. Recall the memory of all existing things.

These names were probably given to the instruments from the special songs which each accompanied

* Ambros Gesch, d. Mus. p. 20, v. 1.
† Amiot Abrege Chron p. 201.

Tcho-yung, a successor of the preceding emperor, is said once to have listened to the songs of the birds, while the empire was in a state of profound peace, and their singing caused him to invent a music which penetrated every where, speaking to the intelligence, calming the passions of the heart, causing perfect equilibrium in the emotions, facilitating and improving the use of all the senses, and prolonging the life of man.

The name of this music was *Tsie-ven*—" Temperance and mercy."

This beautiful legend of the birds, seems almost Greek in its poetry, but there exists yet another mythological bird in the Chinese tales, which is extraordinarily like the Egyptian Phœnix. The *Foang-hoang* was a bird whose nest and abiding-place was wrapt up in mystery; it appeared in China only at the birth of a good ruler, and its coming was always a happy presage to the nation. The Chinese mythology, so far as it relates to music, is evidently a traditional history, and poetically relates actual occurrences, showing that, in all probability, their music existed, and was highly esteemed in pre-historic times.

The authentic history of Chinese music may be said to begin with Fo-hi, the first of the Ty dynasty, and the founder of the Chinese empire. He reigned about 2950 B. C.* All good qualities seem to have been united in this beneficent ruler; in all ways he sought to benefit his race.

* Chinese annals claim that their empire was founded 80,000 or 100,000 years B. C. Fo-hi's reign is fixed by some at about 2,250 B. C.

It was not as an amusement, but as a means of popularizing his thoughts on all sciences, that he regulated and arranged the system of music. His first song celebrated his triumph over ignorance and barbarism; soon after he composed the "Fisher's song" in which he relates how he had taught modes of fishing to the natives. He invented the kin, a stringed instrument in the style of the modern zither, but with cords of silk, and in it he symbolized all manner of things.

He rounded the upper part to represent Heaven; he flattened the lower part to resemble the earth; one part of the instrument was called "The abode of the dragon" (representing the breezes of Heaven); another part was entitled "The nest of the Poang-hoang" (to betoken the seasons of the year). By means of this instrument he could regulate his heart, and curb his passions.*

"Those who would play the Kin," says the Chinese commentator, "and draw sounds from it which can charm, must have a grave countenance and well regulated interior, they should pick it lightly, and give a tone neither too high, nor low."†

Many Chinese writers attribute some of the inventions which are credited to Fo-hi, to his wife Niu-va, a supernatural personage who was regarded as a holy and miraculous virgin in the Chinese annals.‡ The truth about Fo-hi seems to be that

* Amiot De la Mus. des Chinois, p. 54.
† Amiot, p. 57.
‡ It is singular that a similar personage exists in the Hindoo mythology.

he was a remarkably good man and a benefactor to his race, and therefore many useful inventions, and wonderful adventures are attached to his name, which cannot be authenticated. Some writers consider him a myth, which is scarcely a tenable position; others have endeavored to prove him to be neither more nor less than the Noah of the Bible. There is little doubt that he made improvements in Chinese music, and, by exaggeration, was called its inventor. A Chinese writer in giving to the invention a greater antiquity, beautifully says " Music had its cradle in the heart of man."

Chin-noung, successor of Fo-hi, was also a good ruler; his chief works in music seem to have been some alterations in the *Che* (a sort of *Kin*) and he was able by his playing to turn the heart of man, from intemperate life, to celestial truth.

Hoang-ti, the next emperor, had music scientifically investigated and established natural rules to the art. The reign of Hoang-ti is supposed to have been about 2,600 B. C. In his day music though practised, was not understood in its natural elements.

The Chinese even at that day, based all other sciences on music, and sought to make this art (in a mystical and hyperbolical way) the foundation of all others. The emperor therefore ordered Ling-lun to give his attention to the development of the laws of music. The fables on the subject of his researches are innumerable; he travelled to the north-western part of China and took up his abode on a high mountain, near which was a large growth of bamboos. Ling-lun took a bamboo, which he cut between two knots; he removed the pith, and blowing in the tube, a sound resulted which was of the exact pitch of the human voice when in its normal state. Not far off was the source of the Hoang-ho, and Ling-lun found that the tone of his tube was similar to the sound given by the waters of that river in bubbling from the earth; thus was discovered the first *Lu*, (or Li) the fundamental tone.

Ling-lun was pursuing his investigations further, when the Poang-hoang appeared with its mate and perched upon a neighboring tree. The male bird sang in six different tones, while the female also used six, but different from the preceding. The first note of the mystical Poang-hoang, was precisely in unison with the reed which Ling-lun had cut from the bamboo.

On ascertaining this, the fable continues, Ling-lun cut twelve pieces of bamboo and pitched them according to the notes of the two songsters; he found by alternating the sounds of the male with the female bird, that he had a chromatic scale. The six tones of the male were called the *li-yang* (masculine tones) the other six *li-yn* (feminine tones), and throughout all Chinese music, the distinction between the male and female tones of the scale still exists. This was the first Chinese discovery of the proportions of sound, the first step in the science of Acoustics, and though covered over with fable and allegory, it really preceded the discoveries of Pythagoras by many centuries; Ling-lun went back to the emperor's court and there measured and fixed the pitch of the Chinese scale forever. Bells were also made of the official pitch, that it might easily be perpetuated.

Hoang-ti also had immense trumpets made which imitated " the voice of dragons," and drums which sounded " like thunder." This monarch was as great and good in all arts and sciences, as he was in music. He seems to have been a Chinese " king Alfred." After him, came Chao-hao, at whose accession the Foang-hoang again appeared, intimating thereby another prosperous reign in this line of good and musical emperors. Chao-hao invented the idea of marking the divisions of the night by strokes of a drum, and also had founded a set of twelve copper bells, to represent the twelve months of the year. He used all his efforts to make music popular, and invented new modes of playing, making the *yang* and *yn* less distinct from each other, that is uniting the more powerful tones (male) with the weaker (female). It is said that he first introduced songs in honor of the ancestors, which play a very important part in Chinese music, and that these hymns were performed for the first time, in honor of the amiable emperor Hoang-ti.

The emperors next following, all protected and encouraged music. The first songs, that is of a secular style, were composed about 2456 B. C. At this time also, many new instruments were invented, and old ones improved. With the reign of Yao, 2357 B. C., the chronological record of Chinese emperors and their doings becomes much clearer. Under this emperor, China had a season of great peace and prosperity. He invented the instrument of musical stones, called the *king*, (to be described later) and received the stones specially adapted to its manufacture, as tribute from various provinces.

Chun, who succeeded him, though of low birth (he was nominated to the throne by Yao) continued to advance the progress of music, and used it, as the Greek philosophers did later, to prepare himself for public business.

"It was to the sound of the *kin*," says the Chinese historian,* "that the great emperor Chun prepared to deal with the affairs of the empire, and to the melody of the *kin* is due the love and care which he constantly gave to his people." Chun composed the following song, words and music, on the above instrument; it may be taken as a specimen of very early Chinese improvisation.

"The breeze of midday brings warmth and dispels sorrow; may it be the same with Chun; may he be the joy and the consolation of his people. The breeze of midday causes the grain to grow, which is the hope of the people; even so Oh, Chun! be thou the hope and the wealth of thy subjects," etc.

* Quoted by La Fage, Hist. de Mus., p. 47.

Chun also wrote a song in praise of agriculture. In the year 2284 B. C., he established uniformity of weight and measure, as well as a fixed diapason throughout the empire, and endeavored to have all the bells made in just proportions to each other. He also caused to be composed, a melody celebrating the nine principal virtues; it was accompanied with dances, in nine parts and contained nine modulations; it was named *Siao-chao* from the instruments which the dancers held in their hand.

Chun established five grand ceremonials, in each of which music bore a part. First, a ceremony of rejoicing, in honor of Chang-ti (the supreme being) and of the celestial spirits. Second, a festival in honor of the ancestors. Third, a military celebration, in honor of the former dissensions of the empire having given way to a tranquil peace. Fourth, a feast dedicated to courtesy, when the beauties of concord and goodwill were sung. Fifth and last, a ceremony in which the inter-dependence of man was remembered, and the manifold blessings accruing by mutual beneficence, chanted.

Chun also appointed a superintendent of music, who was to see that the art was always exercised in its proper direction.

Kouei was appointed censor, and the instructions of the emperor to him, are full of good sense. "Music should follow the sense of the words." "It should be simple and unaffected." "Music is an expression of the soul of the musician;" such sentiments as these show a keen appreciation of the art, which seems all the more singular when we think of the peculiar music to which it relates. The music of the time of Chun, is rapturously eulogized by Confucius.

Yu, the great, only followed the example of his predecessors in setting to music the most moral precepts and praising virtue, in song. It may perhaps have been this association of high thoughts and ideas, the noble character of the poetry, which gave music such a charm in the eyes of the ancient Chinese. Yu made use of some primitive instruments, in a new and very laudable manner;* desirous of being easily accessible to all his subjects, he caused to be placed at a gate of his palace, five instruments of percussion, which were to be struck by any applicant, according to the nature of his business with the emperor.

A large bell announced a person who desired to complain of an injustice; a drum signified a communication respecting the manners of the empire; and a small bell, private or confidential business; a *tam-tam*, a public or private misfortune; a tambourine, an accusation of crime which was appealed from some lower tribunal to the adjudication of the emperor.

This kindly emperor, regulated what was still deficient in music, and did it so thoroughly that no further changes were necessary until the Hia dynasty became extinct. The last of the above

* La Fage. p 50.

mentioned dynasty was (for a change) a most vicious emperor. Kie was, according to the chroniclers, a sort of Mongolian Caligula, and his memory is execrated.

The next dynasty, called Chang, after a prosperous series of emperors, also ended with an atrocious tyrant called Tchow, who invented a luxurious style of music, and is said to have first established the feast of lanterns. He was deprived of throne and life by violence.

Ou-wang a later ruler, is chiefly celebrated for his military music, for which he seems to have had a *penchant* and of which he composed considerable. One of his pieces was intended for performance while the army formed itself in order of battle.

In his day, the discipline of music was very thoroughly attended to. Every ceremony and rite had its appropriate music attached; the musicians had to undergo two examinations each year, and all innovations either in composition, or in the shaping of musical instruments was jealously guarded against. No special features appear in the musical history of China during the next few reigns.

In the reign of Koang-tsee, a valuable treatise on music was published, which is still highly esteemed. At this era also were established Mandarins of music and of the dance. At this epoch flourished the great Kong-fu-tsee, or Confucius, the leader of Chinese thought and philosophy.

This sage's name was simply Kong, but his disciples added the title, *fu-tsee*, which makes the meaning of the whole, Kong, the instructor, or master. This was Latinized by the Jesuit missionaries into Confucius. This philosopher cultivated the study of music and seems to have esteemed it as highly as the Greek philosophers did a century later. He revised and arranged many of the old books on musical ceremonies and rites. He learnt the art in a distant province, as in his native place music was but little known.

While in the kingdom of Tchi, Confucius heard some of the ancient music of the days of Chun performed. The effect on him was so marvellous, that for three months he scarcely could eat, for thinking of it. "I should never have believed," he said, "that composers could reach such a pinnacle of perfection."*

It is also said that Confucius was an excellent performer on the musical stones of the *king*. Once while playing on this instrument a passer by struck with the beauty of his performance, paused to listen, and exclaimed " surely one who can play thus, must have his soul occupied with great thoughts."

In the later days of his wanderings, when he was reduced to the extremity of poverty and starvation, he sang and played as usual, showing no signs of depression or despondency. One of his disciples ventured a reproach, asking how he could sing when they were all famishing; he replied; "the wise man seeks by music, to strengthen the weakness of his soul, the thought-

* Amiot de la Mus. des Chinois, p. 11

less one uses it to stifle his fears." The facts relating to Confucius, his wanderings and life are full of anecdotes relating to his extreme love of the art, and are probably authentic. The family of Confucius still exists in his native province, having passed intact through sixty-eight or sixty-nine generations; they are honored by special privileges and distinctions and are the most notable hereditary aristocracy of China. It may be mentioned here, that all the philosophers and literati of the empire were musicians as well: in this respect strongly resembling the sages of Greece.

The theatre began to progress greatly in this era, (sixth century B. C.), and one emperor was censured for devoting too much time to his comedians, and too little to the worthy celebration of the ancestral feast. The arts received a severe check when the Tchin or Tsin dynasty obtained control of the entire realm. These were in reality the first who united the various provinces under one rule, and who bore, with right, the title of Hoang, or emperor. It is from this dynasty that China takes its name (Tchina or Tsina). One of this set of conquerors, Tchi-chi-hoang-ti, desirous of obliterating the memories of former glories, which might prove prejudicial to his own, attempted, in 245 B. C., a proscription of all science and art.

He commanded all ancient books to be burnt, and especially caused strict search to be made for the books which Confucius had collected and revised. Only works on agriculture and medicine were to be spared. A large number of literary persons who had concealed part of their books were put to death; yet many continued to risk their lives to preserve the fruits of ancient culture. Books were hidden in walls of houses, in tombs, and buried in the earth, whence they were long afterward recovered. The emperor in proclaiming this war on literature gave as his reason that the ancient books did not suit that era, that they were a hindrance to progress, that they caused the people to neglect agriculture which was the only substantial happiness of a nation, and that they gave to the people liberty to censure the sovereign, and by consequence, fostered disobedience and rebellion. Of course in this universal persecution, music did not fare better than the other arts. All instruments were ordered to be destroyed and made over after new models. The bells which had given the standard pitch up to that time, were melted down, and many of them used for the purpose of founding colossal statues to deck the entrance of the imperial palace. But, according to La Page,* it was much easier for the musicians to evade the emperor's decree, and save their instruments, than for the literati to save their precious books. There were few instruments and they were less rigorously sought after, and it was an easy matter to conceal bells or the *kings* (musical stones) by burying them in the earth whence they could be exhumed intact at any later

* P. 63. Mus. des Chinois.

period. Therefore in spite of the exertions of the emperor, the ancient traditions and arts could not be wholly extinguished; a spark still remained from which the torch of science and art could be re-lit.

It was this despotic emperor, however, who built the *Wan-li-chang* or great wall of China, therefore his influence upon the empire was not wholly exerted for evil, but rather directed towards the establishment of himself and descendants as permanent rulers of China. The rule was short however, for in 206 B. C. the *Han* dynasty governed the empire. The first of this family, named Kao, endeavored to repair the ravages made in the field of learning by the Tsin despots.

He caused extensive search to be made in order that the ancient pitch, division of tone, and system of modulation might be discovered. It was partially unavailing, for we learn that though music was established in all its splendor under the subsequent reign of Vow-ti, yet many writers of that era (about 140 B. C.) assert that the art of regulating the heart by means of music, was irretrievably lost, and that it only seemed to inflame the baser passions.

In fact at this time, music was chiefly an adjunct of the theatre, and each day brought forth new comedies, concerts, or ballets. A terrible scandal was created in the reign of Tching-ti (an emperor who reigned shortly after) by that sovereign taking one of his beautiful *corps de ballet*, to wife.

These ballet dancers seem also to have been talented singers, and were of similar station, though far inferior in talents, to the *Hetaræ* of ancient Greece. In the time of the last named ruler, there were found on the bank of a river, sixteen ancient musical stones or *kings*, and the fact that the sovereign esteemed this one of the most glorious events of his reign, shows how earnest and persistent was the endeavor to reclaim the old school of music from oblivion.

Between the years A. D. 8, and 23, many books relative to music were written; the Chinese, however, assert that all of these were founded on a false system and contained many errors. About A. D. 60, the president of the tribunal of rites and music, made great efforts to collect the remains of ancient knowledge, and place music once more upon its old, pure basis. The work written by him was highly esteemed by the literati but unfortunately, the musicians had become used entirely to the newer, and less pure style of music, and were too lazy to care about learning any new modes; therefore all manner of difficulties were placed in the way of Pao-yé, and the reform was unsuccessful.

Tching-ti, A. D. 280, had at his court ten thousand women, who were all proficient singers and players. Ngai-ti, one of his successors, tried to remedy the luxury and effeminacy which had crept into every department of music. He dismissed all his musicians, except those who performed at sacred rites, or in military music (these being countenanced by ancient usage) and all the troupes of singing girls were also broken up. The poor musicians thus thrown out of employment numbered four hundred and forty. The singing girls were yet more numerous.

These reforms seem to have been of short duration, for almost always, after an emperor who enthusiastically attacked these abuses, came one who with equal fervor, protected them.

One sovereign, A. D. 289, had at his palace five thousand actresses, and the fourth successor of the reformer who dismissed his musicians, named Tsin-ou-ti, although a lover of music, was also a great lover of luxury. His greatest delight was to enervate the officials of high rank by inviting them to carousals which he would extend far into the night, and when the censors remonstrated with him on his course, he heard them patiently; he would then invite them to dinner for the same day, and there cause them to drink so copiously that they had to be carried home.*

An emperor who reigned about 503 A. D. banished comedy and music from the palace, and also established the funeral festival in honor of Confucius, in which sacred music played a part.

Tay-tsung, who ascended the throne A. D. 626, was an active and thorough reformer in music as in all other arts which needed his helping hand. In the year 640, he turned his attention, after having brought the empire to a state of peace, to bringing music back to its ancient and pristine

---

* La Fage 69. De Mailla 191.

glory. In pursuance of this design, he ordered that everything relating to ancient music, books as well as instruments, should be sent to his court. An immense quantity of books, fragments, memoirs, old and new instruments, etc., were discovered and collected, which were handed over to a committee of *savans*, whose duty it was to retain the good, reject the bad, and systematize the whole. Much was discovered by this means; books were printed and the art of music received a strong impetus; but still the Chinese held that the full beauty of the ancient art could not be unearthed, perhaps because they could find nothing in it equaling their expectations: but Tay-tsung for his efforts in the matter, was ever after held in the highest esteem by the Chinese, who rank him with the great and good rulers, Hoang-ti, Yao, etc.

Tay-tsung also composed, or caused to be composed, a war dance, accompanied with the appropriate music; it was intended to inspire the soldiers with virtue and courage, and to make them emulate heroes.

Under the emperors who came immediately after, comedy and theatrical representations flourished. The musicians were always kept within the limits of their caste however. A chief comedian once permitted himself to make an allusion to state affairs, in a play; the emperor listened to him with much attention, (the Chinese politeness is such that they will accord the most respectful attention to a person whom they would like to strangle,) but after the performance called the actor aside and told him that he kept his troupe to amuse, not to advise him, and sent the poor fellow into exile.

Another time a very talented musician committed a murder, and was sentenced to death therefor; several officials endeavored to obtain his pardon, and a number of musicians presented a a petition to the emperor acknowledging that the culprit was very guilty and fully deserved his fate, but that his talents in music could not be replaced, and that therefore his life should be spared. The emperor's reply was a worthy one, " you fear damage to the art of music " said he, "but I fear damage to the laws and government of the empire." The sentence was executed. One emperor dared to raise a musician to special rank, and thus defied the strong respect for caste, which existed in China.

Y-tsung, the causer of this great scandal, had in his service a great performer, named Li-ko-ki, who was an especial favorite. One day when Li-ko-ki had composed a specially agreeable song, the emperor, without considering his profession, gave him the post of captain of the guards. It caused an immense excitement among the sticklers for etiquette, for all previous emperors, when they gave office to their musicians, first caused them to renounce their profession, while Li-ko-ki still continued in the practice of music; the emperor however carried his point. Y-tsung also showered other unusual honors upon the members of this profession, for it was his custom to give a dozen festivals each month, when the musical *corps* were allowed to eat at his own table.

In travelling, of which he was very fond, he rarely took along less than five hundred musicians.

Under the last prince of the Tang dynasty there came many disasters upon the Chinese empire, and the successful inroads of the Tartar invaders, were most of all prejudicial to music; at one time the emperor was forced to fly from the capital, his palace was pillaged, and the musical instruments in it, either destroyed, or carried off to Tartary. When peace had been concluded and tranquillity reigned again, there was an earnest effort made to manufacture new instruments, but in doing this, great obstacles had to be surmounted, the models were dispersed or lost, and the official pitch was uncertain. A great search was made for the set of bells which represented the authorized ancient scale, but in vain; large sums were offered to the Tartars if they would make restitution of those which had been carried off at the sacking of the imperial palace, but these savages, after long delays, replied that they could not ascertain what had become of the captured instruments.

Thus another disturbing influence was imported into the Chinese music; but it was still as highly-prized an art as of old, for soon after these calamities came rulers who were passionately devoted to it; Tchowang-song, gave two provinces to a pair of favorite musicians; and a subsequent emperor *(a la Nero)* took to the stage himself, in spite of the horror of his remonstrating censors.

Music and art took a new impetus under the Song dynasty (A. D. 960 to 1279), and very many books were written, on music especially, but alas! there was now so much uncertainty in the field of ancient (and therefore in Chinese eyes correct) music, that the commentators fell into the same pit which engulfed the modern decipherers of ancient Greek music, i. e., they speedily came to all kinds of varying and irreconcilable conclusions. One thing they resolved however, which was that the bells which gave the official scale were not correct; they therefore founded a new set, which were so satisfactory to the emperor and his advisers, that the former ordered his own official bells to be given to the founders for recasting. The musicians were very ill pleased with the new system, although obliged to conform to it, and yet determined that all trace of the ancient scale should not be lost. They managed by connivance with some officials to save a complete set. The bells were indeed removed from the tribunal of music and rites, but instead of being thrown into the furnace, they were with the tacit consent of high authorities, buried in a court-yard of the palace, and long afterward exhumed.

Tsai-yu, one of the later emperors, studied deeply to place music on a secure footing,[*] and it

---

[*] Amiot de la Mus. de Chin, p 83.

is remarkable that his researches into the proportions of tones, led him to the same results that were *afterwards* discovered by the best acousticians of Europe.

Kang-Hi, in the year 1678-9, worked for the art in an extraordinary manner; he founded an academy of music, and made his third son president of the institution; he wrote a work, " The true method of the Ly-lu," in four books, and had a fifth added "*concerning European music.*"* In a proclamation concerning the diminution of the number of court-musicians, Kang-hi says, "Music has power to quiet the heart, and therefore was beloved by our sages. They also could while enjoying themselves at its practice, benefit themselves, because the fundamental principles of government are contained in the art of music. But such a comparison scarcely is suitable to virtuosity. Why, therefore, expend money on it? I approve of the action of Ngai-Ti, (a former emperor) in discharging them."

The knowledge of European music, which this emperor attained, in opposition to all previous custom in China, came through the Jesuit missionary Pereira, a Portuguese by birth; and Grimaldi, a missionary of the Propaganda. He found it (contrary to the custom of the Chinese) quite to his taste.† He was particularly astounded by the ability of Father Pereira to set down in notes, and

---

* Ambros, Gesch, der Musik, p. 27, v. 1.
Ambros, Gesch. d Mus. p. 82.

sing any melody, after a single hearing. He begged his two guests to prepare a work containing the elements of European harmony, and on their completion of it, he had it printed at his palace in a sumptuous manner, and as an especial honor, he had his own name added to it as their coadjutor. He now forced his musicians to learn and to play French, German and Italian music; they did so quite exactly, but most mechanically and with much unwillingness, for it was contrary to all their ideas of art or propriety. Kang-hi saw that the effort would be useless unless he used severe measures in enforcing his reform, and like a wise man he yielded and allowed his performers to return to their own beloved style of music. But the spirit of reform was yet in him, and so far as he was able, he introduced many innovations and many alterations into all departments of Chinese music.

He made a proclamation saying that the old instruments though very good were quite worn out, and that as new ones were necessary, he had prepared a list of the ones required. One of these *instruments*, can scarcely be called a musical one, as it was simply a flag, which was to be displayed during the continuance of the musical performance.

Kang-hi is spoken of with much rapture by the Jesuit missionaries, for he was not only European in his taste for music; he not only tolerated, but greatly favored Christianity, and at one time it was feared by his court, that he was about to embrace that faith. The real secret of his intimacy with the Catholic missionaries, seems to have been only a great desire on his part, to acquire new information.

He was greatly interested in the mechanism of a clavichord, which the fathers brought with them to China, and ordered two of his musicians to take lessons from them, upon the instrument; the pupils made very little progress, as they were rather unwilling students.

It was not only in the emperor's court, at this epoch, that European music began to be known; many persons throughout all the empire, sought to pave the way to Imperial favor by studying the new art. The method of Father Pereira had been sent into each province by the emperor, and the ancient *Li* were for a time eclipsed by the *Do, re, mi,* etc., of the "western barbarians." It might have been a permanent reform, but for the fact that the Chinese had always been accustomed to associate their music in a peculiar manner, with virtue and morality ; each tone represented some moral precept, each species of the eight varieties of sound represented to their mind some high thought or noble virtue; it was this association of ideas, which evoked the eulogies of Confucius, and it was this time-honored custom which prevented European music from obtaining any foothold among them. When, a short time after, Amiot endeavored to ingratiate himself with the Mandarins by means of his music, he failed utterly, through the same cause.

He thus relates his effort: —

"I understood music passably well; I played the traverse flute and the clavichord: I used all these little talents to make myself welcome to the Chinese. On different occasions during the first years of my stay in Pekin, I never failed to endeavor to convince those who heard me, that our music, excelled that of their own country."

It is to be remembered that these were educated persons, able to compare and to judge; persons of the first rank, who honoring the French missionaries with their kindness, came often to their abode to entertain themselves with them, with various matters relative to the sciences or arts cultivated in China.

"The cyclops," "The savages,"* the most beautiful sonatas, the most melodious airs of the flute, none of these made any impression on the Chinese.

"I saw upon their countenances only a cold and vacant look, which announced to me that I had not touched them in the least. One day I asked them how they liked our music, and begged that they would tell me frankly what they thought. They answered in their politest way, that *our melodies were not made for their ears, nor their ears for our melodies*, it was not therefore surprising, they could not find beauties in our melodies, as they could in their own."

"The melodies of our music," said a distinguished doctor (in the service of his majesty,

---

* Pieces for the Clavichord in the style of Rameau

the emperor); the melodies of our music pass from the ear to the heart, and from the heart to the soul. We feel them, and we understand them; those which you have just played, have no such effect upon us. The airs of our ancient music were something quite different; one needed but to hear them, to be ravished with them. Our books give to them the most pompous eulogies; but they tell us at the same time, that we have, in a great measure, lost the excellent method by which the ancients produced such marvellous effects."* It is interesting to place these remarks beside the reiterated opinion of many writers that the Chinese music is not worthy of being called " music " at all; and then to turn to that most proper definition of the art,—" Music is the art of moving the feelings by combinations of sounds."

The same obstacles exist to-day against change in the music of the Chinese, as in the days of Kang-hi.

This emperor, in his later days added to the long list of his musical efforts, a volume treating of dances, and also a collection of the most celebrated ancient songs. The missionary who mentions this latter work,† assures us that he dares not translate it, lest he should be accused of placing the sentiments of the most noble psalms in the mouth of the Chinese.

During Kang-hi's reign the flute became quite fashionable in China, the people becoming

*Amiot. Mus. des Chinois, p. 3.
† Cibot Essai sur les Caracteres Chinois

infatuated with it; Kang-hi himself became proficient in its use, but on finding, later, that he had not benefited himself in any way by its use he gave up the practice.

Young-tching, his successor, published new rules for music and assigned a special music in honor of agriculture and husbandry, which was to be performed each year. He did not take to the Jesuits as kindly as his predecessor, for from A. D. 1724 to 1732 he was busily engaged in expelling them from China.

Khian-long, his son, succeeded him in 1736. There is nothing remarkable in the history of Chinese music from his day to the present time.

Lord Macartney's embassy (1793) took place during the long reign of this emperor. Many persons were attracted to the embassy's rooms by the European band which each evening gave a concert. Among the most assiduous of these visitors was the chief of the emperor's orchestra; charmed with the sound of some of their instruments, yet absolutely refusing to accept of them as a present, he sent several painters to take designs of them on paper. These artists laid clarinets, flutes, bassoons, etc., on immense sheets of paper, on which they traced the exact shape and size of each, while underneath they wrote remarks giving the exact dimensions of each aperture, valve and tube.

The chief announced his determination of making similar instruments from these models, but in different proportions, which he proposed to fix for himself. The result of the experiment is unknown.

The later emperors have all had long reigns, and left music in *statu quo*, the last emperor Hien-fung being only remarkable for his constant drunkenness. Let us now examine more minutely the order of music which has inspired such disgust to European ears, and such rapture to the Chinese from the earliest ages down to the present time

CHAPTER XII.

CHINESE MUSIC AND MUSICAL INSTRUMENTS.

The Chinese have from the very earliest times divided musical sounds into eight classes, and imagined that in order to produce them, nature had formed eight kinds of sonorous bodies. They divided them as follows: —
1. The sound of skin, produced from the tanned skin, or parchment of various animals. 2. The sound of stone. 3. Of metal. 4. Of baked clay. 5. Of silk, used in the form of strings as we use cat-gut, or wire. 6. Of wood, used often in instruments of percussion. 7. Of bamboo, used in flutes. 8. Of calabash, a species of gourd, out of which a peculiarly constructed instrument was manufactured.

Of the skins of animals, many different instruments are made, all of which may be designated under the general name of drums, but the Chinese possess various kinds of drums of all shapes and sizes.* The most ancient variety of these was the *Tou-kou*, which siginifies earth drum, so called because its body was made of baked clay, over each end of which was drawn the skin. An instrument of this description was both fragile

* Amiot de la Mus. de Chin, p. 85.

and unwieldy; its disadvantages soon caused the clay to be replaced by wood, out of which all subsequent drums were made, the size and shape being varied according to the uses for which they were destined. Nothing is said in the ancient writings as to what varieties of wood were used in the manufacture of the earliest drums, but tradition has it, that at first the wood of the cedar and mulberry, as also sandal wood, were the most used.

The Chinese possess eight kinds of drums. 1. The *tsou-kou*, which had the shape of a barrel, and was fixed upon a pole which ran through its body. 2. The Yn-kou, similar to the above, but the body more elongated, and the staff or pole which supported it usually thrust into the earth to keep it firmly in position, while that of the tsou-kou stood upon a cross piece at its base.* 3. A variety of the *tsou-kou* called hinen-kou, of very large size; on each side of this drum is attached a small drum, in shape like a kitchen pot, one of which is to be struck lightly, the other heavily. 4. The kin-kou, another keg-shaped drum mounted upon a pedestal; it is about six feet long, and six feet in diameter. It receives different names according to the way it is decorated; thus, if it bears on its case paintings of storms, it would be called lei-kou; but if it is ornamented with birds of good omen, such as the *foang-hoang*, or white swans, it is called *lou-kou.*†

† Figures 2 and 3, pl. 1, Amiot. des Chin
* Figures 4 and 6, pl. 2. Amiot.

5. The great tao-kou, which is still used to give the signal for the commencement of a song, is about one foot in length and diameter. 6. The little tao-kou, a cross between a drum and a baby's rattle, is about seven inches long, mounted upon a stick, and through the centre of its case a string is passed; at each end of this string are knots; when this drum is played, the performer twirls it about rapidly, the knots fly against the skin, and produce a sort of rattle or drumming. This drum is used to show the completion of a verse or division of any musical composition. It is also used in funeral processions and at commemorative ceremonies.* 7. The *ya-kou*, a small drum which is filled with rice grains. The skin of this drum is not only tanned but is boiled afterwards in pure water. The sound of this instrument is soft and pleasant. 8. The *po-sou* is a drum of cylindrical shape, and is placed upon a small table; it is played sitting; in all other respects it is like the *ya-kou*.

These are the eight varieties of drums known to the Chinese; many of them are still in use; there are also some varieties of military drums which do not differ much from the preceding.

It is customary to cover not only the case, but the faces and sticks of the drums with paintings.

Drums are used in China to give the hour at night, to announce persons desiring audience, at some palaces, and for many other purposes as well as for music. The Chinese also sometimes muffle their drums (in all religious ceremonies which

---

* Figure 7, pl. 2, Amiot

take place in presence of the emperor) effecting this not in our manner, but by covering the instrument with ornamented draperies of cloth, which absorb part of the sound.

OF THE SOUND OF STONE.

The custom of making a systematic use of stone, in music, is peculiarly a Chinese institution. In the *Chouking*, one of the most ancient of Chinese chronicles, we read that already in the almost mythological days of Yao and Chun, the Chinese had observed that certain kinds of stone were adapted to giving out musical sounds, and that these tones occupied the place between the sound of metal and of wood, being less sharp and penetrating than the former, and more sonorous than the latter, and more brilliant and sweet than either.

Even in those days they carved and shaped the stones, in order to extract from them the regular notes of their scale, and made instruments of them which even to-day are used in China, and are named *king*.

These musical stones were highly valued, and received as tribute as early as 2250 B. C. Those found on the surface of the earth, and near the banks of the rivers, were most esteemed, as it was supposed that their exposure gave clearness and purity to their tone.

These stones, called *Yu*, are found near the mountain streams and torrents of Yun-nan. They are of extreme hardness and are polished in the same manner as agate and precious stones. Large specimens are extremely rare; those which Amiot saw at the Imperial palace, were three feet by one foot eight inches in size, but they were considered unique.

Their weight (specific gravity) is also very wonderful, for stones which seem to be not too heavy a burden for one man, require four men to move them.* Those in the palace were of many colors, milk-white, sky-blue, indigo-blue, yellow, orange, pale green, sea-green, red and gray. Those most esteemed were of a single color throughout, though when five colors blended, it was considered a valuable specimen. It may be mentioned in this connection that the number five seems to acquire a mystical significance among the Chinese, for their music has five principal tones, they recognize five elements, five virtues, five senses, five duties, and five principal ceremonies.†

Some of these stones resemble marble, and others seem to be petrifactions of some sort. We are unaware whether those belonging to the emperor have been examined by any recent geologist. The Duke de Chaulnes in the last century, came to the conclusion that the stone was marble, but that its organization differed in some respects from ours; and that iron entered into its composition.

It is very difficult to complete an octave with

* Amiot, Essai sur les pierres sonores.
† L'Abbé Roussier, Annotations sur Amiot

the best of musical stones. In carving and ornamentation they require most skillful manipulation lest the pitch be endangered.

Under the Han dynasty a most harmonious *king* was presented to the emperor. The designs traced upon the stones were not quite satisfactory to that potentate; on endeavoring to alter slightly the fashion of the stones, the pitch of the instrument was irrevocably lost, and its harmony destroyed forever.* The *king* has from time immemorial been played by striking the stones with a stick or mallet of hard wood. The skill of the player is shown in the degree of shading he can impart to the tones, by varying the force of his blows. Of all instruments, the Chinese claim that the *king* blends best with the human voice. The entire Chinese chronicles teem with praises of this peculiar instrument. Confucius was thrown into ecstatic bliss on hearing it for the first time. The musical work entitled *Li-ki* says: "the harmonious sound of the *king* invites the sage to think of the end of life. When he hears it, he thinks of death, and fortifies himself in his love of duty." But this passage refers only to the great *king* made of *Yu* (the finest melodious stones), which was only played on great religious occasions; it is not singular that this instrument should be associated with religious thoughts. There were other kinds of *kings* which were used on lesser occasions. In the imperial palace were several of

---

* The chronicle says "it was mute forever," but this was meant as hyperbole.

smaller size, called *pien-king*, which were composed of sixteen stones each. The *tse-king* consisted of one large stone, and is used to give the pitch to other instruments, to signalize the commencement of a tune, and according to some writers, was anciently used to beat the time throughout a composition.

The shape of the stones is much like a carpenter's square; and if sixteen of these tools were suspended from a clothes horse, the shape at least of the *king* would be attained; but in the most ancient specimens the stones are shaped with much more diversity, fishes, bats, and other quaint forms appearing with much ingenuity in the different pieces. The only modern instrument of similar style to the *king*, which is known to American readers, is the glass-harmonica, where short strips of glass, being struck by a mallet, give out a melodious, but not very manageable tone, and any person performing on the *musical glasses*, not by friction, but by percussion, can give a fair representation of the music of the favorite instrument of China.

OF THE SOUND OF METAL.

Bells have been in China from the earliest ages the most esteemed of instruments. At first their duty was to be a sort of tuning fork; one bell being made for chief or fundamental tone, and eleven others giving the various semitones. These bells were much different from our church and tower bells; they rather resemble large hand bells, but were of somewhat greater weight. The smallest bells were used in an instrument called *Pien-tchoung*, which consisted of sixteen of them, tuned in unison with the sixteen stones of the king. We have already spoken of the efforts made to suppress the bells, and through them, the authentic pitch of Chinese music, by one of the conquering emperors.

OF THE SOUND OF BAKED CLAY.

Of this the Chinese made a deep-toned whistle, with five to seven apertures called *Hiuen*. This was probably the primitive instrument in China, as it is mentioned as already existing before the reign of Hoang-ty, about 2637 B. C. An ancient Chinese Dictionary speaks of the two varieties of these, saying, " the larger hinen should be of the size of a goose egg, the smaller, of that of a hen."

OF THE SOUND OF SILK.

Under this head come all Chinese stringed instruments, for where we use catgut, the celestials use silken cords. Even in the semi-mythical age of Fo-hi, they made a simple instrument by extending threads of silk upon a board of light wood. Little by little the board was shaped to its purpose better; gradually also, the strings were laid with more precision and exactness, and the cords gave out tones deep or high, according to the tension to which they were subjected, or the number of threads of which they were composed; **thus** by insensible degrees came into existence the *kin*, the leading stringed instrument of the Chinese empire. In size, it is larger than all Eastern stringed instruments except the harp, its length being five feet, six inches. It has seven cords which are tuned as follows: —

      do,   re,   fa,   sol,   la,   do,   re,

giving it only five tones. The pentatonic character of this instrument is observable in all Chinese music, and causes a slight resemblance between that music and the Scotch. There are several varieties of the *kin*. The large, medium, and small, only differ in their size, and have each seven cords, but there is a much larger instrument of the same species, which is called the *che*, which has twenty-five strings, and is nine feet long; it is said that in ancient days there were *ches* made which had fifty strings.

Both the *che* and *kin* were, in true Chinese fashion, made to convey numberless morals and symbols. The breezes of Heaven, the four seasons, the five elements, and the universe were all in some manner dragged into the formation of these instruments. The *kin* represented life, the *che* death, and before performing upon either, the player went through certain ceremonies to fit himself for the task, and lighted some perfumed tapers, which were kept burning throughout the performance. To perform on the *kin*, the Chinese held that one must be well advanced in wisdom and sagacity. Of the *che*, there exist four different kinds, the great, medium, small and very small;

all these differ in size but not in their number of strings, each possessing twenty-five. Amiot* found the *che* to be a more agreeable instrument than any known in Europe in his day (1750 circa), as the softer sounds of the silken cords were preferable to the metallic sound of the wires of the clavichord.

We have no instrument in our music which corresponds to the *kin*, or *che;* but the zither if trebled in length, and strung with silk instead of wire would give a very exact idea of this finest of Chinese instruments.

THE SOUND OF WOOD.

The Chinese have from remotest antiquity, used wooden instruments of percussion; it is most natural that the earliest of instruments used by man, should have been of wood, but it is also natural that most nations should have laid aside these primitive and toneless instruments. Not so the Chinese however; their wooden instruments are still used as they were four thousand years ago; for the historians date their invention from the mysterious reign of Fo-hi.

These instruments are the *tchu*, the *ou*, and the *tchung-tou*, all of which celebrate and typify the most profound moral precepts, *a la Chinois*.

The *tchu* is a plain wooden box, about a foot and a half deep, in which a hammer is fastened; by introducing the hand into a small aperture,

---

* De la Mus. des Chin. p. 60.

made for that purpose in the side of the instrument, the hammer is agitated, and swaying from side to side, produces a sort of tattoo on both sides of the box. This scarcely can be called *music* for it is doubtful if the sound is even rhythmic; but it is not the sound alone which captivates the Chinese ear, the symbol attached to it moves the Chinese heart, for the sages assure us that this clatter represents (in some mysterious way) the advantages of the social intercourse of men, and the mutual benefits of society. The *tchu* is placed at the *north-east* of the other instruments and is played at the commencement of a composition.

The *ou* is an image of a sleeping tiger, and is a symbol of the power which man has over all other creatures. It is placed at the *north-west* of the other instruments, and is played at the close of a piece of music. Along the back of this image is a row of pegs; when the instrument is well played, six tones can be extracted from these wooden pegs, but usually the performance is ended by the player running the stick, by which the pegs are struck, swiftly along the whole row, and finishing with a couple of blows upon the tiger's head. This is repeated three times as *finale.*

The *tchung-tou* cannot really be classed among musical instruments, since they are only the wooden plates upon which music was sometimes written; their moral is obvious; they bring back to memory the great invention of communication by means of written characters. But they also participate somewhat in the general clatter produced by the other wooden instruments; they are about fourteen inches long, and one inch wide, are twelve in number, to commemorate the twelve sounds of the scale, and serve to beat the measure of the music, by being struck lightly against the palm of the left hand. The twelve pieces are attached to each other by means of cords.

There is besides, a military instrument of wood (though also scarcely to be classed as musical) which is carved in the form of a fish, and is suspended in front of the general's tent. When any person requires to see that official, he has but to strike this fish with two wooden sticks which are lying near by, and the audience is immediately granted; so greatly have the Chinese reduced language to various musical sounds, that by the mode of striking with the sticks, the applicant intimates, in a general manner, concerning what description of business the audience is requested.

There also exist in China a few other instruments of wood, from which regular series of tones can be produced, and upon which tunes can be played, but these latter seem not to be really Chinese in their origin, and are spoken of by the musical commentators of the country, as "strange instruments which have come into use in China."

THE SOUND OF BAMBOO.

It seems, at first sight, as if this class of instruments should be placed under the head of "wood;" but the Chinese draw a very wide distinction between wood and bamboo, holding the latter in especial esteem, as being of all vegetation, the most useful to man; and they claim that nature in producing it, fitted it especially to the art of music. It is true that it required no great inventive faculty to extract tones from the hollow sticks of bamboo, and it is possible that music drawn from the bamboo was the earliest of the Chinese empire. One of the most famed of instruments made of this reed, is called the *Koan-tsee*. This is simply a set of pan's pipes, arranged according to Chinese tonality; the superior (male) tones, called *yang* being given to one instrument, and the inferior (female) called *yn* to another, so that to have a melody in any modulations performed, two instruments and two musicians were required. This arrangement was too awkward to last forever; finally the two instruments were united in one, and instead of being weakly bound together by cord, as were the twelve pipes of the *koang-tsee*, two strips of thin board held the tubes in place; the number of pipes was also increased from twelve, to sixteen, and the new instrument called the *siao*.*

Of course the Chinese possess flutes, as well as other instruments of bamboo. The *yo* and *ty* are in some respects similar to our flutes, save that they have usually but three holes, and the tones have therefore to be produced by a more skillful use of the breath than is required on the European

---

*There are two kinds of *siao*, the great and the small. The latter has the same number of tubes, but pitched an octave higher.

flute. An instrument of the flute family the use of which has become somewhat obsolete, is the *tche*. This is different from all other flutes, and is now but little played in China. The *embouchure* is exactly in the middle, both ends are stopped, and on each side of the *embouchure* are three holes. It was considered the most difficult of all flutes to play.

THE SOUND OF CALABASH.

The calabash is a gourd of pumpkin shape, but somewhat smaller. In the instrument which we are about to describe, we shall see that the calabash (called *pao* by the Chinese) really emits no sound, but serves only as an air reservoir for one of the most wonderful instruments of ancient times. The *cheng*, which is the only instrument in which the calabash is used, is in fact a *portable organ*, and when we consider that this intricate instrument was invented about four thousand years ago, we are lost in astonishment that the invention did not lead to greater results; yet the Chinese have frequently, in other sciences as well, advanced to the threshold of great discoveries.

We will not detail to the reader, all the legends, symbols, and mythology attached to the *cheng;* suffice it to say that animal, mineral and vegetable nature is represented by it, and that to each part of it is appended some mystical meaning. The gourd is pierced and cleaned, and an aperture made for the air to enter, then the ends of from thirteen to twenty-four pipes of bamboo are inserted into a many holes cut in the gourd; each of these pipes contains in it a tongue of copper or gold, the vibration of which causes the sound; beneath this is a hole cut in the bamboo, through which aperture the air rushes without giving any sound, but when the hole is stopped by pressing a finger upon it, the air having no other outlet, is forced up the pipe, and striking the metallic tongue, gives out an agreeable reed sound. A curved mouth-piece through which the performer is to blow, is introduced at the centre of the gourd. The *cheng* contains all the elements of the reed organ, and it would be a simple matter to produce harmonies with it, and yet with this instrument in the world for four thousand years, it remained for moderns (comparatively speaking,) to discover the art of combining different sounds; but the invention of so well-conceived a reed instrument in such remote ages, certainly entitles the ancient Chinese to the utmost respect of their unconscious imitators, the Europeans.

MISCELLANEOUS INSTRUMENTS.

There exist in China, some instruments which are not classed with either of the above eight kinds of tone. These we have thought best to group under the head of "miscellaneous," though they are quite as important as any of the preceding, except perhaps, the *king*, *cheng*, and *kin*. The Chinese have long possessed a peculiar variety of fiddle, which at first appearance much resembles a mallet with cords stretched from the head to the handle; but the head of this primitive fiddle is hollow, and holds a sounding board, though a very small one, of gazelle's skin. The sounds drawn from this oriental fiddle are said to set one's teeth on edge; it is said to be the most execrable of all Chinese instruments. The invention of this fiddle cannot be ascribed to the Chinese, as it probably came from India originally. There also exist several Chinese instruments of a kind much resembling our guitars or banjos. The number of strings on these are variable.*

From remote antiquity, the Chinese have understood the ductility of metal, and it is not surprising that the trumpet is, with them, one of the oldest of instruments. These trumpets are made of all sizes and most peculiar shapes.† It appears that they are intended to give but two tones each, although being made of all sizes, a complete scale can be arranged by collecting ten or twelve of them. The music of them (as with the ancient Greeks) is judged only by the degree of loudness with which it is given, and even when several play together, there is no attempt at harmony, but each trumpeter repeats his two notes with vigor and persistency; the result is said to be most distressing to European ears. Yet it is possible to extract beautiful music even from single-toned trumpets, for in Russia, most exquisite melodies are rendered by bands of trumpeters, each of whom performs but one

* Fetis Hist. Gen de la Mus. VI. 1, p. 66-67.
† Fetis, p. 73

note, in the same manner as troupes of bell-ringers give whole pieces of music with small hand bells.

Tom-toms and gongs also appear frequently in the music of the empire; these are chiefly used to keep the time of the orchestra; there is also an instrument analogous to these, which consists of a series of metal basins, (usually of copper) from eight to ten in number, set in a frame. The whole instrument looks not unlike a cooking range with all its utensils. These basins are struck with a mallet, and produce sounds similar to, but less harsh than the gongs. The name of this unique apparatus is *yin-lo*.

THE SOUND OF THE VOICE.

Singular to relate, the Chinese have in their classification of eight musical sounds, utterly omitted to make any mention of the sound of the human voice. In all their great ceremonies, such as hymns of praise to Heaven, and commemoration of the ancestors, songs are used, but never, on these occasions are female voices allowed. In fact, the female, in music, occupies about the same position in China, as she once did in ancient Greece; the better class of respectable matrons do not study any art whatever; and the less respectable and the slaves, are allowed to perfect themselves in many arts of pleasing, among which a study of the lower branches of music, as well as a certain degree of general education is included. A slave is far more marketable with musical talents than without. But women always participated in orchestral music, and in a manner rather astonishing to us; they sometimes played the wind instruments. The singular custom of allowing the weaker sex to play the part requiring the strongest lungs was quite universal among ancient nations, and the Chinese may be regarded as a nation who have kept their ancient usages almost intact. It is seldom however, that women assist in any concerts whatever; the instrumental playing as well as the singing being almost always wholly rendered by men.

Few travellers have heard a musical Chinese lady sing, and those who have enjoyed this rare event, say it is the most torturing of all Chinese music; from the *nose* and throat issue the most droning and hideous sounds, and they seem to pile Ossa upon Pelion in the way of unnatural tones.

Although the female voice is therefore lacking in the concerted music of this singular people, the parts sometimes run very high for male voice and the singers for these parts are procured in the same manner in which the papal choir in the last century, procured its highest male voices.*

Of the divisions of the vocal parts in singing, very little is as yet known, although many books must exist upon the subject, which have hitherto been inaccessible to foreigners. The natural voice of the Chinese is rather high, and very high tenors are not at all rare in the empire.

* " Les Chinois ont remplacé les voix des femmes par celles des casrats Les chirurgiens Chinois sont arriveés a pratiquer l'operation avec une addresse singuliere et presque sans souffrance pour le sujet." La Fage, Mus. des Chin, p. 150

The voice in China is trained to much flexibility by the exigencies of the language, for the Chinese is in one sense, the most musical of languages, as a word acquires half a dozen different significations according to the pitch of voice, or inflection with which it is pronounced.

The number of different words in the whole Chinese tongue does not exceed three hundred and fifty; all the additional ones, are simply variations of these by lowering, or raising the voice. This leads the foreigner into endless complications and misunderstandings; for example, the word *tchu* pronounced clearly with the vowel of medium length, means "master," but by extending the vowel a trifle it signifies "hog;" it also means "column," and "cookery." The syllable "*po*" has eleven different meanings— "glass," "boil," "captive," "prepare, etc., each of which must be pronounced with a different pitch and inflection.* Among the original words are some which decidedly are taken from nature, such as " *tchung*,"—" bell," " *miaou*,"—" cat," but these are very few.

Some authors have endeavored to show from these facts, that the Chinese is in all respects a musical language, but this can hardly be conceded, for the inflections spoken of, are so slight as to escape the European ear, which surely would not be the case if they were really musical notes, since we have seen that Father Pereire, in the last century, was able to note down at first

---

*La Fage, Mus. des Chin. p. 241.

, and imitate any Chinese song. The
in conversation give the voice a flute-like
but this has scarcely arisen from any
musical quality in the language itself

CHAPTER XII.

CHINESE MUSICAL COMPOSITIONS AND CEREMONIES.

The most ancient music with the Chinese as with all people, seems to have consisted of hymns to the Deity, rendering thanks to Him for the benefits given to man in the various departments of labor. These were divided according to the class which used them, into agricultural, military, piscatorial, etc. Very soon after these, there came into existence that reverential ceremony in memory of the ancestors, which is so characteristically Chinese, and which became, of all their festivals, the most important and the most musical.

This ceremonial as conducted by the emperor is as follows. In the vestibule of the hall are retainers who bear a particular kind of standards, which show that the coming of the sovereign is expected. Here also are seen bells, drums, and musicians, as well as officers of the guards, all standing in symmetrical figure, and motionless in their position. On entering the hall one sees, right and left, the performers on the *cheng* and *king*, and the minor instruments, all arranged in their proper order. In the middle are placed the dancers, in uniform and each holding in hand the instrument which they are to use in their evolutions. Near the end are placed the players of the *che* and *kin* as well as the performers on the style of drum called the *po-sou*, and the singers. Finally, at the lower end of the hall are seen the representations of the ancestors themselves, either in the form of portraits, or of simple tablets bearing the name of each. Before these is a table on which stand flowers and libations. Each performer and instrument is placed in an allotted position. For example, the bell is at the south-west, the *cheng* at the north-west, the drum at the south-east, the flute at the north-east, and the table at the south; and this arrangement is never departed from.

When the signal announcing the approach of the emperor is heard, the singers and musicians, slowly and with great majesty, begin the hymn of honor, while the emperor, with stately and dignified tread, advances to the table at the south of the hall.* It is a moment of holy awe (somewhat akin to the instant when the Host is elevated in Catholic churches) for the spirits of the departed are supposed at this time to come down from Heaven to their descendants. We give here an English paraphrase of the words of part of this hymn, which we have translated from the version of Father Amiot.

---

* Amiot Mus. des Chinois, p. 179.

Hymn to the Ancestors.*

When'er I think of you
Oh ancestors so great,
Then to the highest Heaven
My soul I elevate.
There in th' immensity
Of the eternal springs
Of Fame which cannot die
And constant happiness
Are your immortal souls.
The vision transport brings
Your valor has reward
Your virtues Heaven doth bless
Around your joyous souls
Each new delight it flings.
Ineffable your joy
Your constant happiness.
If I in spite of faults
And of insufficience
Am called on by the high
Decrees of Providence,
To fill upon the Earth
The very highest place
'Tis but because I am
Descendant of your race.
Although I never may
In your great footsteps move
Yet I will care display
Throughout my life's high course
That every act of mine
Shall to descendants prove
That I lived not in vain
And need not feel remorse.

*In singing this the chorus speaks in the name of the emperor.

In giving this, necessarily weak, translation of the opening part of the hymn, we have endeavored to preserve the short Iambics of the Chinese version; but in the Chinese there are only eight lines to the first division, therefore four lines of the translation correspond to one of the original. After the chorus has sung as far as this, which is only an exordium, or manner of worthily preparing for the following exercises, the emperor prostrates himself three times, touching his forehead to the earth each time, and then taking the libations, offers them up to the departed: meanwhile the chorus sing the second part of the hymn, still in the name of the emperor.* In this he again alludes *per* chorus, to his noble descent, and thanks them for leaving their abode of bliss to visit him, and humbly prostrated, begs to render homage to them, and entreats that they will accept the libations offered, as a testimonial of profound respect and perfect love.† After offering these, the emperor prostrates himself nine times to the earth, and then resumes his position in front of the table, while the chorus sing the third part of the hymn. During this final division of the music, the spirits which descended at the first part are supposed to be reascending to Heaven. In the third part the emperor (still by proxy) states how mean and pitiful he feels, after such illustrious predecessors, and tells how heavy

---

* Amiot des Chin, p. 180.

† The offerings are viands, libations, and perfumes, the latter being burnt as incense by the emperor.

the burdens of state are to him, and thanks his ancestors for their spiritual assistance. He concludes with the statement that he can do very little to testify his appreciation of all their benefits, but what he is able to do he has done.

"Three times with respect, have I offered the triple sacrifice; not being able to do more, my vows are satisfied." The hymn being finished, the emperor retires with his ministers and *cortege* in the same order in which they entered the hall. The music continues until he has reached his own apartments. Dancers participate in this ceremony and are sumptuously clad and really assume a *role* of much importance. As with the ancient Greeks and Romans, they are not to be thought of as being jumpers or twirlers; they express by their motions the sentiments which actuate the emperor as he eulogizes his ancestors, expresses his own unworthiness, his gratitude, pride, and other emotions. The music of this august ceremonial, is entirely written in whole notes, without any change of rhythm whatever. It is rather monotonous than distressing to our ears.

This is not the case with other vocal compositions of the Chinese; nearly all travellers agree in saying that their music, in this branch especially, resembles far more the cries of the nocturnal cat than the human voice. The composers seem to have an aversion to progression by degrees, in their songs, and a decided *penchant* for long skips. We do not intend a slur upon the Scotch music when we say that there are points of resemblance between the Chinese music and the former. Some Chinese airs (given by Irwin and Barrow*) show this resemblance startlingly. Although the Chinese understand the division of the chromatic scale perfectly well, yet they never use it; five tones are all they ordinarily employ; these are

FA, SOL, LA, DO, RE,

omitting even the semitone of our diatonic scale. Some of their most eminent theorists have maintained that the notes pienkoung (si) and pienche (mi) are as useless to music as a sixth finger would be to the hand.

It will be observed that the semitone progression is not used in China, and though known, is universally proscribed and avoided; it is this which occasions the peculiarities of Chinese music. On this subject we cannot refrain from re-quoting an article on Chinese music, which appeared in the "China Mail," a Hong-Kong newspaper, in 1845.†

"One possessed of a musical ear, and at all conversant with the musical art, cannot fail, on his arrival in this country, to be struck with the peculiarities of what is esteemed music here. He notices at once, that the characteristics of western melody, are almost wholly wanting. Nearly every note seems out of place, and there is neither beginning, middle nor end, to the airs he listens to. Instead of a theme which is developed and embellished by the whole performance, he hears a hurry-skurry of notes, appar-

---

*Copied by Ambros, in Gesch d mus. v. 1, p. 34-5

† Quoted by Fetis, Hist. Gen. de la Mus v. 1, p. 62.

antly flung together without link or **affinity**; and even the confusion of sounds to make it worse, instead of finishing in a quiescing cadence, passes beyond what is looked for as the last note, and sometimes ends with what we should call a **flatted keynote**, leaving the listeners in a most uncomfortable state of suspense and uncertainty as to what may follow. For my own part, I have not been able as yet to discover whether the Chinese recognise such a thing as a keynote among the parts of song, or whether their composers begin, continue, and end their tunes *ad libitum*."

We have inserted the above that the reader may judge how strongly the music distresses the musical European at first hearing; but it is also not to be forgotten that the Eastern, (Hindoo and Arabian) music had a similar effect upon persons who a year later were obliged to acknowledge that they had begun to find beauty, and take pleasure in it.

Of other court musical ceremonies, the emperor's birthday, the harvest sacrifice, the feast of agriculture, and the fifteenth day of the first moon, are the most important. The first occasion is described by Lord Macartney, who heard it on the 17th of September, 1793. It began with a slow majestic sound of deep-toned bells and muffled drums, in the distance. This impressive music was occasionally interrupted by sudden pauses; with equal suddenness the whole force of singers and instrumentalists would burst out with their utmost strength, while the entire court bowed their faces to the earth as often as the refrain was sung:—"Bow down your heads ye inhabitants of the earth, bow down your heads before the great Kien-long."

The emperor was not visible during these ceremonies.

Among the secular pieces, collected by Amiot, is one which demands especial notice; it is an instrumental representation of a battle. It will be recollected that fifty years ago, many popular European compositions took this shape. "The battle of Navarino," "the battle of Prague," "Waterloo," etc., were the out-crops of this mania: the Chinese certainly have better instruments than we had, wherewith to represent the din of combat.

In the accompaniment of songs, the Chinese seem to stand, as regards their harmony, about where Europe stood in the middle ages, for they use as sole and only harmony, when playing on the *kin,* a succession of *fourths and fifths.**

The constant use of instruments of percussion, in slow and monotonous songs, is one of the most tiresome institutions of the Chinese music; almost all the tunes are taken at an *andante* or *adagio* pace, and it is but just to say, that the Chinese chiefly dislike European music because it is often played quickly.

"To what purpose" they ask, "should one dance and hurry in this manner, and how can such

---

* Amiot, p. 171.

things penetrate to the soul? With us" they add proudly, "all is done calmly, and without precipitation.*"

It must be acknowledged, that the Chinese love, and take pride in music, that is, in their own kind. In every great state ceremony, in theatres, in religion, it everywhere plays the leading *role.*

One of the nine tribunals which have charge of the general affairs of the empire, is charged with the care of music, rites, and ceremonies; and the mandarins of music are considered of much higher rank than the mandarins of mathematics, and have their college in the enclosure of the imperial palace.

The fondness for the art is apparent in all classes, and music is used on almost every occasion of festivity, high or low. The streets of the cities are full of peripatetic musicians, who earn their living by catering to the general public, somewhat as the organ grinders do with us.

The feast of lanterns is the greatest of all popular Chinese festivals; it takes place on the fifteenth day of the first moon, and corresponds to a New Year's feast. On this occasion every part of the immense cities of the empire glows with the light of innumerable lanterns, while fire-works and decorations are seen on all sides. In the streets are seen large *Lantern Theatres,* that is to say, edifices made of paper; on the inside, which is brightly illuminated, is a stage whereon actors and singers give plays and con-

* La Fage, des Chinois, p. 269.

certs. Another great festival, where music plays a leading part, takes place on the fifteenth day of the eighth moon. On this evening the Chinese imagine that a *hare* is seen in the moon, and to the sound of many instruments, the entire population turn out to look at it. It is customary for friends to send each other cakes, on which the figure of a hare is moulded, in sugar. Concerts are an important accessory to this festival with both rich and poor; the former make every effort to secure the best singers and performers for their entertainment on this holiday; the latter, not being able to have the more delicate instruments content themselves with a clatter of basins, pots and frying-pans, and make with these a sort of burlesque concert.

At each full moon there takes place a festival in which gongs and cannons rather than musical instruments are heard. Besides these festivals which are celebrated throughout the empire, there are also local ones, which are numberless. The richest class generally keep their private troupe of musicians, whom they own almost as slaves. Often also they educate young children of both sexes, in the musical art with the utmost care, in order that when grown up they may swell the ranks of their musical retinue. Among these are often special artists whom they will not allow to appear on ordinary occasions, but reserve to perform before their own family, or intimate friends to whom they wish to show especial honor: at such times, the ordinary performers are sent away.

CURIOSITIES OF MUSIC.

Among the strolling musicians, there are many who make their living by going to private festivals of the middle classes, such as weddings, birthdays, and other rejoicings, even when uninvited; these are similar to our ball room musicians, but also bear some resemblance to the itinerant performers of early Eastern nations. In Poland there still exists a similar class.

For the poorer class, there are also, numerous blind musicians, who travel from house to house, sometimes in bands, sometimes alone. We have already compared these to our own organ-grinders, but they differ from them in one particular; they do not rely so much upon making music indiscriminately, but go, with much tact, to those places where their services are likely to be required.

In China the custom of celebrating the birthday anniversary is universal; these wandering minstrels recollect the date of the birth of each individual for miles around, with unerring exactness, and when a birthday *fete* occurs in any family, they may calculate with some degree of certainty that the music will come without being sent for.

There are other occasions, where these shrewd disciples of the muses can turn an honest penny; if a skillful physician has saved the life of the wife or child of some rich man no higher compliment can be given to him (besides his fee) by the grateful nabob, than to invite him to a great feast, and to send an escort of eight musicians to convey him thither, besides bringing him numerous presents.

Music is employed at funerals, but the friends of the deceased, are not allowed to perform it; for months after, etiquette forbids their touching any musical instruments.

The mourning for a parent, or grandparent is very strict and protracted. In China filial love and obedience are the virtues most insisted upon. If the descendants give forth any musical sounds at all it is only to howl dismally a chant respecting the virtues of the defunct; there are many of these compositions, or "lamentations" in existence, of which the poetry is by no means despicable. When the funeral ceremony is taking place, some trumpets and a drum placed at the door, announce the arrival of visitors who come with their condolences to the afflicted family. After the body is buried with the ancestors, the *bonzes*, (Chinese priests) chant the office of the dead, for nine days, and in the procession itself drums, trumpets, tam tams, flutes, etc., play a discordant dirge.

We have already mentioned the wooden fish suspended at the tent door of military commanders to summon them to audiences concerning public and private affairs. Mandarins have, in like manner, a drum in the outer hall of their palaces, by means of which they can be summoned to give audience to any applicant; they are obliged to give immediate attention to the complaint of any person beating the drum, but woe to the audacious drummer who does not have some very especial wrong to complain of; he is immediately soundly bastinadoed.

At eclipses of the moon, the Chinese use their musical instruments in a purposely hideous manner. This is done to frighten away the dragon which is supposed to be eating up the orb of night. Instruments of percussion are chiefly used on this occasion. The same instruments (i. e. gongs, drums, trumpets and tam-tams) are used to aid the marching of the army.

The *musical language* such as we use in directing the movements of cavalry and artillery, is much more extended, though differently used in China; such musical signals are used in commanding civil as well as military personages. Various trades have their especial songs also, which they sing at their work.

But the music of China, although extending into every department of social and official life, is totally incapable of any advancement. Musical martinets are continually exclaiming against the changes in style of composition, which innovators are constantly introducing into *our* art,* but it is these changes which give the surest signs of real life and intrinsic merit to modern music.

In China, precisely as formerly in ancient Egypt, no such changes are possible; the music for each and every event is as carefully mapped

---

* First it was Haydn, then Handel, then Mozart, then Beethoven and to-day Wagner (a few years ago, Schumann) whose bold eagle-flights dismayed the more timid owls.

out and adhered to, as is the cut of the garments, or the exchange of civilities among this precise people.*

If ever change takes place in their musical system, it will assuredly be a gravitation towards the European, as they have in a certain measure a comprehension, theoretically at least, of our system of semi-tones, but could by no means conceive of, and accurately produce the third and quarter tones of Indian music. We have already related the ineffectual movement towards western style, made in the last century; during the embassy of 1793, Macartney observed many indications of inclination for our system, such as the use of the violin,† the notation of music upon ruled paper, and interest in the band concerts given at his rooms each evening. He also found in the emperor's palace at *Yuen min-yuen*, an English musical clock, made by Geo. Clarke, Leadenhall Street, London, which played many selections from the "Beggar's Opera."‡ It is certainly not too venturesome to predict, in spite of the jarring of their music upon us, that they may yet develop a taste for some of the coarser branches of ours.

*"Among the Chinese themselves, society chiefly consists of certain stated forms, and expressions, a calm, equal, cold deportment, hypocritical attentions, and hyperbolical professions." Barrow's Life of Macartney, v. 2, p. 414. The curious reader will also find a very full description of Chinese social etiquette, in the " *Description de la Chine*," by Pere Du Halde, pages 115 to 154, vol. 2. Rules are given for set formalities, even on the slightest occasions, such as, the opening of a conversation when visiting (p. 126), the exit, the rising from table after meals, (135), etc., etc. It is possible, that in the customs of this people, we may see a living reproduction of some traits of the ancient Egyptians ' Barrow's life of Macartney, v 2, p. 231. ‡ Ibid, v. 2, p. 217

CHAPTER XVI.

THE CHINESE THEATRE AND DANCES.

Although the Chinese are passionately fond of plays, yet they do not possess a good fixed theatre in their chief cities; for those edifices which are regularly used for this purpose are never of a good class, and many of them are even considered disreputable. The cream of the theatrical troupes are reserved for private entertainments; when a number of people of the middle class desire a comedy, they club together and engage a troupe. The upper classes, as already stated, have always their private comedy company. They have also their private halls for dramatic representations.

The Chinese, have like ourselves, Comedies, Tragedies, Farces, Ballets, etc., and the music attached to them is always of the style of the play. There is an excellent description of the ceremonies and social etiquette used at a private dramatic entertainment, given by Du Halde.* He says, . . . "It was then, four or five of the principal comedians were seen entering the hall, in rich costumes; they made a profound bow all together, and struck the earth four times with their forehead. . . . They arose and their chief

---

*Desc. de la Chine. T. II. p. 132. In La Fage's quotation the page is given as 112, probably an oversight, or a later edition.

addressing one of the principal guests, presented to him a book composed of long tablets, on which were written, in golden letters, the names of fifty or sixty comedies, which they knew by heart, and any of which they were ready to perform on the spot if desired; from this book they begged the guest to make a choice. The guest excused himself and handed the volume politely to a second guest, with a sign of invitation; the second guest passed it to the third with the same ceremonies, the third to the fourth, etc. All excused themselves, and finally the book was returned to the comedian, who yielded at last, opened the book, and ran his eye over the list a moment, and then decided upon a comedy which he thought would prove agreeable to all the company. Should there be any inconvenience in producing any particular play, the comedian-in-chief is expected to announce it; one of these inconveniences would be, for example, that one of the chief characters of the play bore a name similar to that of one of the guests. After the choice the comedian shows to the guests the name of the play which he has chosen, and each one signifies by a nod of the head, his approval. The representation begins with some music which is essentially Chinese and noisy. It is performed with metal basins, drums flutes, fifes, and trumpets. The play is often performed at a banquet, and after the guests have finished their meal, the comedians take their places at the table; after a short refreshment the guests are recalled and the play proceeded with.

or a new farce is chosen and performed as dessert."

Many of the plays are not destitute of poetry and plot. It may not be uninteresting to give a short sketch of the style of incidents woven into their plays by Chinese authors.

The following is an outline of the plot of a play performed before the English embassy, Lord Macartney's, in the latter part of the last century; it was given in a private theatre, by a private troupe.

"An emperor of China and his empress are living in supreme felicity, when on a sudden his subjects revolt. A civil war ensues, battles are fought; and at last, the arch-rebel, who is a general of cavalry, overcomes his sovereign, kills him with his own hand, and routs the imperial army.

The captive empress then appears upon the stage, in all the agonies of despair, naturally resulting from the loss of her husband, and her dignity, as well as the apprehension of that of her honor. Whilst she is tearing her hair, and rending the skies with her complaints, the conqueror enters, approaches her with respect, addresses her in a gentle tone, soothes her sorrows with his compassion, talks of love and adoration, and like Ricnard the Third with Lady Anne, in Shakespeare, prevails, in less than half an hour, on the Chinese princess to dry up her tears, to forget her ueceased consort, and to yield to a consoling wooer. The piece concludes with a wedding and a grand procession."*

* Account of Lord Macartney's embassy, by Sir George Staunton.

Engel, who quotes the above plot, well says* "how interesting would it be to the student of national music, to possess an exact notation of the music belonging to this scene '(the empress complaints)' and to ascertain in what manner the intense emotions and vehement passions represented are expressed in the Chinese musical compositions."

The above plot is curious in its Shakespearian resemblance, and seems to be a drama of the superior order, for Lord Macartney was shown the highest and best side of Chinese life and art; the comedies of the people are less refined and of broader touches. We give as companion piece to the above, a comedy plot which is a favorite one with Chinese authors as well as the public.

The emperor Vouti, having lost one of his wives, whom he tenderly loved, had recourse to a celebrated magician, who assured him that his spouse was not dead as supposed, for she had bought of him the elixir of immortality; she still existed, but lived chiefly in the moon from whence the magician promised he could cause her to descend as often as desired. The emperor caused to be erected, under the superintendence of the magician, a very high tower, to facilitate her descent; he also often assisted at the incantations of the wizard, but as the fair immortal did not respond, the imposter, fearing the anger of his royal master, invented a new stratagem to avert this unpleasant conclusion. He wrote upon

* Musical Myths and Facts, vol. 2, p. 168.

a piece of silk a counterfeit letter from the dear defunct, giving various pretended reasons as to why she could not return personally to the royal lover; this letter is given by the sorcerer to a cow, who is then led by him to the emperor to whom he confesses that some involuntary crime has, for the present, interrupted his intercourse and influence with the immortal beings, but that in the stomach of the cow he has perceived something; Vouti commands that the animal be opened on the spot, and the silken message is discovered; the magician is already enjoying his triumph when it is perceived that the characters of the communication are in his own handwriting. He is at once condemned to death, and the emperor thenceforth renounces magicians, immortal elixirs, etc., etc.*

It is well known that the Chinese often give, on the stage, a representation of the life of the hero of the play from early infancy (sometimes even *from birth*) to death, and these representations last weeks in their performance; every action being done deliberately; for example, if a performer smokes a pipe, he does not give a whiff or two and then go on with the action, but calmly and placidly smokes it out to the last puff.

Fairy spectacles, the Chinese also possess, in which Genii appear and disappear, as well as birds and beasts endowed with the power of speech. Their farces are of a much broader character, and often in these, the clownish, awk-

*La Page Mus. des Chinois T. 1. p. 302

ward character is a European or an American; they heartily enjoy all his mishaps, even his manner of lifting his hat and bowing, being held up to ridicule; it is very much the same kind of pleasure as we "western barbarians" enjoy in seeing such farces as "*Ici on parle Francais*" or "The Perplexed Dutchman," where the habits of a Frenchman, and German, are the mirth-provoking element; or of a piece with the character of Sir Hugh Evans and Dr. Caius, in Shakespeare's "Merry Wives of Windsor."

There is another point of resemblance in Shakespeare, to the Chinese drama: his following of the life of Henry VI. so closely and extensively (through three parts) suggests the more extensive life-history-dramas of the celestial empire. But the Chinese also give the "outside barbarians" a thrust, *au serieux;* for in their plays the devil often appears, dressed as a European.

In the music of their dramas, the Chinese are decidedly Wagnerian, for not only do they use a great many loud instruments (chiefly of percussion) but they illustrate with them the action of the drama; when an actor enters into a combat at arms, the orchestra pound away at their instruments with redoubled vigor. The characters often sing long *arias* to the accompaniment of these voice-drowning instruments.* There is much spoken action as well as song in these dramas, which therefore approach more nearly to our *vaudevilles* than any thing else.

* Leit motiven however the Chinese have not!!

Choruses are few in Chinese pieces, but sometimes the air is sung by many voices, in order to emphasize it, and make it more plainly perceptible above the racket of the orchestra.

The Chinese have also many tragedies and comedies wherein no music whatever is employed. The actors in these, assuming the ordinary conversational tone.

Conjugal infelicity and infidelity, form a staple plot with these, and the same inappropriate and ludicrous entering into detail is apparent in them.*

Movable scenes are not used, and the most infantile devices are used when a rapid change is necessary; a general having to depart on a distant expedition, mounts a hobby horse, or even a cane, and using a small whip with one hand, imitates riding, (three or four times around the theatre being sufficient) and then, announcing that he has arrived at his destination, goes on with his speeches without any embarrassment. This is but one example of the many where the dramatists draw heavily upon the imagination of their audiences.

The actor on entering (in the play) begins by announcing his name and telling the audience why and wherefore he has come; this is done to simplify the following of the action, as in some dramas there are hosts of characters and one player often assumes many *roles.*

Such puerility is caused partly by the small size of the stages, which would not admit a host of performers, and partly by the fact that many of

* De Guignes Voyage a Peking v. 2, p. 325.

The characters in a Chinese play are comparatively unimportant, appearing once, and then vanishing forever; in fact at the end of some of the Chinese dramas, one is considerably mystified as to the fate of many of the characters, as the author, unlike the European and American dramatists, who make everybody (except the villain) happy in the last act, only deems it necessary to follow out closely the career of his hero and heroine, and they being once dead, the other characters are allowed to wind up in a very sudden and, to us, very unsatisfactory manner. The musical part of these dramas is often quite long, and whenever the actor desires to express much feeling, he falls into music. Sometimes it is introduced in a most unnatural manner; in one tragedy, a wife having murdered her husband is sentenced to be *flayed alive;* after the execution of the sentence, she returns to the stage wholly bereft of her skin, (this is depicted with true Chinese realistic effect, the body of the performer being painted in exact imitation of nature in such a hideous plight) and she then and there sings a song to excite the pity of the infernal spirits. The song is full of screeches and howls, and lasts half an hour.* Let us not be too hasty in smiling at such absurd stage effects; there is an opera still performed on our own stage, where an innocent Jewess is boiled in oil, as *finale,* and as to the inappropriateness of a long song, under such circumstances, there is a

---

*It would however, be as unjust to judge average Chinese plays by this one instance as to judge of the Shakesperian drama by "Titus Andronicus."

long chorus in a French opera of the last century, where the mayor of the village having fallen into the water, the anxious choristers sing for many minutes, that " he will be drowned unless he is speedily helped out;" decidedly we must not smile too broadly at the Chinese, as yet.

Sir John Barrow* speaks of the theatre, which he visited, as a mere " Shed of Bamboo." He says: " In the farther division of the building, a party of comedians were engaged in the midst of an historical drama, when we entered; but on our being seated they broke off, and coming forward, made before us an obeisance of nine genuflexions and prostrations, after which they returned to their labors, keeping up an incessant noise and bustle during our stay. The heat of the day, the thermometer standing at eighty-one degrees, in the open air, and at least ten degrees higher in the building, the crowds that thronged to see the strangers [this was in 1792, when Europeans were great rarities in China] the horrible crash of the gongs, kettle drums, trumpets, and squalling flutes, were so stunning and oppressive that nothing but the novelty of the scene could possibly have detained us a moment."

"The most entertaining, as well as the least noisy part of the theatrical exhibition, was a sort of interlude, performed by three young women, for the amusement it would seem of the principal actress, who sat as a spectator, in the dress and character of some ancient queen, whilst an old

---

* Voyage to Cochin China, p. 295.

eunuch, very whimsically dressed, played his antic tricks like a scaramouch, or buffoon in a Harlequin entertainment."

"The dialogue in this part, differed entirely from the querulous and nearly monotonous recitation of the Chinese, being light and comic, and occasionally interrupted by cheerful airs, which generally concluded with a chorus. These airs rude and unpolished as they were, appeared to be regular compositions, and were sung in exactly measured time. One in particular attracted our attention, whose slow, melancholy movement breathed the kind of plaintiveness so peculiar to the native airs of the Scotch, to which indeed it bore a close resemblance." [We have before spoken of this resemblance, which proceeds from both scales, Chinese and Scotch, being pentatonic, or five toned.] "The voices of the women are shrill and warbling, but some of their cadences were not without melody. The instruments at each pause gave a few short flourishes, till the music gradually increased in loudness by the swelling and deafening gong. Knowing nothing of the language we were of course as ignorant of the subject as the majority of an English audience is at an Italian opera." Thus speaks Barrow of his first impressions of a Chinese theatre, but he probably fell into two errors; the *women*, whom he mentions were in all likelihood, eunuchs; and the theatre itself, being public, was of inferior style to those private establishments which are the pride of the rich mandarin class.

It is singular, however, that the noise of the gong, tamtam, trumpet, etc., are inseparable from all Chinese dramatic performances: although the noise is deafening, and the voices of the actors are sometimes drowned in spite of their shouting themselves hoarse, yet this pandemonium only gives tranquil delight to the Chinese spectator whether he be of high or low class. It is so extraordinary a fact that physiologists and anatomists have endeavored to prove that the cause is due to a peculiar formation of the Chinese ear.*

Certain it is that the Chinese are so passionately fond of the drama, that they will sometimes pass many hours in succession in this noisy entertainment.

There is a tremendous number of comedians in China; most of them are purchased in early infancy by the chiefs of troupes, and by them trained in music, singing, declamation, pantomime, and dance. It is a species of slavery, not very unlike that of old Rome, but is not always life-long.

Some comedians, especially the chiefs, acquire large fortunes in the exercise of their calling, but the caste is so looked down upon, by the general public, and the facility of confiscating their fortune is so great, that they seldom attempt to leave the profession, or make any display of their wealth, lest it should be seized under any pretext

---

* In like manner physiologists at one time endeavored to account for the peculiar singing of the Tyrolese peasantry (called the "yodel") by the theory that the Tyrolese throat was shaped differently from throats in general. Anatomy exploded the assumption.

by some mandarin, in which case (in spite of the theoretical justice of China) it would probably be beyond recovery.*

We may mention here, a peculiar mode of paying actors, in Cochin China.

The occasion described is an entertainment, the expenses of which were borne by the Quong, or provincial governor. An Englishman who was present, thus speaks of the affair,—" The Quong was there squatted on a raised platform in front of the actors, with a small drum before him, supported in a diagonal position, on which he would strike a tap every time any part of the performance pleased him; which was also a signal for his purse bearer to show a small string of about twenty *cash* to the actors. To my taste this spoiled the effect of the piece; for every time the *cash* fell among them, there would be a silence, and the next moment a scramble for the money; and it fell so frequently as almost to keep time with the discordant music of the orchestra.

The actors were engaged by the day, and in this manner received their payment, the amount of which depended upon the approbation of the *Quony*, and the number of times he encored them by tapping his drum. I could see that many of them paid far more attention to the drum than they did to their performance; though I suppose the amount thrown to them is equally divided. Sometimes the string on which the *cash* was tied, unluckily broke, and the money flew in all direc-

* La Fage, Mus. des Chinois, v. 1, p. 311.

tions; by which some of the by-standers profited, not being honorable enough to hand it up to the poor actors.*

This was a public performance and took place in a large shed, before a numerous audience. Often the theatrical performances are allowed to take place in the Joss-houses or houses of worship, the *bonzes* or priests being wise enough not to offer any obstacles to a mode of amusement so thoroughly loved and appreciated by all the Chinese.

It is somewhat singular, and yet in keeping with the custom of the most ancient nations, that the Chinese should at the same time enjoy the drama so keenly, and despise the performers of it. The comedians are kept as thoroughly within their caste as musicians were in Egypt, four thousand years ago. Parents in China have almost unlimited power over their children (filial love and obedience is the highest of Chinese virtues,) they may sell them as slaves, or in some instances kill them, but they are not allowed to sell them to the troupes of strolling comedians, or to magicians. Any person so selling them is punished with one hundred blows of the bamboo, and any go-between or middle-man, in such transactions, receives a similar dose; any person of free parentage, marrying an actor or actress, is punished in the same manner, in spite of the precedent of several emperors. The crime of intimacy with actresses is punishable with sixty blows, but this is easily

* Edward Brown, Adventures in Cochin China, p. 221, quoted by Engel Mus. Myths and facts, vol. 2, p. 157.

eluded, and the law seems to be obsolete. This punishment is not attended with much infamy; the bastinado is in fact the lightest of Chinese punishments. When the number of blows does not exceed twenty, there is no disgrace whatever attached to the infliction: it is then considered only a paternal chastisement; the emperor himself often orders this correction to be administered to high officials for slight faults, and afterwards treats them as if nothing had happened. After such paternal punishment is inflicted, the victim goes on his knees to the judge, bows his head three times to the earth, and *thanks him* for the care he has given to the education of his subject.*

It is significant that the " State Gazette " of Pekin, which will often enter into details concerning the death of a private soldier, and give eulogies to the military valor of the most humble, does not even mention the decease of the most brilliant and well-known comedian, no matter how much applause may have been accorded to him while living.

In such a country as China, it is easily imagined that there exists a large troupe of " comedians to the emperor." These although not more superbly costumed than those of some rich mandarins, are clothed in a peculiar manner. Of course it would not be allowable to turn their backs upon the emperor, and yet often the action of the play, might demand that they turn around. This dilemma is overcome by allowing them to wear

* DuHalde, Description de l'emp. de la Chine. T. 2, p. 156.

two masks, one on the face, the other at the back of their head, and thus, Janus-like, they can always face the emperor. Their clothing is in consequence different from that of ordinary actors, having two fronts and no back.*

The *corps* of singers, declaimers and musicians of all kinds belonging to the Imperial court, is of course very large.

The dances of China, are as with all Eastern or ancient nations, purely pantomimical, there are few pirouettes and skips as in our *ballet.* The names and subjects of some of the earlier dancers, will show this conclusively; "The labors of Agriculture," "Joys of the Harvest," "The fatigues of War," "The pleasures of Peace," "The skill of Hunting," etc. These all show a primitive style of the art, and are not far removed from the dances we shall find in vogue among the most crude children of nature, such as the Australians, the Bushmen, or the Tasmanians. The Chinese possess (as did the Egyptians) a number of gymnastic performances similar to our clog, ballet, and comic dances, but these come a long way after the dance proper, in the estimation of the people; the word *ou* which signifies dance, does not apply to them. We cannot be surprised if from earliest times the regulation of the dance has been a matter of State legislation.

The ancient emperor was allowed eight dances, with eight performers to each, his full troupe containing sixty-four members. Kings of Prov-

* LaFage, Mus. des. Chin, T. 1, p. 313.

...ces had six dances of six performers, thirty-six in all; and thus through all the upper ranks, literary doctors being allowed only two dances of two performers each. Only certain instruments were allowed as accompaniment, and the direction of the whole was always to be in charge of various musical doctors. There also existed dances which were called "little dances," as they were taught to children at a tender age; the names of some of these are interesting; "the Dance of the Flag," danced in honor of the spirits of earth and the harvests, so called because the dancers waved small banners; "The Dance of the Plumes," in honor of the spirits of the four quarters of the world, in which the young dancers carried a plume of white feathers, attached to a short stick; "The Dance of the Poang-hoang," which was danced to induce the assistance of the mysterious bird (already described) in times of drought, and in which the dancers held plumes of feathers of five colors; "the Dance of the Ox Tail," in which each dancer swings an ox tail; "The Dance of Javelins," where this weapon was brandished in honor of river and mountain spirits; and finally, "the Dance of Man," in which the hands were quite free, no accessories being used.

The "Javelin Dance," was not altogether pleasing to the great philosopher Confucius. He condemns it as being too war-like, and the gestures accompanying it, as too savage; as a whole he thought it liable to inspire cruel sentiments. He preferred the "Dance of the Plumes," as containing all the chief elements of the "Javelin Dance" without tendency to cruelty. In the palace, the sons of the emperor only, were permitted to the " Dance of the Plumes."

At the epoch, when these dances were at their zenith, the emperors had a peculiar way of showing by them their approbation, or condemnation of their viceroys. When the viceroy was presented at court, if his administration seemed good to the emperor, he was welcomed by numerous and lengthy dances; if, on the contrary his government seemed worthy of censure, the dances were both short and few.

The following were the customs observed in presenting them:—Long before the dance began, a drum was sounded " to dispel from the minds of the spectators any thoughts unsuited to the occasion." On the arrival of the performers, they took three steps forward and put themselves in an attitude, calculated to impress the beholders; a sort of *tableau vivant.* The entrance was always accompanied with a slow movement of the music, which gradually augmented both in speed and volume, until the *finale,* when the climax having been reached, the music had attained a presto movement, and the dancers retired with precipitation in order that the interest might not have time to flag.

Sometimes the dancers carried a small shield with bell attached.

The Chinese sages deeply regret the loss of these ancient dances; (for like all excellent customs the modern writers claim that they were at their best in "the good old times,") it seems that the ancient Chinese, endeavored in the dance, to reproduce an easily-comprehended allegory of the natural actions of men; the movements, gestures, attitudes, and evolutions, all to be natural and easily understood by the spectators. Since the days of Confucius, this simple style of dancing has fallen greatly to decay.

In those days many of the emperors of China studied and understood the art of dancing. History shows many such "Davids" (although not so well known as Israel's royal dancer) in the dynasties of the empire. Autumn was the favorite season for the study of dancing, as the "feast of ancestors" takes place in the Spring, and the pupils were ready to exhibit their proficiency at that great event. The ancient practice of imperial dancing, was continued even as recently as 1719, when one of the sons of Kang-hi, of the age of twenty, performed before the emperor and his court. There are also mandarins whose duty it is to dance before the emperor; the pantomime of these is especially graceful and dignified. They advance slowly two by two, their limbs and bodies moving gently to the time of a tranquil music; they turn around without quitting their relative positions, and after a series of gestures made in perfect unison, and some symmetrical evolutions, they make the salute of honor, and retire. This dance seems to be only a formal expression of homage to the emperor. The dress of these officials is uniform, and elegant, fine silk capes, caps, etc., the only difference of costume being the buttons, with which the top of the caps are ornamented; the different color of these being indicative of greater or lesser rank. This corps of dancers is recruited from the wealthiest and greatest families of the empire.

In the dances, every detail is strictly systemized and observed; the very positions are calculated according to the points of the compass; thus one dancer is always placed at the north-west, another at the north-east, the entrance is to be made from a fixed cardinal point, the exit at another; all is rule and precision.

The number of dancers is not at present limited to that given above (sixty-four for the emperor, thirty-six for viceroys, etc.) as the ancient standard. At times of great festivity, the dancers of the Imperial court are reckoned by hundreds. Such *grandes ballets*, are almost always symmetrical and in concerted movements; but there are also *solo* dances; in these *pas seuls* the dancer often accompanies himself with both song and instrument. This proves how slow and majestic the motions must be.

In dances, females very often appear, but in private only. Mandarins frequently own female dancers and singers, whose performances are reserved for their own families. It is but rarely, and as a mark of especial honor, that they allow some intimate friend to view the dancing of these slaves.

Spectacular pantomimes, such as delight the theatre-goers at Christmas time in Europe and America, find also a congenial atmosphere in China; a most beautiful one was performed in the presence of the emperor, and Lord Macartney, in 1793. In this representation the object seemed to be, to illustrate upon the stage, the wonders and fertility of the world, or an allegory of the intermarriage of earth and ocean. The earth gave forth in this pantomime, a large number of its animals, and products; elephants, tigers, dragons, ostriches and eagles, as well as oaks, pines, bamboos, and other specimens of vegetation appeared upon the stage; while upon a lower stage, the ocean sent forth whales, dolphins, porpoises, and also vessels, rocks, weeds, sponges, and coral. Each of these creations was true to life, and in many of them were concealed actors who represented the motions and habits of the animals in a manner quite natural. After these products of earth and sea had performed several evolutions separately, each division moving in a separate circle, all united and came to the front of the stage, where a farther series of movements was enacted; suddenly the entire mass of actors divided, moving swiftly to the right and left in order to give place to the whale, who seemed a sort of commander in chief. This immense fish then advanced to the front of the stage, opposite the box in which the emperor was seated; on arriving here, he lifted his head and spurted an enormous mass of water, amounting to many barrels full, into the pit of the theatre;

where (holes having been bored to receive it) it swiftly disappeared.*

This performance seemed to give the greatest delight to the Chinese part of the audience. The music attached to this spectacle, was as usual of the most deafening character.

Of the lower order of dances, such as tumbling, harlequinades, etc., the Chinese have a vast variety; even puppet shows *(marionettes)* are greatly used by them, and plays with simple plots, very skilfully given by their means. This is the story represented at one of them;—An unfortunate princess is kept prisoner in a castle surrounded by dragons: to her comes a bold warrior, who after many combats with dragons, wild beasts and other horrible creations, succeeds in killing, vanquishing and dispersing them. He is recompensed by receiving the hand of the grateful princess, and the whole concludes with processions, tournaments and other festivities.†

As to the musical part of all these lesser performances, it is nearly always present, and ever of the peculiar style which has filled every traveller (so far as we know *without exception)*, with utter distaste. The juggling performances, of which there are many, both public and private, are accompanied throughout with the above described orchestra. Feats of skill, performed by troupes of children are especially admired by the Chinese, and

---

* Barrow's life of Macartney, v. 1, pp. 341-2

† Ibid, p. 337.

much sought for. The children begin their training in these arts, very young.

Boat races have also their music, which is evidently intended to inspirit the oarsmen. The following is a description of such an event, (so far as it relates to music).

"On each side of the little mast that supports the national flag, are two men, who leave off striking the tum-tum, and executing rolls upon the drum, whilst the mariners leaning over their oars, row on vigorously, and make the dragon junk, skim rapidly over the water.

Whilst these elegant boats are contending with each other, the people throng the quays, the shore and the roofs. . . . They animate the rowers with their cries and plaudits; they let off fireworks; they perform at various points, deafening music, in which the sonorous noise of the tum-tum, and the sharp sound of a sort of a clarinet, giving perpetually the same note, predominate over all the rest. The Chinese relish this infernal harmony."*

We have dwelt with some detail upon the music of the Chinese, for we consider these people, musically as well as ethnologically and philologically a series of contradictions, and especially differing from all our conceived notions of right and propriety: a nation where music is heartily loved, and taught to youth,† and yet where

* Ainsworth, around the world, p. 102.

† The following is a short synopsis of Chinese education. "When choosing a wet-nurse, the mother must seek a modest, virtuous, affable

musical progress is almost unknown; where goodness and love are taught in the most beautiful writings, and where greater cruelties are practised than anywhere else on earth. They differ from us on almost every point. We mourn in black, they in white; we respect crowns as badges of honor, they the boots; we build solid walls, they make them hollow; we pull a boat, they push it; we place the orchestra in front of the stage; they behind it; with us children fly kites, with them, men; we scratch the head when puzzled, they, the antipodes of it, etc, etc.*

A nation so strange cannot be judged flippantly or speedily; only a short time since we held the Japanese in the rank of the semi-civilized; now they are making giant strides on the highway of

discreet, respectful, exact and prudent woman. When the boy can carry his hand to his mouth he is weaned, and taught to use his right hand in eating; at the age of six, teach him the simplest numbers, and the names of most important parts of the globe; at the age of seven separate him from his sisters, and let him neither eat nor sit with them; at the age of eight teach him the rules of politeness and civility, which he must observe when entering or leaving a house, or when he is with his elders; at nine teach him the calendar; at ten send him to the public school and give him no more cotton-stuffed garments, they will be too warm for his age. The school-master is to give him knowledge of reading, writing and arithmetic. At thirteen, let him study music, that he may sing poetry, and that the wise maxims contained in the verses, be engraven on his memory. At fifteen he is to learn archery and riding. As for girls, when they have attained the age of ten years, they are not to be allowed to go out of doors; teach them to speak sweetly, to have an affable air, and to understand all household duties." Book of ancient rites quoted in Pere du Halde's Descrip. de la Chin. T. 2, p. 438

*Ainsworth, p. 102.

progress. Who dare say that the Chinese may not yet experience a similar awakening? At present their heaviest drawbacks, in music, as well as in all civilization, seem to be, a senseless clinging to ancient usages; an education of the head, and not of the heart; an etiquette which becomes both ludicrous and burdensome in its requirements;* a totally false position of woman; and a theoretically competitive, but practically

---

*A good example of the ludicrous side of this over politeness, may be given here. The host in China will constantly press his guest to accept of things which the latter is *expected* to refuse; the host is also required by etiquette to depreciate himself and extol his guest, which the latter returns in kind. An English gentleman having resigned himself to his interpreter, the following dialogue (like that in Kinglake's "Eothen,") takes place:—

Interpreter His excellency has long looked forward to this day.

Chinese Dignitary. I meet him now as an old friend, and request to know his honorable age.

Int. His excellency has profitlessly passed ——— years.

Chinese Dig. The ears of his excellency are long, and betoken great ability.

Int. Ah! oh! he is unworthy of the compliment.

Chinese Dig. You have had an arduous journey.

Int We deserved it, etc.

A similar "call" is described in Ainsworth's "all around the world," p. 106.

"At last we begged to take our leave, and began violently to "tsing-tsing," a ceremony which consists in clasping your hands before your breast, and making a crouching baboon-like gesture; it is the equivalent of shaking hands, only one shakes one's own hands . . Our host insists on following us to our chairs. We remonstrate; "stop! stop! we are unworthy," say we "What language is this" he replies. "We are really unworthy" we reiterate. "You are in my house," he insists; and so we back to our chairs, perpetually imploring him not to accompany us, which he vehemently resists, until at last, when we are in our chairs, he reluctantly consents to return, apologizing to the last, for being so rude as to leave us even then"

corrupt public service. There have recently been unmistakeable signs of progress, and, once begun, it is more than probable that the reform will be thorough and swift as it has thus far been with their neighbors. In such case, China will be of far higher interest to the world than she has been to us in our describing her as—a curiosity shop.

CHAPTER XVII.

MUSIC OF JAPAN.

It is a singular fact, that while the Japanese have in all ages given a great deal of attention to poetry the kindred art of music has been suffered to remain almost neglected. Their musical system has never been carefully formed or elucidated, and although they may vie with the Chinese in the beauty of their poetical effusions, in the field of music their research is nothing, when compared with the immense patience and study which the latter people have given to the subject.

Although there are few treatises on the art, yet the practice of music is now deemed an essential part of the education of a Japanese young lady, for contrary to Chinese custom, we find that in Japan, the female sex are proficient in the art.

Although at first glance there seems to be much affinity between Japanese and Chinese music, (so much so, that it seems natural to suppose that the former was an outgrowth of the latter) yet, upon closer analysis, these resemblances are found to be few, and the contradictions many and irreconcilable.

The Japanese songs do not appear to have been founded on the Chinese pentatonic scale, but rather upon the *chromatic*.

It is very possible, that the music of Japan had its rise long ago, within the limits of the island. Unfortunately, in this branch of history, we can as yet, come to no definite conclusion; the absence of all knowledge of the system (if there be one worthy of the name) on which their melodies are formed, and the very slight knowledge of the ancient history of the people, confine us altogether to conjecture and inference. That China exerted some influence upon the musical style of Japan, is undeniable. In the year (A. D.) 57, an embassy was sent from the island, to the Emperor of China, with presents. The return of this expedition, brought to the (at that time) totally rude and uncultivated people, the fruits of the older Chinese civilization, and it was probably at that epoch, that the Chinese instruments, which still exist in Japan, were introduced.

The instruments of Japan, though resembling, are much cruder than their Chinese, prototypes. The *che*, of China, is found under the name of *koto*. It is larger than the *che*, but has fewer strings; the latter are of silk, lightly lacquered. The *sam-sin* is a guitar, with a very long neck, and has three strings. These instruments are among the indispensable articles of the wedding outfit of every bride.*

Of wind instruments they have many styles of flutes and a trumpet, made of a conch shell.† The *cheng* (small mouth organ) is also possessed

* Japan, Aime Humbert, p. 173.
† Ambros, Gesch. d. Mus. v. 1, p. 88.

by them. It is called in Corean dialect *sainy-hwang*.* Gongs, tamtams, and noisy instruments of percussion, the Japanese possess in profusion; they have also a curious instrument, quite like the Egyptian sistrum,† formed of two sonorous metallic rings upon a light frame work, which give forth a tinkling and jingling upon being shaken, or struck with a small stick.‡ The *ko-kiou* is a kind of violoncello played with a bow; the *birva* is a similar instrument, which is picked with a *plectrum*. The same plectrum is used in performing upon the *sam-sin*. The clarionet is used very frequently; it is made of bamboo, like the flute. There is also an eight-holed flageolet. Among the instruments of percussion, are wooden rattles; stone drums like bowls, which stand on low frames; a musical drum made of leather; the *tam-tam*, or portable tambourine; gongs of all shapes, such as shields, fishes, tortoises, etc., producing all tones grave and piercing; bells, and kettle drums.

The tambourines which accompany the character dances, are sometimes played two at a time; one being held under the arm, the other in the left hand.§ There is a picture extant, representing a Japanese concert, in which there is one melodious instrument (a flute) against *six* instruments of percussion, such as bells, cymbals and drums.‖

* Ibid, 39.
† See Article on Egypt.
‡ Fetis Hist. de la Mus. v. 1, p. 84.
§ Humbert's Japan, p. 174.
‖ Siebold Pantheon of Nipon, part C, plates

The Japanese ladies not only play the various instruments, but study singing, assiduously. The language is well adapted to vocal efforts, being one of the most melodious and soft of the East; it approaches the Italian in its smoothness; it is monosyllabic,* but not varying with the pitch of the voice, as the Chinese does. (The written characters have been derived from the Chinese.) The very alphabet, or the nearest Japanese approach to it, is converted into a short song, which is characteristic of the materialistic views of the people.

The poetic setting of the "Irova" (as this is called) runs thus:—

"Color and light pass away
In our world nothing is permanent
The present day has disappeared
In the profound abyss of nothingness.
It was but the pale image of a dream;
It causes in our bosoms no regret."†

Nothing can give a stronger picture of the philosophy of Buddhism and its influence upon the Japanese mind.

Buddhism was so well suited to the temper of the people, that upon its introduction into the country (A. D. 552) it almost absorbed the ancient style of worship (Sintuism), and has, at the present time, so altered that superstition, that the prevailing aspiration of one branch, even of that creed, is an escape from trouble into nothingness. The mode

* Or more properly, agglutinate.
† Humbert, Japan, p. 42.

of worship is exceedingly simple, and in the main, joyous; there is no thought of supplication to their deities; for as they regard these as being in a state of bliss, they deem that the sight of any person in distress, must be painful to them, and therefore, when in trouble, they avoid going to religious exercises. In fact on the days of religious festivals, they behave in a manner which we should call decidedly immoral, but they do it with the best of motives, for they argue that nothing can please the gods more than to see mortals enjoying themselves heartily; and on this plea, both Buddhists and Sintuists indulge in all kinds of excesses on holidays.

Music does not play a very important part in the religious ceremonies of Japan. The Sintuists, who worship the Kami, or demi-gods, employ choirs on some occasions, and bear in all their ceremonies, some resemblance to the Catholic rites; this resemblance is yet more striking in the Buddhist religion; so much so, that a pious divine* on beholding their customs, came to the conclusion that the whole was a parody by Satan, upon the Catholic church.

The annual *fetes* instituted in honor of the chief Kami, consist almost wholly in ceremonies of purification. On the day before the chief solemnity, the priests march in procession, with tapers, to the temple where the arms and other objects which belonged to the demi-god, are kept in a reliquary called *mikosi*. According to the

* Abbe Huc, Travels in Thibet.

priests, the *mikosi* is the earthly dwelling place of the *Kami;* a sort of terrestrial throne, for occasional inhabitance; and each year it must undergo a thorough purification, in order to be acceptable to the hero. The reliquary is emptied and brought to the river; a certain number of priests carefully wash it, while others kindle a series of huge fires, to keep away the evil *genii.* The *kagoura,* or sacred choir, play soft and pleasant music, in order to appease the Kami, who is temporarily deprived of his earthly dwelling; they make as much haste as possible to restore it to him, which is done by placing the relics again in the reliquary.

The temple itself undergoes a purification lasting several days, at the same time. Sometimes the Buddhists send out collectors for their temples, who sing and play, quite musically, in front of the doors of persons from whom they expect to obtain a gratuity; they continue at each door until the heart of the proprietor is softened, or his patience gone, when the door is opened and the singers rewarded civilly.*

In order that the similarity of the Buddhist and Christian rites may be remarked, we give the description of the interior of a temple during worship, as seen by a European traveller.†

"A hundred kneeling devotees were present; a large shrine, with a gilt image in its recess; two large globular lamps, and two burning candles.

* S. Osborne, Japanese Fragments.
† Mr. Oliphant, in Elgin's Mission to Japan.

immensely long and thick; as also numerous gold and porcelain vases, holding lighted tapers, and surrounded by a forest of artificial flowers, were the objects that most riveted his attention. On both sides of this magnificent and richly gilded shrine were two smaller ones, each illuminated with lighted candles and perfumed tapers, burning with colored flame; the effect of which was very beautiful. In front of the principal altar, within an enclosure, knelt six shaven-headed priests (the latter, and physicians shave the whole of the hair off their heads), robed in crimson silk, and white crape; the centre and chief of whom engaged himself in striking a small saucer-shaped bell, while four more of the number performed a similar duty with padded drumsticks on hollow vessels of lacquered wood, which awoke a dull, monotonous sound. They kept good time, playing in unison, and toning their prayers to their music in chanting. At the conclusion of this singing and drumming they bent their foreheads to the floor, after which they arose and repaired to the smaller shrines, where a ceremony made up of gesticulation and a solemn reading of prayers, took place. In the meantime, the audience knelt, with their eyes directed to the ground, and gave some time to silent prayer."

Music bore a part also in the funeral ceremonies of some sects in Japan. The priest sang a eulogy of the dead, just before the funeral pile was set on fire.*

* Thunberg, Voyage to Japan, p. 351, Sherwood's Edition.

The order of "mountain priests" use a few instruments of sound (rather than music) in their wanderings. They have a staff with a copper head, to which are fastened four rings, also of copper, which they shake on uttering certain words in their prayers. They also carry a shell called *forano-kai*, to which a tube is attached, and which they use as a trumpet. They blow a blast upon this instrument (which in tone resembles the horn of a cowherd) whenever they see any travellers approaching, as a summons to them to give some charity to the order.*

There also exist several orders of a semi-ecclesiastical character; among which may be mentioned the society of blind men. One branch of this society gives the following legend as to its origin. Kakekigo, a general much renowned for his valor and supernatural strength, fought under a prince, named Feki, against the famous hero, Joritomo. In a great battle Feki was killed, and Kakekigo taken prisoner. Joritomo, far from desiring to put him to death, sought by every means to attach him to his own army. One day, when he was pressing him very close to enter into his service, upon whatever terms he pleased, the captive general returned him the following resolute answer:—" I was once the faithful servant of a kind master. Now that he is dead no other shall boast of possessing my faith and friendship. I owe even my life to your clemency; and yet such is my misfortune, that I cannot set my eyes on you, but

* Kaempfer, Hist. of Japan (Pinkerton), p. 745.

with a design, in revenge of him and me, to cut off your head. Therefore, these designing instruments of mischief, I will offer to you, as the only acknowledgement of your generous behavior towards me which my unhappy condition will allow me to give you." Saying this, he plucked out his eyes, and presented them, on a salver, to Joritomo; who, astonished at so much magnanimity and resolution, instantly set him at liberty.

Kakekigo then retired into the province of Fiuga, where he learned to play upon the birva (a musical instrument mentioned above), and founded the society of the Feki-blind, of which he himself was the first head. Many of the members of this society apply themselves to music, in which capacity they are employed at the courts of Princes and great men, as also upon public solemnities, festivals, processions, weddings, and the like. The society does not solicit charity, but its members all strive to be self-supporting, as well as of mutual assistance to each other. Whoever is once admitted as a member, must remain so for life.*

The Birva, mentioned above, is a great favorite with the masses, especially when played by the Feki musicians, who still make it their chief instrument. It has been known in Japan for twelve hundred years;† and one of the most beautiful lakes in Japan, near Kiota is named Birva Lake, from its shores resembling the outline of that instrument.

* Kaempfer Hist. of Japan, p.
† Dr. Muller, Journal of the German Eastern Asiatic Society.

The religious chanting of some of the larger sects, is quite impressive. Mr. Sile, Professor of History and Philosophy at the Imperial University of Yeddo, says:—" Some of the chants are very impressive; especially those of the Buddhists; they have a kind of sepulchral solemnity about them, and when performed responsively by large companies of Bonzes, on either side of a gloomy temple, in front of a shadowy half-illumined shrine, they sound like the mournful wailings of prisoners, not of hope, but of despair."*

The peculiarity of the performance lies in this: every man chants, not on a given key, but on that which best suits his natural voice. The time is well kept, but the key notes are as various as each voice that sings; as each one is allowed to choose his own pitch. The effect is good; it giving that blurred and massive sound, which is observed when a large congregation repeats the "Lord's Prayer" together; but the inflections and intervals are more marked and effective. Instrumental music is also sometimes present. The bonzes clad in heavy, sacerdotal vestments, officiate to an accompaniment of gongs and tambourines.

The solemn entry of the high priest into the choir, makes an immediate diversion in the monotony of the service. This grand dignitary is clad as richly as the bishops and arch-bishops of the west; red cloak, green silk stole, and white embroidered robes. He is followed by a young

* Letter to the "Leisure Hour," June 9. 1877.

acolyte, dressed chiefly in white, who accompanies his master, step by step, to offer to him, at an understood signal, a cup of tea from a portable vessel which he carries with both hands.*

Some of the Buddhist bonze-houses are celebrated for their luxury, the number of their priests, their magnificent attire, and the theatrical grandeur of their religious ceremonies. There are also endless numbers of retainers, heralds, grooms and porters, attached to the monasteries. The bonzes often give theatrical spectacles, in which dancers and comedians appear. A very curious piece is given on the fifteenth day of the sixth month. It is a sword dance, or military pageant, performed entirely by the priests. Buddhism in Japan has been a most flexible and conciliatory religion. It has succeeded so easily against the older Japanese religion of Kami, or hero-worship, because its introducers saw what customs had become rooted in the Japanese heart, and retained them. Thus we find the worship of heroes, tolerated in the Buddhist faith, as well as every spectacle and sound, calculated to please the senses of the people. It also steered clear of the rock upon which Christianity split (in Japan), that is, the alienation of the people from their rulers or sovereign.

Players of secular music, are numerous everywhere in Japan, but few of them have any idea of time or notation. Blind musicians (of the fraternity above mentioned, and of another called

*Humbert, Japan, p. 248.

the Buffetz) are numerous and much encouraged by the people, probably on account of their infirmity. Women and girls form the bulk of the secular players and singers. Most of these have been brought up to this from childhood, and (as with the ancient Greeks,) the possession of a musical and literary education often goes hand in hand with considerable laxity of morals.

The practice of music is, therefore, not held in any great esteem among men, as the few males who devote themselves to it are chiefly itinerants. The secular songs are often plaintive in character, but at times also quite stirring and fiery.

In Japan, as in some other Eastern countries, it is not unusual to find persons among the upper classes, who, while disdaining to study the art themselves, yet are very fond of listening to the performances of hired musicians. The taste seems to run entirely in the direction of melody, and not at all towards harmony; although they have a knowledge of a rude kind of harmony, consisting of melodies played upon two or more instruments tuned a fifth apart, thus forming an endless succession of consecutive fifths. This harmony, or a plain melody played in unison, they prefer to the finest (or, in fact, any) European music. Our readers will recollect the answer made by the Chinese mandarin to Pere Amiot, relative to his opinion on the respective worth of Chinese and European music. A similar reply was given by a Japanese nobleman to Dr. Müller, when asked to give an opinion on our music,—

"European music may please women, children, and common people, but Japanese gentlemen may not endure it."

In singing, the Chinese custom of using falsetto tones, obtains also in Japan. One peculiar taste for Western music exists among the Japanese; they like, and purchase many of our music boxes, and many are made in Switzerland especially for the Chinese and Japanese market. These contain two Chinese airs; but it is said that the people would enjoy them even more, if there were no harmonies attached. The entire instrumental music of Japan, partakes of a tinkling character, suggestive of a music box.

Secular singing is an indispensable adjunct of banqueting and feasting. These are frequently enlivened by songs and the sound of stringed instruments.*

The Japanese have a great *penchant* for excursions, banquets and lively enjoyments; they have been, not inaptly, called the "Parisians of the West;" hence it is not surprising to find houses of entertainment scattered broadcast throughout the realm. In these tea houses, every kind of dissipation, from the most innocent, to the reverse, is found, often under the same roof. The most aristocratic of these resorts, have a numerous staff of attendants, among which are singers, dancers, and guitar-players. Although these establishments appear disreputable in European eyes, yet the Japanese gentleman does not hesitate to take his

* Caron's Account of Japan (Pinkerton), p 633.

wife and children thither, for a pleasure jaunt. When we consider that the Japanese are the most careful people in the world regarding the education and behavior of their wives and children, we cannot attribute this seeming incongruity to negligence.

In tea houses of an inferior rank, when female dancers and musicians are not among the assistants, they may be sent for, and engaged by the hour. These women never enter the lower class of tea-houses, unless thus sent for. In this respect, as well as by the correctness of their behavior, they are to be distinguished from the lower order of street musicians and dancers at fairs. These are not allowed to perform in private houses; the law compells them to confine their music to such places as are subject to police regulations. Theatres being included in this category, they often appear there, at the request of performers in the plays, in order to figure in the ballet.*

In Yeddo, many of the tea houses are built along the banks of the river; and in this case, they have large family boats or gondolas attached, which they let out by the hour, to such parties (and there are many) as desire to take their recreation upon the water. Guitar players and refreshments are furnished with these boats.

The lower classes are passionately fond of listening to story tellers and singers, and these, as 'n other Eastern countries, give open air perfor-

---
* Humbert, Japan, p. 295

mances, trusting to their ability to delight their audience, for a voluntary recompense.

Every day at the close of working hours, one may see groups of artizans, and laborers, as well as many women of the working classes, either at the door of the workshop or at a street corner, arranged in a semi-circle around the story-teller.

National legends and romances are usually given only by those women who have made a profession of music and singing. This branch of street singers forms a large class; they are less roving than the others, and sometimes of rather a high order of talent, as compared with their more itinerant associates. The most distinguished of them have three or four musicians as accompanists, and do not themselves play upon any instrument. The effect of these combinations is said sometimes to be very charming, when heard and seen on a summer's evening, in a light bamboo frame work, hung round with vines, and lighted with paper lanterns.

Humbert has given the subject of some of these legendary songs, and they are found to be of a most sensational description: A few examples will suffice to prove this.

"Asahina-Sabro charges a troop of enemies, and passes through them, lifting with his right hand, a soldier wearing a casque and cuirass, and spinning him round in the air, while with the left hand he kills two equally redoubtable warriors with one blow of his mace."*

* Humbert, Japan, p. 258

"Nitan-nosiro, the dauntless hunter, astride on the back of a gigantic wild boar, which has flung down, and trodden under its hoofs, all the companions of the hero, holds the furious monster between his knees, and plunges his cutlass into its shoulder."

"Sonsige, one of the horsemen of the Mikado, finds his comrades squatting around a checker board; he spurs his horse, and with one bound, it stands in the centre of the board, as motionless as any bronze equestrian statue."

"Tame-tomo desired to conquer the island of Fatsisis. As he mercifully desired to avoid bloodshed, he set about convincing the islanders that resistance was useless. He therefore summoned the two strongest men of the race of the Ainos (the ancient inhabitants of Japan) and, seated calmly upon a mass of rock, he presented his bow to them, holding it by the wood and ordering them to try and bend it. Each seized it with both hands, and setting their heels against the wood of the bow, they leaned back with all their weight, and pulled the string with all their strength. Every effort was in vain; the bow only yielded when Tame-tomo took it delicately between the finger and thumb of his right hand, and shot an arrow which was immediately lost in the clouds."

It must be remembered, however, that these highly spiced romances are the especial pabulum of the lower classes; and it may be ranked considerably higher than the musical recreation of the working classes of China.

The laborers of Japan, sometimes sing while at their toil, in a measured but cheerful manner.* Before leaving the subject of Japanese songs, it may be interesting to note that in the days of Kæmpfer, the Japanese were as curious about our songs, as we are to hear those of barbaric nations; for the emperor and his court, insisted upon that grave historian dancing, and singing before them.† On one of these interesting occasions the historian basely deceived the imperial Japanese searcher after knowledge; for on being commanded to sing, he sang to the emperor, a love ditty, which "he had formerly composed for a lady, for whom he had a particular esteem;" and upon the emperor inquiring the meaning of the song, he answered that it was an ode of praise, in honor of the emperor and his court.‡ Let us hope that the Japanese will not lead our investigators astray in such a manner.

The court of Japan had, at that era, musicians attached to its service, though by no means on the grand scale of the Chinese court. The empress had her private band, consisting of players upon the birva, the koto, and the samsinn. Theatrical representations were sometimes added to music. A corps of young comedians played little operas, or executed character dances, some grave and slow, in which a long mantle was worn; others lively and playful, the dancers appearing suddenly

---
* Thunberg, Voyage to Japan (Sherwood's Ed.), p. 298.
† Kæmpfer's history of Japan, p. 815 (Pinkerton's).
‡ Ibid, p. 818.

and with appropriate movements, in the disguise of birds or butterflies.

The court ladies had their private boxes at the theatre and at the circus of wrestlers; many of these customs still exist at the Japanese court but not with the spirit and life of former days.

Processional music is, in Japan, similar to that described in " Chinese Music," noisy and distressing; but it is by no means so generally used as in China. In some processions it is not present at all. The emperor formerly appears to have had no music in his pompous cavalcades, for a description of one of these pageants (written in the seventeenth century), thus concludes:

"It is at the same time in the utmost silence that the procession proceeds. No one is heard to speak a word. Neither the spectators in the streets, nor those who form the procession, make the least noise. It can only be perceived by the sound of men's footsteps, and the tramping of horses."*

At the ecclesiastical processions, which take place on days devoted to special *Kami*, (similar to the saints days of Europe), and called *Matsouri*, the music consists of the fifes, drums, and gongs of the bonzery. Of course these processions vary in proportion to the popularity of the special Kami or saint. The greatest *Matsouri* which takes place at Yeddo, is that given in honor of Zinmou, the founder of the empire. Even those who do not believe in Kami-worship, attend this

* Caron's Account of Japan (Pinkerton's ed.), p. 611, v. 7.

feast to show respect to their country, and it has become a patriotic as well as religious occasion. Over a million of spectators, annually view this procession. In the ranks appear an image of the patron of sacred dancing, borne on a large drum; and the sacred gong of the priests. The band on this occasion is large, and flutes, trumpets, big drums, cymbals, gongs, and tambourines are among the instruments carried. The expenses of the lesser *Matsouri* are often defrayed by the people of a street or quarter which is specially devoted to the *Kami* in whose honor it is held.

Many of the customs above alluded to are sensibly losing their hold on the populace, since the recent introduction of our civilization; this is especially the case with such customs as come under government surveillance. The military music for example, has been remodelled on the European plan; regimental bands in French style (that is with a preponderance of drums), are now attached to the Japanese national army. The trumpet calls are said to be played with much aptitude by the Japanese performers, but in the matter of time-keeping by the band, and keeping step to the music by the soldiers, exactness is yet far from being attained.* In the theatre and its music, there is, as yet, not so great a change from former days, yet there are many European customs to be found there (though probably not all derived from Europe), and the theatre differs from that of China, in having a curtain in front of the stage;

---

* Dr. Muller; paper read before the German Asiatic society.

in being often built upon a permanent site; and in other particulars.

The plays although sometimes quite as minute in details as the Chinese, are much shorter, lasting usually about two hours; and are often much wittier.

There has been a peculiar manner of presenting these plays; if five plays are to be performed in one day, the following mode has sometimes been adopted.*

The performers go through the first act of the first play, then the first act of the second play, and so on until the five *first acts* have been given. They then take the *second* act of each play in succession, and so on, until all the last acts are given. The object of this custom is to enable spectators to see one act, go away, and come again in time for the next act.

Often, however, the spectators remain throughout the entire day, and in that case refreshments are openly consumed. It is also thought correct for ladies to change their dress as often as possible during the day, so that there is as much change of costume, in front of the stage as upon it. In the Japanese comedies there is generally a large amount of love making. The tragedies deal chiefly with the exploits of the mythological heroes, and are expressed in verse, sometimes declaimed, sometimes sung.† The terrific combat is an acknowledged essential of this order of plays.‡

* Wood's Natural History of Man, v. II, p. 849.
† La Fage, Hist. gen. de la musique, v. I, p. 376.
‡ Wood's Nat. Hist. of Man, v. II, p. 850.

The effect of the martial scenes is much increased by a bass drum, called "taiko" (after a celebrated ancient warrior), which is sometimes played with a smaller one called "kakko."*

The building where these plays take place is very plain. The theatre at Matsmai, the capital city of the Island of Jesso, is thus described.†

"It is a large and pretty high building; at the back is a stage which with us, has a raised floor. From the stage to the front wall, where the entrance is situated, two rows of seats are placed for the spectators. In the middle where we have the pit, there is a vacant space in which straw mats are laid down for the spectators. As this space is much lower than the stage, those in front do not intercept the view from those behind. Opposite the stage, where in our theatre the galleries and chief boxes are situated there are only a bare wall, and the door for entrance.

There were no ornaments in the interior; the walls were not even painted. The dresses and decorations are kept in a separate building."

In Yeddo this is far different and keeps more pace with civilization, and, as Yeddo supplies the surrounding provinces with both actors and plays, the change is spreading throughout the empire. The plays begin at six or seven, P. M., and last (without the before-mentioned alternations) until one or two o'clock in the morning. Theatres are exceedingly numerous in the city; each has its

* Dr. Muller, German East. Asiatic society.
† Japan and the Japanese. Capt. Golownin, v. II, p. 149.

own arms or design, by which it is called; and these are painted upon banners and lanterns, which are hung from a tower upon the roof of each establishment. We give as complement to the above description of the Matsmai theatre, the following picture of a leading theatre at Yeddo.

"The interior of the theatre forms a long square. There are two ranges of galleries, the upper containing the best places in the theatre. Numbers of ladies are to be seen there in full dress, that is to say, covered up to their eyes in crape dresses and silk mantles.* The whole of the remainder of the house is occupied exclusively by men.

The floor of the house as seen from a distance, resembles a draught board. It is divided into compartments containing from eight to twelve places each, most of which are hired by the year by the citizens who take their children regularly to the play. There are no lobbies. Every one walks to his place on the planks which enclose the compartments at the height of the spectators' shoulders, who squat on their heels, or crouch on little stools. There is neither a ladder nor staircase, by which to get down into the midst of them. The men hold out their arms to the women and children. The settling of the audience in its place forms a very picturesque part in the preliminaries of the representation. Tobacco and refreshments are served during the whole evening

* Worn one above the other. Sometimes six or seven dresses are worn in this manner by one fair fashionable.

by koskeis, or servants, along the before-mentioned gang planks. On two sides of the pit are two bridges of planks, which also communicate with the boards of the stage; the first is nearest to one of the doors; the second, which is four planks wide, forms an angle with the extremity of the boxes. On this bridge certain heroic or tragic comic personages perform their part, and the ballet is danced. The house is lit by paper lanterns tied to the galleries; there is no chandelier from the roof, which is perfectly flat, the cupola being unknown in Japanese architecture. Large lanterns are however, sometimes held up to the roof, in order to light up the performance of the acrobats, especially that of the "flying men," who cross the theatre by means of cleverly contrived mechanism.

The curtain which hangs before the stage, is ornamented by a gigantic inscription in Chinese characters, and surmounted by a target with an arrow in the centre. This is a symbol of the talent and tact which the actors are about to display, and signifies that they expect to "hit the bull's eye" of the audience's wishes.*

The performance generally lasts till one o'clock A. M., and usually consists of a comedy, a tragedy, an opera with a ballet, and two or three interludes of acrobats, wrestlers and jugglers.

The tragedy we have already partly described as of a mythological sensational type. In the comedy it is often customary for the audience to

*Humbert's Japan, p. 336.

address the actors, and the latter answer in kind; thus frequently a brisk fire of *repartee* is kept up which delights the audience far more than the play itself. It is very rare in any of these pieces that more than two actors are upon the stage together. In the ballet the performers are richly attired, and sometimes wear several dresses of light silk, one above the other; as they dance they detach a few of these vestments and allow them to hang from their waist, a cloud of airy texture seemingly voluminous, but in reality very light.* The Japanese plays are sometimes preceded by a prologue in which much of the action is described (*a la* Greek chorus) but not the *denouement*.† The performance of the jugglers is most to the popular taste, for it is not unusual to find the restaurants (with which each theatre is surrounded, and which cater to the same class of custom) quite crowded during the entire performances, but the moment that the gong gives the signal for the commencement of the juggling, they are at once deserted, every one hastening back to his seat in the theatre. The principal parts of the performance are announced not with a bell or with music, but by striking a small wooden stick upon the stage.

Sometimes the actors pass through the audience on their way to the stage, in order to give the spectators an opportunity to admire their appearance and costume, as closely as possible.‡ The

---
* Thunberg.
† La Fage, Hist. de la Mus. v. I, p. 375.
‡ Engel Mus. Myths and Facts, v. II, p. 164.

appearance of infernal personages on the stage is always accompanied with lightning.

The principal characters of the drama are accompanied on the stage by a couple of attendants, each carrying a long stick at the end of which is a lighted candle. The use of these candles is amusing; they show to the audience what they ought to admire. If the actor's facial expression be peculiar, his attitude graceful, his dress fine, or his weapons elegant, the candle is at once held to the part, to attract attention.

With regard to the literary merit of the Japanese drama, not enough is yet known whereon to base a detailed analysis, but it is safe to say that the art is yet in its infancy. It is singular, that, while we regard some of the situations in their plays as exceedingly indelicate, they, on their part, condemn our drama as totally immoral, and would not tolerate such plays as "Hamlet," "School for Scandal," etc.

The key to the enigma is this,—they allow every license to unmarried ladies, but the married state is with them inviolable. They therefore tranquilly witness plays which would put "Camille" to the blush, but allow nothing which involves post-marital intrigue. Some of their actors are quite skillful; there is one at present upon the Yeddo stage, who performs the part of a man possessed with the soul of a cat, and the blending of human and feline character is said to be marvelous.

The caste of actors, as in China, is rather low;

the comedians being in least repute. Although the theatre is so well patronized, yet it is only by the middle and lower classes; very few aristocrats even of the lesser nobility ever attending, and these even disguise themselves.

Of course, it was to be imagined that the Jesuits would not (at the time of their mission in Japan) neglect so straight a road to the popular attention, as the drama. In their church at Nagasaki (more than two centuries ago), they represented a play in the style of the mediæval miracle plays, representing the birth of Christ. The parts were taken by the neophites and native students at the college of the order. Everything passed off in the best possible manner, as well in the appointments of the theatre, as in the ease and smoothness of the acting, and it would have been applauded in any European theatre."*

It may be interesting to the reader to peep into the green room of a Japanese theatre, during performance. It is thus described,—

"In these places none but men are to be seen, excepting from time to time some servants, or the artists' wives who bring refreshments to their husbands, or come to give the last touch to their toilet before they go on the stage in the costume of either sex. In the midst of the general disorder we find some very characteristic groups. Here are musicians occupied in refreshing themselves, and indifferent to everything else until the signal to return to their posts shall reach them; there,

*La Fage, Hist. de la Mus. v. I, p. 876.

two actors are rehearsing together the attitudes and gestures which in a few moments are to delight the spectators; and another sitting on his heels, before a looking glass placed upon the floor, is painting his face and adjusting his feminine head-dress. A young devil beside him, has thrown back his mask, with his horns and mane over his shoulders and is fanning himself, while the chief of the wrestlers, is tranquilly smoking his pipe, in the midst of the acrobats.

. Among the crowd, carpenters are coming and going, carrying the screens and partitions for the next scene; the machinist is working a trap through which a whirlwind of flame is about to escape; and the piece is going on outside to the accompaniment of drum beating, amid the conversation of the public in the house, and that of the disengaged actors."*

Such briefly, is the condition of music and the drama in Japan, but such astounding changes are taking place throughout every part of the life of this enterprising people, that a description which is appropriate at present, may be a record of past customs, ten years hence. Already there is a tendency in upper circles towards Western music, but this may be rather a result of fashion (which is being rapidly *Europeanized*) rather than of genuine appreciation; even the present empress of Japan has, it is said, a real taste for European music and instruments. She is a good performer upon the piano-forte.

*Humbert, Japan, p. 887.

As with the Chinese, the customs in general of the Japanese are at total variance with our own; to show respect we take off our hat, they their shoes. We get up, they sit down, (it is the height of impoliteness to receive a visitor standing.)[*]

We turn the back as a mark of incivility, they as a token of respect;[†] their mixture of the truest modesty with the greatest license, must ever remain an enigma to us. Since then, we cannot in other respects, judge this remarkable people, it behooves us, in the field of music, to study them without preconceived ideas of the art. That music is in an undeveloped state with them, is undoubtedly true; the absence of treatises and system proves it; but what direction the art will take in its development can only be settled by time. That it will not remain stationary in the midst of change, is a foregone conclusion.

[*] All Round the World, p. 206.
[†] Thunberg, p. 307.

CHAPTER XVIII.

MUSIC OF SAVAGE NATIONS.

The music of savage tribes, should properly begin a chronological account of the music of the world. It can scarce be doubted that the strains which to-day delight the ears of the rudest peoples, were similar to those which gave pleasure to the uncultivated denizens of the earth in pre-historic times. The scientific inquirer, even to-day, finds unexpected points of resemblance in music of nations and tribes, separated from each other in distance, custom, climate and religion; resemblances which are so numerous that they can only be accounted for by the hypothesis that the strains have come down from an earlier, homogeneous race. Of course the earliest efforts of primitive man were rather rhythmical than musical, and even at present the music of the least civilized races is altogether rhythmical. The ease of the discovery that a regular clapping of the hands, or stamping of the feet, or striking two pieces of wood together, could produce a pleasing effect, is so apparent that it puts all discussion as to the origin of music, out of sight; a fortunate occurrence, since there are enough points of dispute yet left for our wiseacres to contend over.

The discovery of drums and horns also came

almost directly from nature; and here the musical instruments of primitive man stopped; and here also (in drums, clappers of wood, and trumpets) the catalogue of musical instruments, of the more savage peoples, of the present, ceases.

But among the more advanced tribes of savages, we shall find instruments that will cause us to coincide with Solomon's opinion, that "there is nothing new under the sun."

With these, who did not stop contented at the rude percussion and trumpet instruments, the next step was probably to cut reeds of various lengths and to discover that the length regulated the tone. Here was the first real discovery in music, for no sooner were high and deep tones known than pleasant alternations would suggest themselves, and as a consequence, melodies (however uncouth) sprang into being. Possibly at the same mystic era, the tension of the sinews of some animal, left exposed to the breeze, would fore-shadow string music. Then a thought was required to find that the sounds varied with tension of the sinews, and that a frame on which several threads and sinews were extended in different degrees of tension, could be made to give the same variety of tones, but of different quality of sound *(timbre)* from the reed pipes. This already made demands upon the inventive faculties, and in the infancy of music, as in the modern orchestra, stringed instruments take the lead.*

*Ambros, Gesch d. Musik, v. I, p. 4.

It is improbable, however, that all nations went the same road in these discoveries. Accident had much to do with it. The conch shell, among a tribe near the sea, the horn, with a hunting people, and, with people situated near the bamboo forests, the "pans pipes," would be the first of instruments. Instruments of the order of flutes, were also of easy fabrication, and the knowledge that they are so wide-spread among savages all the world over, is internal evidence that they were "natural" instruments.

Without sketching further the probable progress of musical invention, we shall now describe some of the instruments and songs used by the people of the world who are yet in a state of nature. But first let us mention some instruments, which have been handed down to us from an immensely remote and ante-civilized period.

The antiquarians in classifying the progress of pre-historic races from their earliest emergence from barbarism, have called that age, when the use of metal became first known,—the Bronze Age; as at that time smelting not being known, the use of iron was not understood, and metal implements were fashioned of copper, which could be beaten by the hammer (of stone) into the required shape, even when cold.

Of this mysterious epoch, a most interesting relic has been discovered, in the shape of a musical instrument. In a sepulchre, in a deep ravine, in Schleswig, were found very recently, a number of ornaments of bronze and gold (silver as well as iron, was not then used), and also the horns of many oxen. In the midst of this, lay a very large *trumpet* of bronze; a sure token of the existence of manufactured musical instruments, thousands of years ago. This unique instrument when blown, gives forth a deep, grave, and sonorous tone. In common with all the barbarian trumpets, it has but one tone. It is at present in the Museum of Copenhagen, but was exhibited at the Paris Exposition of 1867.*

The second of these instruments is more ancient still. The age preceding the knowledge of the uses of metal by early man, is called the Stone Age. At this period the rude implements of use and ornament were made either of soft substances, such as wood, ivory, and horn, or else of stone. Even in this crude epoch, instrumental music seems to have existed, and not in its rudest form, for a specimen has fortunately been preserved, which, if authenticated fully, will show a degree of musical taste at a most unexpected period. In an ancient *dolman*, or sepulchre near Poictiers was found a partly completed *flute* made of a stag's horn. The distances of the holes, and shape of the mouth-piece, show an aptitude of construction and an experience in acoustics; but the instrument evidently belongs to the later period of the Stone Age.

But the third instrument is more interesting yet. It was discovered by M. Lartet in a ravine, along with bones of animals now extinct in

* Comettant, Mus. et Musiciens, p. 586

France. It is also a flute (straight, and with mouth piece), with finger holes.* It is made of the bone of a reindeer, which seems a proof positive of its being made at a time when the climate and zoology of France were totally different from the present. From the skulls found in tombs and caves of this period, it appears impossible that man could have been developed sufficiently at that time to construct an article of pleasure, such as this. The skulls are said to greatly resemble those of the present natives of Australia. Yet their possessors must have had a vastly superior intelligence to the latter.

It is no great leap in fact, although it may be in time, to leave the savages of our own ancient race, and describe the musical customs of the savages of another, and inferior one. Therefore, we will leave the discussion of the above three instruments and their makers to Anthropological and Ethnological societies, and pass on to the examination of the barbarian of the present age.

One of the most curious facts in savage music is to be found in New Zealand. It is almost universally conceded that harmony was unknown to Europeans until the tenth century; yet in New Zealand for unknown ages, a combination of simple thirds in a short vocal strain† has been known. It only illustrates the assertion of the force of accident, in the rise of music.

Here was a savage tribe of cannibals who came

* Fetis Hist. gen de la Mus., v. I, p. 26
† Ambros. Gesch. d. Musik, p. 10, v. I.

upon a most important musical idea (to be sure, in a crude state, but still the germ of the Harmonic theory) probably long before its acceptance among civilized nations.

Another strange savage song is that which was sung by the aborigines of Canada, at the time of Cartier's taking possession in the name of the King of France (A. D. 1537). The curious fact here, was not in the music, but in the words, in as-much as the word "Alleluia" occured in it. This strange coincidence made some early writers conclude that the inhabitants were Hebrews,* probably the lost tribes; it is needless to say, that the surmise, was not borne out by any further researches.

In describing the music of barbarian races, we find that its sister art, dancing, is closely connected with it, and that it is impossible to separate the two. In the lowest tribes, the dance is the most prominent part of the musical efforts of the people. The Australians, who are considered, from the conformation of their skulls, and legs, to be nearest to the brute creation, have many interesting dances. The most important of these is the "Cobbongo Corrobboree," or great mystery dance. It is performed by the inhabitants of the far interior of the island. We subjoin the account of a witness of this event.

The time selected for this great event is every twelfth moon, and during her declination. For several days previous, a number of tribes, whose

* See Fetis Hist.gen. de la Mus. v. I, p. 15.

territories adjoin one another, congregate at a particular spot, characterised by an immense mound of earth, covered with ashes (known amongst the white inhabitants as "a black's oven"), and surrounded by plenty of "couraway" or water holes.

To this place, they bring numbers of kangaroos, possums, emus, and wild ducks, and a large quantity of wild honey, together with a grass from the seed of which they make a sort of bread.

"Upon the evening on which the 'corrobboree' is celebrated, a number of old men (one from each tribe) called 'wammaroogo,' signifying medicine-men, or charm-men, repair to the top of the mound, where, after lighting a fire they walk round it, muttering sentences, and throwing into it portions of old charms which they have worn round their necks for the past twelve months."

"This is continued for about half an hour, when they descend, each carrying a fire-stick, which he places at the outskirts of the camp, and which is supposed to prevent evil spirits from approaching. As soon as this is over, during which a most profound silence is observed by all the men of the tribe prepare their toilets for the 'corrobboree,' daubing themselves over with chalk, red ochre, and fat."*

*The effect of this in some Australian dances, is said to be very striking The favorite device, is to draw the outline of a skeleton, on the front of the body, with white paint. As the dancers twirl round, the pattern is plainly perceptible when their faces are turned toward the spectator, but when their black backs are turned, the whole vanishes, and gives the impression of a number of ghastly skeletons.

"While the men are thus engaged, the gentler sex are busy arranging themselves in a long line, and in a sitting posture, with rugs made of possum skins, wound round their legs, and a small stick called 'mulla mulla' in each hand. A fire is lit in front of them, and tended by one of the old charmers. As the men are ready, they seat themselves, cross-legged, like tailors, and in regular serried file, at the opposite side of the fire to the women, while one of the medicine-men takes up his position at the top of the mound, to watch the rising of the moon which is the signal for 'corrobboree.'"

All is now still; nothing disturbs the silence, save the occasional jabber of a woman or child, and even that, after a few minutes, is hushed. The blaze of the fire throws a fitful light along the batallion-like front of the black phalanx, and the hideous faces, daubed with paint and smeared with grease, show out at such a moment to anything but advantage. As soon as the old gentleman who has been "taking the lunar" announces the advent of that planet, which seems to exercise as great an influence over the actions of these people, as over many of those amongst ourselves, the "corrobboree" commences.

"The women beat the little sticks together,* keeping time to a peculiar monotonous air, and

alternately appearing and disappearing, by the dim flicker of the firelight.

*Here we see one of the earliest traits of primitive music. The use of a plain, rhythmic accompaniment, without tune.

repeating the words, the burden of which may be translated in this manner,—

> ' The kangaroo is swift,
>   But swifter is Ngoyulloman;
> The snake is cunning,
>   More cunning is Ngoyulloman, etc.'

Each woman using the name of her husband, or favorite in the tribe."

" The men spring to their feet with a yell that rings through the forest, and brandishing their spears, and boomerangs commence their dance, flinging themselves into all sorts of attitudes, howling, laughing, grinning, and singing; and this they continue until sheer exhaustion compels them to desist, after which they roast and eat the product of the chase gathered for the occasion, and then drop off to sleep one by one."*

We have already expressed our opinion that the dance (pantomimic) first sprang into existence when some savage finding his own limited language (perhaps even, he had none) inadequate to describe to his companions, some deed of hunting or war which he had performed, reproduced the feat in actions, to give a more perfect understanding of it. If song be as old as speech, dancing may be said to be as old as gestures.

We are not surprised, therefore, to find among the Australians, dances which represent such events. In the "frog dance," the performers paint themselves as usual, and then, squatting upon their haunches, jump around in a circle

---
* From the "Illustrated London News," Oct. 8, 1863.

imitating the motions of the frog. The "Emu dance" represents the chase after that swift running bird. The performer who takes the part of the Emu, imitates its fleet, long strides, and gives out the low rattling drumming sound which is the bird's only note.

In the "canoe dance" men and women stationed in two lines, imitate the graceful motions of paddling a canoe.

There is a dance "with partners" prevalent in the southern part of Australia. Both sexes participate in it. Each man carries a belt of possum skin, or human hair, which he keeps stretched tight, holding one end in each hand. The men all sit down in a circle while a woman takes her place in the middle; one of the men then dances up to her, jumping from side to side, and swaying his arms in harmony with his movements. The woman also begins swaying and jumping in time with him, as he approaches her, and after a short *pas de deux* they dance back to their places, while the centre is occupied by a fresh couple.

A strange dance was celebrated by the Tasmanians at each full moon. The various tribes assembled at some trysting place, and while the women prepared the fire, and fenced off a space for the dance, the men retired to adorn themselves with paint, and to fasten branches of bushy twigs to their ankles, wrists and waists. The women being seated at the front of the space, one of the oldest among them, strode forward, calling by name, one of the performers, whom she reviled as a coward, and challenged to come forward and meet her charge, and answer it.

The warrior was swift enough in his response, and, bounding through the fire, into the circle, he recounted his deeds of valor in both chase and war. At every pause he made, his female admirers took up the list of his praises, vaunting his actions in a sort of chant which they accompanied with extemporized drums, made of rolled kangaroo skins.

"Suddenly upon some inspiring allegro movement of the thumping band, thirty or forty grim savages would bound successively through the furious flames, into the sacred arena, looking like veritable demons on a special visit to *terra firma;* and, after thoroughly exhausting themselves, by leaping in imitation of the kangaroo, around and through the fire, they vanish in an instant. After this, the old lady who was the origination of all the hubbub, gave a signal, upon which, all the females rose, and quite unadorned, gave a series of acrobatic performances around the fire, that were strange and wonderful to behold. The main point being however, with each of them, to outscream her sister singers."*

In the dances of Australia and Tasmania, only the rudest instruments of percussion are used, and the chants are not musical, though sometimes (rarely) the attitudes are graceful. A far more musical and poetical people, are the New Zea-

* Wood's Nat. Hist. of Man, v. I, p. 68

landers who as we have already mentioned, intuitively knew of harmony before the Europeans. Many of their love, war, and religious songs have real sentiments of beauty in them, and the gift of improvising poems and songs is much prized among them. Singular to state, they (unlike all other savage races) do not use the drum in their accompaniment. The *pahu* (drum) is only used by them to give military signals.* Their chief instrument is the flute, which is usually made from a human thigh bone; often that of a fallen enemy. When this is the case, the instrument is more than ordinarily prized, and is worn around the neck. It is played through the nose, by placing the nostril against the aperture, and blowing; stopping the other nostril with the finger.

The native New Zealander sings in all his sports and labours, and in spite of his *penchant* for human flesh, is of a light and joyous temperament. Every incident of war, chase or love is commemorated by an extemporized song. Sometimes these songs live for generations after their signification has passed away; and thus it is, that in many of the songs of this people, words are found, of which, neither the singers nor audience understand the meaning. One song *(E' Haka)* is accompanied with much mimicry; when giving this, the performers sit down in a circle, throw off their upper mats, and sing in concert, making meanwhile the wildest of gestures, and turning up their eyes so that only their whites are visible.

* Meinicke, Inseln des Stillen Oceans, v. I, p. 329.

Their canoe song is very animating, and is often accompanied by the primitive nose flute mentioned above.

The words (improvised) are such as "pull away! pull away! pull away." "Dig into the water." "Break your backs," etc., and are shouted with stentorian lungs, but not unmusically.

But their greatest song and dance is the wardance. In this they far excel all other savage tribes the world over. Their movements although extremely violent, are made with a precision and unity, to which all other races are strangers. A description of this unique performance speaks of it as follows.

"They begin by smearing the whole of their clothing and painting their faces with scarlet ochre, so as to make themselves as hideous as possible. When they assemble for the dance they arrange themselves in lines usually three deep, and excite their naturally passionate dispositions to the highest pitch by contorting their faces, and thrusting out their tongues as an act of defiance, interspersing these gestures with shouts, yells and challenges to the enemy. The dance itself begins with stamping the feet in perfect time with each other, the vigor of the stamp increasing continually, and the excitement increasing in similar proportion. Suddenly with a yell, the whole body of men leap sideways into the air, as if actuated by one spirit, and as they touch the ground, come down on it with a mighty stamp that makes the earth tremble. The war song is raised, and in accordance with its rhythm, the men leap from side to side, each time coming down with a thud, as of some huge engine."*

The New Zealander often entertains himself with sham fights,† but nothing has so intense an effect upon him as the music and action of this rhythmic war-dance. Even when actual war is not impending, he will enter into it with a vigor that is terrible. It transforms him for the time into a monomaniac, and absorbs his whole nature; even when the dance is given in honor of a stranger, it is dangerous to go too near the Maori (native New Zealander) until he has become more tranquil.

On one occasion a party of New Zealanders, visiting a European ship, were requested to give an exhibition of their war-dance on board. They did so, beginning without much excitement, but gradually their leaps became so fierce and powerful that the captain was afraid that they would break the deck; he begged of them to desist, but in vain; he might as well have spoken to a whirlwind. His voice was drowned in the shouts and singing of the frenzied warriors. The chief of the party, showed the influence of its charms, in a ludicrous manner :—

He had been presented on his arrival, with a full suit of naval uniform, and he stalked around the deck, in all the dignity of new clothes. He

* Wood's Hist. of Man, v. I, p. 162.
† Meinecke Inseln d still. Oceans, v. I. p. 330.

cheerfully allowed his followers to begin the war-dance, but he himself looked on with conscious dignity; but after the excitement had continued a few minutes, he too was drawn into its vortex. At first a gentle swaying of his body, in time with the music was all; then a little *sotto voce* singing, then he joined in the rhythm stamping, and finally, forgetting his new finery, he sprang into line and danced more enthusiastically than any of them; so much so, that the clothes soon split, and at the end of the dance he presented a very seedy appearance. It is needless to say that the dance could not in any way be checked, and found its conclusion only when all the dancers were reduced to a state of complete exhaustion.

With all savage people, song, dance and poetry are indissolubly united; a fact which goes far to prove the "naturalness" of the old Greek music. In the Malaysian archipelago we find a similar style of music, to that described above; but we find the natural instrument of barbarians, the drum, far more plentifully used.

The Javanese have two kinds of drums, both made of copper, but differing in size and pitch. The sound is like that of a distant bell, and as they are used in sets, the compass often reaches an octave. The larger set, called *Salendro* contains but five tones in this interval; the general effect of this set is *major*. The smaller set, called *Pelog*, contains seven drums to the octave, and is minor in style. The natives themselves speak of the *Salendro* as being masculine, and the *Pelog* as being more tender and feminine in its effect.

The songs of Java (as also of other islands in the Malay archipelago) are strongly suggestive of the Scotch popular ballads, and can readily be reproduced in our scale.

It is not customary to sing the written poems, with an instrumental accompaniment unless there is dancing simultaneously. As in French poetry and song, many letters, usually mute, are sounded, so in the Javanese much license of pronunciation is allowed in song, which would be condemned in prose. There are some traces of inflection and accent, altering the meaning of a word; thus "*boten*" signifies "*no*," but when the accent is placed on the first syllable, it signifies a haughty or peremptory refusal, but when on the latter, a mild and regretful one.

The Javanese have three styles of musical compositions, the great, medium, and lesser. The latter is used for the popular songs, the former for the higher flights of poetry.

Very often one can hear an old native, on a holiday occasion, singing of the great deeds of the ancient princes; the subjects of his ballads, are often borrowed from the *babads*, or popular legends of the country, and he accompanies himself with a species of stringed instrument. He sings of the glories and fall of the kingdom of Pad-jad-jaran, and praises and laments those royal heroes. Many of the love songs of the Malays are written in the form of question and answer, as follows,—

> "Where do the swallows go to bathe?
> They go to bathe in the forest brook.
> What has my loved one promised to me?
> She has promised to chat a little with me," etc.

This questioning and answering is not confined to their music, for the Javanese are passionately fond of conundrums.* The imagery of their poems and songs is of the simplest and most natural description, fields, flowers, trees, rivers, etc., appear *ad infinitum* in their literature.† Their early historical legends are full of Gods in human form, of giants, and miracles; somewhat resembling in this the Hindoo allegories.

Theatrical representations, of course form a large part of both Malaysian and Polynesian popular amusements. In Java, national history is preserved not only by the ballads, but by pantomimic representations; in the latter, little puppets made of leather, wood, or paper, and sometimes masked performers, appear. The performance is accompanied by orchestral music, certain stringed instruments of which are only played by women. Some of the representations are given at night behind a white curtain, and resemble what, with us, are called, "shadow pantomimes;" these are performed mostly by females, and often last all night, breaking up, at times, as late as six in the morning.

---

* A conundrum from Java may be interesting to the reader   Here is one,—
  Q.— What is lower than the knee, yet higher than the mountain?
  A — The road which crosses the mountain.

† De Backer, L'Archipel Indien, p. 185.

At all Javanese *fetes*, music is played, and every native is expected to entertain such wandering musicians as apply to him. A refusal is apt to cost dearly, as the irate musicians stone the dwelling of the obdurate one.*

M. Scherzer, connected with the Austrian Round-the-world expedition in 1857 (in the frigate Novara), was not highly delighted with the Javanese pantomime dancing and music;† he says:

"Conversation was carried on with difficulty, for an incessant and stupefying noise was kept up with the gammelong, or orchestra of bells. Bayaderes, very scantily clothed, and excessively ugly, executed sentimental and religious dances of a most tedious description.

Stiff, slow, and thin, these damsels jumped like forks, with motions as graceful as those of old semaphores. The governor was kind enough to explain to us, that the dance was meant to represent the touching history of four sisters, who, lost in the forest, implored from the divinity the return of their mother.

This was followed by another choregraphic entertainment, a dance of eight warriors, accompanied by the perpetual *gammelong* The same delectable music, delighted the ears of those who were without in the court-yard. Hideous masks, on foot and on horseback, circulated there amidst the crowd; a Mussulman priest was also howling

* De Backer, L'Archipel Indien, p 207.
† Quoted in Ainsworth, Round the World, p. 246

fearfully, as he danced on hot ashes, near to a mass of burning wood; others jumped in and danced away frantically. At last the priest himself joined them, and the shouts and gesticulations became furious. This representation had probably some signification of religious expiation, at least it would have been deemed as such in ancient mysteries."

After this followed conjuring tricks of a wonderful, though sanguinary description, " and then the infernal *gammelong* began again." Then came excellent fireworks. "At last the *gammelong* ceased its stunning noise."

During Captain Cook's voyage round the world, Banks and Solander, two of his best associates witnessed (A. D. 1769) a pantomime in one of the Society islands. It was of a comic nature, and contained music and dancing. The subject was the adventures of a thief, including his capture.[*] In Cook's second voyage, Forster observed a comic opera in the Society islands, which appear closely allied to the above. Actors and actresses appeared in this play, the first act of which concluded with a burlesque beating of three of the participants. The commencement of the second act was announced by the musicians beating their drums.[†]

In the Tonga islands, the actors of these musical dramas recite sentences which are answered by a chorus of singers. There is a great variety in their movements and groupings. Occasionally

---

[*] Engel's Musical Myths, e c., v. 2, p. 150.
[†] A voyage round the World (Cook's) Forster, p. 898, v. 1.

they sing slowly, and afterwards quickly for about a quarter of an hour. Sometimes they form a semi-circle, assume a bending position, and sing in a subdued tone of voice, a soft air, which is soon followed again by a loud and vehement declamation.

It is a singular fact that some of the races most addicted to cannibalism are also much addicted to music. We have seen this already in the case of the New Zealanders; it will be fully as apparent with the most cannibalistic race of the globe,—the Fiji Islanders. With them, music teaching is a remunerative art, and any one who has composed a new song or dance, can earn a large quantity of goods by teaching it. Their musical instruments are poor and few; they consist of pipes, flutes, drums, and trumpets. The trumpets are merely conch shells, blown through an aperture in the side.

The flutes are nose-flutes, played by putting the aperture under one nostril, closing the other with the thumb of the left hand, and blowing. The pipes are a species of pandean pipes made of bamboo.

The dances are very carefully got up, and more resemble military movements than dances, the similitude being increased by the martial array of the dancers, who are all dressed as if for war, their faces painted with scarlet, their bodies powdered black, and their best clubs or spears in their hands. They execute intricate manœuvres, marching in various figures, wheeling, halting, and stamping their feet in exact time to the rhythm of the song, and the beat of the drum.

Sometimes several hundred men are engaged in the dance, while the musicians are twenty or thirty in number. The scene at one of these dances is very picturesque, but it wants the furious energy, which gives such fiery animation to the war-dance of the New Zealanders; the movements, though correct in point of time, being comparatively dull and heavy. In order to enliven it a little more, a professional buffoon is usually introduced upon the scene, who performs sundry grotesque movements, and is usually applauded for his exertions. Music and dancing are always used at the celebration of a marriage.* Mr. Seeman in a recent work† says of the entertainment called *Kalau Rere*, that, " with its high poles, streamers, evergreens, [these cannibals are very tasty in their personal adornments, wreaths of flowers, evergreens, etc., being much used], masquerading, trumpet shells, chants, and other wild music, is the nearest approach to dramatic representation, the Fijians seem to have made, and it is with them, what private theatricals are with us. Court fools, in many instances hunchbacks, are attached to the chief's establishment."

The music of the remaining races of Oceanica, does not differ very materially from the above-described forms. Many of the instruments found in use among the Malays, have had their origin in

---
* Wood's Nat. History of Man, v. 1, p. 285.
† An account of a Government mission to the Fiji Islands, p. 116.

China and India,* and therefore the description of them has not been made so minute as that of the instruments of those countries. Summed up briefly, we find that the taste for rhythm is *every where* prevalent; for instruments of percussion, almost so, (the New Zealanders forming a notable exception here), and that the prevailing impulse of these races, on hearing rhythmic music, is to dance.

We now proceed to the examination of the music of another large division of the human race.

* Fetis, Histoire de la Mus., v. 1, p. 82.

CHAPTER XIX.

AFRICAN MUSIC.

In describing the music of the natives of **Africa**, we will place in contrast the modes of the two extremes of the scale of intelligence.

The Kaffir is certainly as far in advance of the Bushman, as we are in advance of the native Indian. The Kaffir is peculiar in music; very deficient in melody, he is almost perfect in rhythm and time-keeping. He is fond of singing in company, and in fact is a rather convivial person altogether. At social meals, while the food is cooking, the guests often amuse themselves by singing together until the repast is in readiness. The subjects of the songs are various; love songs, and war songs being held in equal favor, but the Kaffir is always specially pleased with any song that relates to the possession of cattle; and being a cattle-owning people, they have many songs celebrating their favorite subject.

Many of the Kaffir's musical effects would seem most ludicrous to us. Sudden contrasts, have, to him, a special attraction, and it is not unusual to hear him give the highest squeaks of falsetto, and the deepest bass grunts, alternately.

Loudness in singing is his great end and aim, and to effect sudden *sforzando* effects, he has a peculiar method, i. e.—the choruses of the songs are usually meaningless, being often a mere reiteration of the words e-e-e-y*u* (which may be called the African "fol de rol de ray"), and when, after shouting with full lungs on the *e-e-e*, the singer desires more power on the *yu*, he effects it by giving himself a sound thump in the ribs with his elbows; this produces a marked emphasis on the syllable, and the result, when two or three hundred singers do this simultaneously is startling. The Kaffir, contrary to our practise, *sits down*, when he sings.

One of their favorite songs, is used at husking festivals. "The dry heads of maize are thrown in a heap upon the hard and polished floor of the hut, and a number of Kaffirs sit in a circle round the heap, each being furnished with the ever useful *knobkerry* (a stick or club, very like a *shillelagh*, but with a knob at one end). One of them strikes up a song, and the others join in full chorus beating time with their clubs, upon the heads of the maize. This is a very exciting amusement for the performers, who shout the noisy chorus at the highest pitch of their lungs, and beat time by striking their knobkerries upon the grain. With every blow of the heavy club the maize grains are struck from their husks, and fly about the hut in all directions, threatening injury, if not absolute destruction to the eyes of all who are present in the hut. Yet the threshers seem to enjoy an immunity which seems to be restricted to themselves and blacksmiths; and while a stranger is anxiously shading his eyes from the shower of hard maize grains, the threshers themselves do not give a thought to the safety of their eyes, but sing at the top of their voices, pound away at the corn cobs, and make the grains fly in all directions, as if the chorus of the song were the chief object in life, and the preservation of their eyesight were unworthy of a thought."*

The war-songs of the Kaffirs are fiery and exciting, though in a less degree than those of New Zealand.

Their poetry is full of metaphor, and alliterative enough to be admitted into the opera of the future. The participants sit in a circle, sometimes three or four deep, with their knees well drawn up, and sing, beating rhythmic accompaniment upon the ground, twirling their *assagais* (javelins), and occasionally enlivening the proceedings with an ear-piercing whistle, or deafening shout.

We give an English version (Mr. Shooter's) of two of these, merely premising that much of the native beauty is said to be lost in the transpositiou to a foreign tongue.

* Wood's Nat. History, v. 2, p. 282.

PRAISE OF DINGAN.
A VERY CELEBRATED CHIEF.

"Thou needy offspring of Umpikazi
Eyer of the cattle of men,
Bird of Maube, fleet as a bullet,
Sleek, erect, of beautiful parts.
Thy cattle like the comb of bees.
O head too large, too huddled to move,
Devourer of Moselekatze, son of Machobana,
Devourer of Swazi, son of Sobuza,
Breaker of the gates of Machobana,
Devourer of Gundave of Machobana
A monster in size,[*] of mighty power,
Devourer of Ungwati of ancient race,
Devourer of the kingly Uomapé;
Like Heaven above, raining and shining."

The other is an Alexandrian lament of the lack of nations to conquer. It is in honor of Tchaka, (a renowned warrior and chief).

"Thou hast finished, finished the nations!
Where will you go out to battle now?
Hey! Where will you go out to battle now?
Thou hast conquered kings!
Where are you going to battle now?
Thou hast finished, finished the nations!
Where are you going to battle now?
Hurrah! Hurrah! Hurrah!!
Where are you going to battle now?"

From the extracts it will be seen that flattery is not confined to European courts; the Kaffir carries

[*] All Kaffir chiefs aspire to obesity as an emblem of rank.

it still further, for in addition to his own proper name (which it is deemed ill omened to speak) everybody of any rank, receives a number of *isi-bonges* or praise-names, alluding to some action or peculiarity. It is customary on all formal occasions, to recite several of these *isi-bonges*, just as a European nobleman on official ceremonies desires to have all his titles proclaimed. In songs, of course, the invention of these is unlimited. Thus the great Panda, a renowned ruler of enormous fatness, is spoken of as,—

"A swallow which fled in the sky,"
"A swallow with a whiskered breast,"
"Ramrod of brass,"
"Thigh of the bullock of Inkakavini."
"Thou art an *Elephant*."
"Monarch who art black," etc., etc.

Such songs of praise are sung with great relish by full choruses. Violent gestures are used to heighten the effect. The songs are in unison, no harmonic divisions being attempted.

The instruments of the Kaffir are few and crude; the whistle before mentioned, although giving but one tone, is a great favorite. It is so shrill that it can be heard above the wildest din of the *ensemble*.

A rude flute or flageolet is also sometimes used; but the most-used instrument, is a primitive harp with *one string* only, and whose tones though light and sweet can scarcely be heard at six yards distance. It is an ordinary bow with a string of twisted hair, and a hollow gourd attached at the centre of the wood to give resonance. A ring is passed along the string, to raise or lower the tone, which is produced by striking the cord with a short stick, or *plectrum*. The bow is about five feet long, and exactly resembles the usual weapon, which however is not used in war by the Kaffirs.

Although the resources of this instrument are so extremely limited, the musicians of this people are content to sit for hours, listening to its monotonous sound.

Let us now turn to the degraded black brother of the foregoing race, the Bushman. His amusements are two;—singing and dancing.

The dance of the Bushman is to European eyes a most uninteresting one; as there is scarcely any motion or gesture at all in it, save that which is made by *one leg*. Standing on one foot, the performer shakes the other, (to which a string of rattles, made from the ears of the spring-bok are attached) occasionally giving his body a twist, and singing vigorously all the while, changing the foot, however, from time to time.

The spectators keep the rhythm by a constant and regular clapping of hands and a monotonous singing.

A water-drum, which is merely a wooden bowl, into which a little water has been poured, and over which a skin is tightly drawn, is struck regularly in time with the movements of the dancer; the latter when partially exhausted, falls upon the floor, but still singing and kicking in time with the music; after a short rest of this description, he jumps up and continues as at first. When utterly exhausted, he retires among the spectators and unfastening his leg-rattles, hands them to the next dancer. The music to this odd performance is *not* in unison; the dancer sings one air, the spectators another, and the drum gives a species of "ground bass" to the whole.

While engaged in this interesting occupation of shaking one leg, the Bushman is completely oblivious of all other considerations, as if he were entranced. Discordant as the music seems to us when annotated by the travellers who have heard it, yet these same authorities are almost unanimous in declaring that the effect is extremely pleasant.

The most peculiar instrument of the Bushmen, is the *goura*, which is shaped like a bow, but has at one end of the string, a piece of quill inserted; this quill is blown upon in the same manner that we use a jew's-harp. Women play upon this instrument, but hold it perpendicularly, and do not breathe upon it, but strike it with a stick, and then catch it up, quickly to their ear, to listen to the tones. When thus played, it is called, a *joum-joum*.

All the airs played upon this primitive instrument seem to come by chance rather than skill, and the performer never seems able to play the same tune twice. But the same or better music could be drawn from a much more compact and portable instrument; therefore the *goura* has now been almost superseded by a European competitor, and the favorite instrument of the **African** Bosjesman now is the *Jew's-harp.*

They also possess a rude banjo-like instrument from which comparatively fair music could be produced, but the Bushmen are content to strum it without method, and take the music as fortune sends it. A drum completes the list of Bushman instruments; it is sometimes played with sticks and sometimes with the fist. It can be heard at a considerable distance.

In contrasting these two extremes of African races, it is singular to remark, that the superiority in music, if there be any, must be conceded to the lower race.

We find much that is curious and worthy of note in the music of those mysterious tribes of central Africa, who have so recently become known to us through the researches of Schweinfurth, Stanley, and Baker.

Among the best known of these tribes, may be mentioned the **Nyam-Nyams**, a set of most inveterate cannibals, whose very name comes from the sound of gnawing at food, and was given them on account of their man-eating propensities. Their chief musical instruments are mandolins or small harps of four strings each, drums (mostly of wood,) bells of iron, whistles and pipes. Many of these instruments are very symmetrically formed, and tastily carved, for in wood, iron, and clay designing the Nyam-Nyams are very expert. Schweinfurth thus describes their music,*—

---
*The Heart of Africa, v 2, p. 29

"They have an instinctive love of art. Music rejoices their very soul. The harmonies they elicit from their favorite instrument, the mandolin, seem almost to thrill through the chords of their inmost nature. The prolonged duration of some of their musical productions is very surprising." Piaggia has remarked that he believed a "Nyam-Nyam would go on playing all day and all night, without thinking to leave off either to eat or to drink," and although quite aware of the voracious propensities of the people, it seems very probable that he was right.

One favorite instrument there is, which is something between a harp and a mandolin. It resembles the former in the vertical arrangement of its strings, whilst in common with the mandolin, it has a sounding-board, a neck, and screws for tightening the strings.

The sounding board is constructed on strict acoustic principles. It has two apertures; it is carved out of wood, and on the upper side it is covered with a piece of skin; the strings are tightly stretched by means of pegs, and are sometimes made of fine threads of bast, and sometimes of the wiry hairs from the tail of the giraffe.

The music is very monotonous and it is difficult to distinguish any melody in it. It invariably is an accompaniment to a moaning kind of recitative which is rendered with a decided nasal intonation.

"I have not unfrequently seen friends marching about arm in arm, wrapt in the mutual enjoyment of the performance, and beating time to every note by nodding their heads."

"There is a singular class of professional musicians who make their appearance decked out in the most fantastic way, with feathers, and covered with a promiscuous array of bits of wood and roots, and all the pretentious emblems of magical art, the feet of earth-pigs, the shell of tortoises, the beaks of eagles, the claws of birds, and teeth in every variety. Whenever one of this fraternity presents himself, he at once begins to recite all the details of his travels and experiences, in an emphatic recitative, and never forgets to conclude by an appeal to the liberality of his audience, and to remind them that he looks for a reward either of rings of copper, or of beads."[*]

With some slight differences these men may be found throughout Africa; almost everywhere they are sought for and their talents enjoyed, but they themselves held in contempt. Among the Nyam-Nyams, their appellation in itself ("Nzangah") implies contempt, being similar to that which is applied to despised and outcast women.

Contrary to the custom of almost all other savages, the Nyam-Nyams delight most in gentle music; some of the minstrels sing so softly that it is impossible to hear them a few yards off. The light Mandolin accompaniment is in good accord with this *pianissimo* style of music.

Their dances, given by male and female performers, are wonderfully swift, intricate and pleasant.

[*] Schweinfurth, Heart of Africa, v. 2, p. 30.

AFRICAN MUSIC. 261

A great "Congo" or dance was given by some of these people to Col. C. Chaillé Long, an American officer on the staff of the Khedive of Egypt, who made a very interesting expedition to the Makraka Nyam-Nyams, and Lake Victoria Nyanza in 1874. He thus describes the scene:—*

"Invitations had been sent to all the Nyam-Nyam lasses, who came even from as far as Parafio, and did honor to the occasion by brightening up their copper and iron fastenings, and in putting on fresh fig leaves. The loose bands that encased their ankles, kept perfect time in loud clanking sound to music really euphonious, and of a symphony that my unmusical ear I regret cannot translate here, evoked from a Sinon-like wooden horse, that was beaten on its sides with drum-sticks, or by parallel banana trees that were traversed by different sized pieces of dry wood, upon which several performers beat successively.

This musical instrument, as well as drums and horns, the latter made of Elephants' tusks, were very similar to those I had seen at Ugunda. . . .

The Sheik, a robust, powerfully developed man, led his brave warriors in the dance, holding in his hand, a curiously-shaped sword, his insignia of office, whilst the round little forms of hundreds of Nyam-Nyam maidens followed, each with giddy swiftness as the "cancan" fantasia became fast and furious. The festivity continued until the 'wee sma hours' of the morning."

The trumpets of the Nyam-Nyam are more generally used as war signals than as musical

* Central Africa, or Naked Truths about Naked people, p. 278

instruments; they are blown through a hole in the side, and not at the end; therefore the mode of performing upon them, rather resembles our style of flute playing.*

Another musical nation of Central Africa is the Karague; travellers who have visited them have given more or less detailed accounts of their instruments and festivities. Capt. Speke had the unusual honor of a serenade from the royal court band. The king after receiving a present of some beads, cloth wire, and a tin box, was so delighted that he sent his own band to give Speke a tune.

The performers used reed instruments (made in telescopic fashion) and marked the time by hand-drums. At first they marched and countermarched, playing meanwhile much in the manner of Turkish regimental bands; but this was soon changed to a species of "horn-pipe," which all the musicians danced, playing furiously meanwhile.†

Another bit of musical ceremony which Speke witnessed, will at once remind the reader of the great "Zapfenstreich" or grand tattoo practised sometimes in the German army. At the new moon the king surrounds himself with numerous drummers (Speke saw thirty-five); these strike up together, gradually increasing to a deafening noise; this is followed by a milder kind of music, similar to that described above. The object of the ceremony is to call in all the king's warriors to renew their

* Wood's Nat'l History of Man, v. 2, p. 498.

† Journal of the discovery of the source of the Nile, by Capt. Speke, page 210.

oath of fealty.* The time keeping is said to be very exact, and the drummers burst forth again and again during the night. The war drum of the Karague is beaten by women.

A kind of guitar exists among this people, and six of the seven strings which it possesses accord perfectly with our own diatonic scale, the seventh string only, being discordant. Their wind instruments are flageolet and bugle, or at least similar to them.

Among the nations adjacent to those already mentioned are the Bongo.

We again quote from the valuable work of the most musical traveller who has visited this section, —Schweinfurth.†

"The Bongo, in their way are enthusiastic lovers of music; and although their instruments are of a very primitive description, and they are unacquainted even with the pretty little guitar of the Nyam-Nyams, which is constructed on perfectly correct acoustic principles, yet they may be seen at any hour of the day, strumming away and chanting to their own performances. The youngsters down to the small boys are all musicians. Without much trouble and with the most meagre materials they contrive to make little flutes; they are accustomed also to construct a monochord, which in its design reminds one of that which (known as the Gubo of the Zulus) is common throughout the tribes of Southern Africa. This

* Captain Speke's Journal, p. 222.
† Heart of Africa, v. 1, p. 287.

consists of a bow of bamboo, with the string tightly strained across it, and this is struck by a slender slip of bamboo.

The mouth of the player performs the office of sounding board; he holds the instrument to his mouth with one hand, and manages the string with the other. Performers may often be seen sitting for hours together with an instrument of this sort; they stick one end of the bow into the ground, and fasten the string over a cavity covered with bark, which opens into an aperture for the escape of the sound. They pass one hand from one part of the bow to the other, and with the other they play upon the string with the bamboo twig, and produce a considerable variety of buzzing and humming airs which are really rather pretty. This is quite a common pastime with the lads who are put in charge of the goats. I have seen them apply themselves very earnestly and with obvious interest to their musical practice, and the ingenious use to which they apply the simplest means for obtaining harmonious tones testifies to their penetration into the secrets of the theory of sound.

As appeals however to the sense of sound, the great festivals of the Bongo abound with measures much more thrilling than any of these minor performances. On these occasions the orchestral results might perhaps be fairly characterised as cats' music run wild.

Unwearied thumping of drums, the bellowings of gigantic trumpets, for the manufacture of which, great stems of trees come into requisition. Interchanged by fits and starts with the shriller blasts of some smaller horns, make up the burden of the unearthly hub-bub which re-echoes miles away along the desert; meanwhile women and children by the hundred fill gourd flasks with little stones, and rattle them as if they were churning butter; or again at other times they will get some sticks or faggots and strike them together with the greatest energy.

The huge wooden tubes which may be styled the trumpets of the Bongo, are by the natives themselves, called "manyinyee;" they vary from four to five feet in length, being closed at the extremity and ornamented with carved work representing a man's head, which not unfrequently is adorned with a pair of horns. The other end of the stem is open, and in an upper department, towards the figure of the head, is the orifice into which the performer blows with all his might.

There is another form of manyinyee, which is made like a huge wine bottle; in order to play upon it, the musician takes it between his knees like a violincello, and when the build of the instrument is too cumbrous he has to bend over it as it lies upon the ground.

"Little difference can be noticed between the kettle drums of the Bongo, and those of most other North African Negroes. A section is cut from the thick stem of a tree, the preference being given to a tamarind when it can be procured, this is hollowed out into a cylinder, one end being larger than the other. The ends are then covered with two pieces of goat skin, stripped of the hair which are tightly strained, and laced together with thongs.

At the nightly orgies a fire is invariably kept burning to dry the skin, and to tighten it, when it has happened to become relaxed by the heavy dews."

A short description of the signal horns of the Bongo is also given by our musical traveller; some of them resemble fifes, and many are made of antelope horns.

Regarding the singing of the Bongo, Schweinfurth is quite descriptive and as the deductions he arrives at are very similar to those we have ascribed to primitive or natural men, we introduce the passage without alteration.*

"Difficult were the task to give any adequate description of the singing of the Bongo. It must suffice to say that it consists of a babbling recitative, which at one time suggests the yelling of a dog, and at another the lowing of a cow, whilst it is broken over, and again by the gabbling of a string of words which are huddled up one into another. The commencement of a measure will always be with a lively air, and every one without distinction of age or sex will begin yelling, screeching, and bellowing with all their strength; gradually the surging of voices will tone down, the rapid time will moderate, and the song be hushed into a wailing melancholy strain.

* Heart of Africa, v 1, p. 289.

"Thus it sinks into a very dirge such as might be chanted at the grave, and be interpreted as representative of a leaden and a frowning sky, when all at once, without note of warning, there bursts forth the whole fury of the negro throats; shrill and thrilling is the outcry, and the contrast is as vivid as sunshine in the midst of rain."

"Often as I was present at these festivities I never could prevent my ideas from associating Bongo music with the instinct of imitation which belongs to men universally. The orgies always gave me the impression of having no other object than to surpass in violence the fury of the elements: adequately to represent the rage of a hurricane in the tropics, any single instrument must of course be weak, poor, and powerless, consequently they hammer at numbers of their gigantic drums with powerful blows of their heavy clubs. If they would rival the bursting of a storm, the roaring of the wind, or the plashing of the rain, they summon a chorus of their stoutest lungs; whilst to depict the bellowing of terrified wild beasts, they resort to their longest horns; and to imitate the songs of birds, they bring together all their flutes and fifes.

Most characteristic of all, perchance is the deep and rolling bass of the huge "manyinyee" as descriptive of the rumbling thunder. The penetrating shower may drive rattling and crackling among the twigs and amid the parched foliage of the woods; and this is imitated by the united energies of women and children, as they rattle the stones in their gourd-flasks, and clash together their bits of wood."

The dances of these people are similar in wildness to their music. The performers wear iron rings, with balls attached, around their ankles, and clash these together with such energy that their feet are often bathed in blood.

The Mittoo tribe rank very high among the African tribes, in their musical attainments; their melodies are quite agreeable to the cultivated ear and the pains which they take in mastering the intricacies of a musical composition, recall to the mind the difficulties which beset the path of the civilized musical student.

We have seen a transcription of one of their songs, which would require but little alteration to transform it into a very fair "slumber song."

Many of them are quite skillful upon the flute, and have been described by Nubian travellers as equal to the best Frankish (European) performers who reside in Cairo.

The Monbuttoo also have a strong passion for music, so much so that the king sometimes dances before his wives and subjects, to the accompaniment of the royal band.

In his court concerts he has horn-men, who can modulate their tones from infinite tenderness to the sound of a lion's roar; and can perform upon a horn so cumbrous that it can scarcely be held, passages of runs, trills and shakes, which would be even difficult upon a flute.

Court fools. jesters and mimics also appertain

to the King of the Monbuttoo—Munza; they have also a sort of national hymn, more noisy than musical. The words are monotonous and much repeated,—

" Ee, ee, tchupy, tchupy, ee, Munza, ee!" will do as a sample line. The king stands up and *beats time*, with all the gravity of a musical conductor. His *baton* is made of a wicker worked sphere filled with pebbles, and attached to a short stick, in fact exactly what we should call a baby's rattle. When he approves the performance or gets excited, he joins in the chorus with a stentorian " B-r-r-r-r——" which shakes the house.

It is singular that music boxes should be popular with Africans who indulge in such noisy effects, yet such is the fact; there is no present so desired by Negro potentates as a music box with bells and drums.

Explorers can find no surer road to the heart of an African chief than by a present of one of these mechanisms. Sir Samuel Baker had great trouble with King Kabba Rega (of the tribe of the Unyori,) about a music box.* Speke and Schweinfurth both found them among the most treasured possessions of the savage chieftains. Kabba Rega's reason for prizing the box above all other musical instruments, is unique; on hearing it play, for the first time, he remarked,—" It is more convenient than an instrument which requires study, as you might set this going at night, to play you to sleep, when you were too drunk to

*Ismailia, By Sir S W. Baker, page 391

play it yourself even if you knew how to do it."*
The national hymn of this monarch, bears considerable resemblance to the first part of the well known air—"Three Blind Mice."†

We have not space to describe fully the rites and music of that curious people, the Abyssinians; two examples of their musical ceremonies must suffice.

A funeral procession (reported by an American eye witness) consisted of about one hundred and fifty people, old and young, preceded by a few priests; every few minutes the *cortege* would halt to shriek and howl. The priests (clad in cotton robes with broad scarlet bands) were acting in a frantic manner; tearing off their turbans, pulling their hair, then folding their hands on their breasts and looking inexpressibly miserable.

They carried Arabic parchment books, illuminated with quaint figures and devices, and now and then chanted prayers to some favorite saint,‡ very dolefully, though with strong lungs and nasal intonation. Numerous genuflections were made, always accompanied with long drawn howls of extreme agony. At the lowering of the body into the grave, they chanted a prayer, of which the following is a translation,—

"Werkena, son of Yasous, who was the son of Tekee, is dead. Rejoice, oh ye people! He has gone to his rest with Abraham, with Isaac, and

---

* Ismailia, p. 355.

† See "Ismailia," p. 372.

‡ It will be recollected that the Abyssinians belong to a sect of the Christian Church

with Jacob. Let us pray for those who still live, and pray for the soul just gone to doom. From vengeance and stern judgment, pray that his soul be delivered. How can the souls be delivered from tribulation? By long prayers. Pray, then, that he be sheltered by Father Abraham, that he may walk in safety by the side of Moses and the prophets, Amen, and Amen!"*

After the grave was closed, the major part of the mourners followed in the train of a musician, who was discoursing lively tunes on an oboe, and one of the priests, who had been mourning so vigorously, offered to show strangers over his cathedral for the consideration of one dollar.

A fitting contrast to this, is the musical ovation tendered to the British Army, after the conquest of King Theodore, April, 1868. The natives came in great numbers to sing praises. They chose for the subject of their psalm, the twenty-second chapter, of the second book of Samuel, (David's song), beginning:—" The Lord is my rock, and my fortress," and they sang it with David's own fervor; and, to make it quite realistic, in imitation of his dancing before the ark, the Abyssinian clergy brought out an imitation of an ark, five yards in length, one yard in breadth, and a foot in height. It was covered with a scarlet cloth, embroidered with gold, and above it was a representation of a mercy-seat of crimson silk, surmounted by a canopy of similar stuff; candlesticks, lavers, priests' robes, hyssops, communion

* Coomassie and Magdala. by H. M. Stanley, p. 310

cups, pixes, chalices, crosses of brass, silver and gold, mitres, etc., figured in the religious paraphernalia employed. The Neophytes kept up a deafening, jingling clang; or, with instruments of wood and brass, one stringed banjoes, clanking brass cymbals kept a rhythmic time, which swelled louder and louder as they drew near the headquarters of the army.

"The priests (out of respect for their office) took the front position, and one of them, with a semi-ludicrous air, struck up the first note of the impromptu stanzas which were to celebrate the British conquest of Abyssinia."

"As he warmed to his theme, and his voice rose to enthusiasm, the motley assembly, at the waving of a crucifix, chimed in with chorus, which, sung with stentorian lungs, had a tremendous effect. After the chorus, six priests clad in cotton stoles headed by the sub-hierarch, took the eulogy up at a very low key, which soon, however, rose so high and shrill in a protracted continuity of sound, that one momentarily expected to hear their lungs crack, ending with a stormy chorus as before. Then, forming themselves into a circle, a hundred of them commenced a dignified sailing round their neighbors, to the right and left, their togas getting inflated with the movement, weaving each into another, until it might have been imagined that they had manufactured some complicated knot, on the gordian principle; but, soon taking the reverse method, they reached their former positions in time. The singing went on louder and louder, and the choragus giving the warning clap, the whole multitude clapped their hands; the women and children struck up the silver-toned "li, li, li," performing a dance similar to the Chinese hop and skip."

"They then formed triplets and massed themselves together, when a shrill note from the boys, sent them into a confused whirl, round and round, the sub-hierarch and his six assistants going faster and faster, as they acquired momentum, clapping their hands, singing louder than ever, the head priest ducking his body lower and lower, and more energetic, until the dance and the excitement which they all labored under, assumed the appearance of a jubilee medley, composed of waltzes, Dervish-dances, sarabands, fandangos, pirouettes and chasses, the three latter performed by the most youthful of the assembly."

"It must not be forgotten, that all this time the ark and mercy-seat — minus the cherubim — (which was totally omitted from this Abyssinian imitation), stood on the ground near the priests, while a choice number of infantine neophites, manfully rang the merriest chimes, and the instruments of Juniper-wood, the one-stringed banjos, and cymbals, made as much discordant music as was possible under the circumstances. The Ethiops before concluding the entertainment, raised* once again the Canto Trionfale."

The effect Mr. Stanley says, had a wonderful charm, and the blending of the mass of women's

*Coomassie and Magdala, page 488.

and children's voices with the larger and deeper tones of the bass, was like the whistling of a gale in a ship's shrouds, blending with the deeper roar of a tempest.

We cannot give a better idea of the hold which music has upon the average native Negro, than by narrating an incident which befell Sir Samuel Baker, in the Shooli country.

He held a review of his troops March 8, 1872, and after a sham fight, firing of rockets, etc., the troops marched up and down a hill, with the band playing. The natives assembled in considerable numbers and viewed the manœuvres with much delight; but the brass band music was the crowning point of their enjoyment. We sub-join his description of its effect upon these children of nature.

"The music of our band being produced simply by a considerable number of bugles, drums, and cymbals, aided by a large military bass-drum, might not have been thought first-rate in Europe, but in Africa it was irresistible."

"The natives are passionately fond of music; and I believe the safest way to travel in these wild countries, would be to play the cornet, if possible, without ceasing, which would ensure a safe passage. A London organ-grinder would march through Central Africa, followed by an admiring and enthusiastic crowd, who, if his tunes were lively, would form a dancing escort of the most untiring material."

"As my troops returned to their quarters, with

the band playing rather lively airs, we observed the women racing down from their villages, and gathering from all directions towards the common centre. As they approached nearer, the charms of music were overpowering, and halting for an instant they assumed what they considered the most graceful attitudes, and then danced up to band."

"In a short time my buglers could scarcely blow their instruments for laughing at the extraordinary effect of their performance. A fantastic crowd surrounded them as they halted in our position among the rocks, and every minute added to their number."

"The women throughout the Shooli are entirely naked; thus the effect of a female crowd, bounding madly about as musical enthusiasts, was very extraordinary; even the babies were brought out to dance; and these infants strapped to their mothers' backs, and covered with pumpkin shells, like the young tortoises, were jolted about, without the slightest consideration for the weakness of their necks, by their infatuated mothers."

"As usual among all tribes of Central Africa, the old women were even more determined dancers than the young girls. Several old Venuses were making themselves extremely ridiculous, as they sometimes do in civilized countries, when attempting the allurements of younger days."

* Ismailia, page 282.

"The men did not share in the dance, but squatted upon the rocks in great numbers to admire the music and to witness the efforts of their wives and daughters."*

Sir Samuel Baker also once used music for quite a different purpose. He was quartered near the town of Masindi, where dwelt Kabba Rega, King of the Unyori, when one evening, he noticed a most unusual stillness in the town, where ordinarily drunken songs and horn-blowing were the rule. Suddenly there sounded the deep tones of a *nogara*, or drum. This ceased in a moment; and then came a burst of terrific noise, which caused every man in camp to rush to his post. It was a din, caused by many thousands yelling and shrieking like maniacs. At least a thousand drums were beating; horns, whistles, and every instrument which could add to the confusion, was blowing and sounding, yet no human being was visible.

The dragoman, on being questioned by the commander, laughed, and said it was "to make him *afraid*, and exhibit the large number of people collected in the town."

Gen. Baker on ascertaining this determined to act as though it were a compliment which he felt bound to return. He ordered the regimental band to strike up, and play their loudest. This nonchalance had its effect, for, after a short time, the bugles, drums, and clashing cymbals of his own band, were the only sounds heard; the tumult in Masindi had subsided, and soon Gen.

Baker ordered his own musicians to cease playing, and all was again perfectly still.*

We close this account of the music of some of the savage tribes of the earth, with a description of a farewell dance, given to Stanley, by the Wanyamwezi of Singiri, which is well worthy of a place, as showing the powers of improvisation of the Africans.

"It was a wild dance, with lively music, four drums giving the sonorous accompaniment, being beaten with tremendous energy and strength. Everyone (even Stanley himself) danced with great fervor, and combined excited gesticulations, with their saltatory efforts. But after the close of this war-like music, came a total change; all dropped on their knees, and in sorrowful accents sang a slow and solemn refrain, of which the following is a literal translation,—

Solo:—"Oh, oh, oh! the white man is going home.
Chorus:—Oh, oh, oh! going home! going home! oh, oh, oh!
Solo:—To the happy island on the sea, Where the beads are plenty, oh, oh, oh!
Chorus:—Where the beads, etc.
Solo:—While Singiri has kept us, oh, very long From our homes, very long, oh, oh, oh!
Chorus:—From our homes, etc.
Solo:—And we have had no food for very long, We are half-starved, oh, for so long Bana Singiri.

---
*Baker's "Ismailia," page 351.

Chorus:—For so very long, oh, oh, oh! Bana
      Singiri, Singiri, Singiri! Oh! Singiri!
Solo:—Mirambo has gone to war
      To fight against the Arabs;
      The Arabs and Wangwana
      Have gone to fight Mirambo.
Chorus:—Oh, oh, oh, to fight Mirambo,
      Oh! Mirambo, Mirambo, etc.
Solo:—But the white man will make us glad,
      He is going home! For he is going
      home,
      And he will make us glad! Sh, sh, sh.
Chorus:—The white man will make us glad!
      Sh, sh, sh.
      Sh—— sh-h-h——, sh-h-h-h-h
      Um-m——mu—um-m-m—sh!*"

Mr. Stanley says that the rhythm and melody were beautiful, and the general effect fine.

It is curious to contrast this quiet and pathetic farewell with the bombastic "Where are you going to battle now?" previously given; and it is also noticeable, that the power of improvisation which is so well developed in the African Negro, is fully sustained by his descendents in America.

It will be an interesting task to the student to compare the slave-music, especially the camp-meeting songs of the American Negroes, with the various descriptions of songs given above. The same fervor of expression, and gradually growing excitement, and the same exaggeration of feeling will be perceived at once.

* Stanley's "How I found Livingstone" page 622.

It is not too much to say, that the Negro race may be, when refined and toned down, the most universally and thoroughly musical race on the face of the globe.

CHAPTER XI

MUSIC OF THE EARLY CHRISTIAN CHURCH.

We now resume the chronological chain of musical history, from the termination of "Ancient Greek music;" for the music of the Christian church took its rise, from the melodies of Ancient Greece. Yet it is probable that the earliest Christian melodies were not according to the classical Grecian type, but rather conformed to the popular in style. This has always been the case in the rise of a new sect with sagacious leaders. The Jews on leaving Egypt, yet sang the popular melodies dear to their hearts, by association of childhood and youth; only at a later period, only when these songs were no longer so endeared to them did David introduce such reforms, as gave to the Hebrew music a distinctive style. So, also, it was with the Christian church in its earliest days; it would have been positively injudicious, at first, to have attempted a reform; and therefore, the old popular melodies of Greece and Rome, were set to new words and exerted a new influence.

Music has been, with every religion, the most powerful accessory of the Faith; but with none more than with Christianity. It had the additional advantage, of being in an advancing state (under the charge of able directors, who fully saw the power of the art when made popular) while the music of the Pagan church was greatly declining. The great emperor Julian, foresaw the result, and used great efforts to secure a better class of music for the Roman sacrifices, but without avail.

With regard to the Christian music of the time of the apostles, we have only tradition, but these traditions have so much probability, that they acquire some degree of authority.

Eusebius assures us that St. Mark taught the first Egyptian Christians how to chant their prayers: St. John Chrysostom affirms (in his sixth homily) that the Apostles wrote the first hymn. In Rome (according to Tertullian) the chants were given in a deep tone, and not in a sustained manner, at one part of the service, and with strong accents, and flexible voice at another. The Fathers of the church almost all bear testimony that the music of the service generally partook of the habitual style of singing of each nation.

Kiesewetter, one of the most careful of the students of Ancient Greek music, maintains that, while the early Christians borrowed much from Greecr, yet from the first, the tendency was rather away from, than in the path of the Greek style. Brendel in his essays coincides with this opinion.*

The cause of this, so far as Rome and Greece

*Brendel. Gech. d. Musik, p. 7.

are concerned, is very apparent. The apostles and their followers, started unencumbered in the musical field. The theory of Greek music was a most difficult one to master, and the converts were at first almost wholly among the humbler classes. It would have been impossible to have trained them in the elaborate Hellenic school, therefore, the more ear-catching melodies were at first used, combined probably with a simple chant. The same cause operated in the foundation of a newer and simpler theory of music; hence, although our modern music is the child of the ancient Greek school, yet it did not go in the same course, or arrive at the same goal which would have resulted, had the old Greek civilization been continued two thousand years longer.

We hold that the Greeks were too much devoted to the plastic arts, ever to have brought music deeply into the inner life.

Before the liturgy had been well established, improvisation was much employed; a result always to be anticipated when uncultivated persons become musical. At the evening meal, the twenty-third Psalm was usually chanted.* Other passages of scripture were also used, such as Exodus xv., and Daniel iii.

When the water was passed around for the washing of hands, each one of the company was asked in turn to praise God in song, and the selection might either be taken from Scripture, or improvised, according to the taste or ability of

* According to Clemens Romanus, a contemporary of St. Paul.

the performer.* Some of the best of these effusions were unquestionably preserved and possibly even admitted into the regular service of the church The songs may have been rough and uncouth, but they were given with a fervor which compensated for any short-comings. They were unaccompanied, for two reasons; first, it would have been difficult to have formed an instrumental accompaniment to such variable and primitive songs, (sometimes a mere intonation of the voice, scarcely to be called music or even chanting); and second, because all the instruments of the heathen were in daily use at the sacrifices and theatres; and it would have seemed sacrilegious to have used them in the celebration of a Christian festival.†

The summing up of the legends, surmises, and few statements concerning the music of the earliest Christians, are well expressed in Ambros.‡

We can conclude regarding the music of the earliest Christian times, that it was at first a species of Folk-song, founded upon the school of music then in vogue, but elevated and impregnated with a new religious spirit. But this simplicity soon was changed: profiting by the experience of the Romans in uniting all art and beauty in their theatres, (whereby the theatre grew, and the church declined;) the early Christians soon found it wise to unite every art, in the service of their

---

*Tertullian, Apologia, 39. Evidently a custom derived from the *skolion* of Greece.

†Ambros, Geschichte d. Musik, v. II, p. 5.

‡Gesch. d. Musik, v. II p. 11

church. It is also probable that much of the music was borrowed from that of the Hebrews. This is more natural when we reflect that Christianity was at first a continuation (or reorganization) of Hebrew rites and the apostles were all well acquainted with the ceremonies of the Jewish church.

The chanting of the scriptures which took place in the latter worship, was undoubtedly transplanted into the Christian service.* Many of the early psalms and canticles were sung in caves and subterranean retreats in which places the proscribed and persecuted worshippers were obliged to seek refuge, and where they still kept up with undeviating regularity the practice of their ceremonies.

Pliny the younger on being made pro-consul of Bithynia was especially charged by the emperor Trajan, to find accusations against the Christians there, the number of whom was augmenting daily. A letter of his, supposed to have been written in the third year of the second century of our era,† contains the following regarding the new religion.

"They affirm that their fault, and errors have only consisted of this;—they convene at stated days, before sunrise, and sing, each in turn, verses in praise of Christ, as of a God; they engage themselves, by oath, not to do any crime, but never to commit theft, robbery, or adultery, never to break faith, or betray a trust. After this they

---

*Marcillac, Histoire de la Mus. Modern, p. 25.
† Fetis Histoire Gen de la mus, v. 4, p. 6.

separate and afterwards reassemble to eat together innocent and innocuous dishes."*

At a later period (the fourth century) all proselytes and new converts were not admitted to sing in the church with the baptized. The new converts presented themselves before the hierarch, (a dignitary who was charged with the duty of classifying the catechumens in different orders) and expressed to him the desire of joining the church. If the questions of the priests were satisfactorily answered, he placed his hand on the head of the applicant and gave him the benediction with the sign of the cross, and afterwards inscribed his name among the number of candidates for baptism. The catechumen had not the right to enter the church. He might linger around the porticos, but was on no account allowed to join in the prayers, except in a low voice, and in the hymns not at all, until he had received the rite of baptism.

The candidates for baptism were divided into various classes. Even after baptism there were three orders of Christians, and those who had fallen into disgrace with the church, were sometimes disciplined by being reduced for a few years

---

*Letters, v 5, p 7.

Affirmabent autem, hanc fuisse summan vel culpæ suæ, vel erroris quod essent soliti stato die ante lucem convenire; carmenque Christo, quasi Deo, dicere secum invicem; seque sacramento non in scelus aliquod obstringere, sed ne furta, ne latrocinia, ne adulteria committerent ne fidem fallerent. ne depositum appellati abnegarent, quibus peractis morem, sibi discedendi fuisse, rursusque coeundi ad capiendum cibum, promiscium tamen et innoxium.

to the rank of auditors at the services. These were not allowed to join in the congregational singing, and were sometimes not even admitted to the body of the church edifice unless called there.

It is presumable that the right to join in the singing was, during the first two or three centuries, highly prized.

Little by little the spirit of improvement crept into the unskilled but soul-felt music of the early Christian church. It seems rather strange to find in the very germs of the religion, a silent, yet real contest between congregational and paid singing; and to find the same evils creeping in with the employment of singers in those early times, that we see in the present days of quartette choirs. In the days of Origen (about the middle of the second century) all the congregation sang together.

St. John Chrysostom says,—

"The psalms which we sing united all the voices in one, and the canticles arise harmoniously in unison. Young and old, rich and poor, women, men, slaves and citizens, all of us have formed but one melody together."*

A better picture of the full congregational singing of the primitive Christians cannot be given. The custom of allowing both sexes to sing together, was abolished by the Synod of Antioch in A. D. 379, and it was then decided that the men only should be allowed to sing the psalms.

In A. D. 481, the council of Laodicea ordained

* Quoted by Fetis, Histoire Gen. d. l. Mus., v. 4, p. 7.

that the clerks only (called canonical singers "*Canonicos Cantores*,") should be allowed to sing during the service.* The abuses which accompany paid singing, appeared even in the second century. Singers found themselves sought after in proportion to their talents, and therefore (in the absence of an exact method of notation) sought to make those talents more conspicuous by an introduction of florid ornaments and cadenzas into their music; they gradually forgot, or disregarded the old traditional style of singing, and sought only to excite the admiration of the masses by exhibiting to the best advantage the power and agility of their voices.

It was, without doubt, to remedy this abuse that Pope Sylvester I, who occupied the pontifical chair, A. D. 320, founded a school in Rome for the formation of singers † At this time also, the choir had its own gallery or place in the church assigned to it, and every art was called into play to impress and enthrall the worshipper. Sculpture, Painting, Architecture and Music combined, as they had previously done for Pagan theatres and amusements, to render the church a beautiful as well as holy resort. Charity combined in some instances with policy; for we learn that a singing school founded in A. D. 350, by pope Hilary, was called an orphan asylum (orphanotrophia), and here the education of clerks for the church, was commenced at a very tender age.‡

* Fetis.
† Marcillac Histoire de la Mus. Moderne, p. 27.
‡ Ambros, Geschichte d Mus., v. 2, p 13.

These schools did much to re-establish a dignified and worthy style of sacred singing. Yet there was great need of a sweeping reform; for as there existed no really fixed system, the differences in singing were almost as numerous as the various existing churches. Before speaking of this reform, we will briefly outline the progress of music in Christian communities outside of Rome.

GREEK CHURCH.

The Greek church, from the very beginning, paid great attention to music in all its details. The first institution of the mass, is attributed to St. James the lesser, first bishop of Jerusalem, who died a martyr in A. D. 62. This mass is still in existence. There are also existing, masses by the two great luminaries of the Greek Church, Sts. John Chrysostom and Basilius, who flourished in the last half of the fourth century.

Although there are doubts expressed as to whether St. John Chrysostom wrote the one attributed to him, yet it is certain that the mass was used in Constantinople (of which city he was the Patriarch) as long ago as the end of the fourth century, and was not materially changed until the eighth century. It is entitled "The mystery of the divine Eucharist."*

The *hymns*, which at first were not used at all in the Roman church, were one of the brightest ornaments of the Greek. The verses and ancient tunes of these hymns were at first well adapted to

---

* Fetis Histoire Gen. de la Mus., v. 4, p. 17.

each other; but, by the constant introduction of embellishments, shakes, and cadenzas, the connection was soon lost.

This taste for ornamentation in sacred music was driven to far greater excess in the Greek church, than even in Rome; the taste for *fioritura* is to-day, and always has been, a characteristic of most Eastern nations. This is driven to such excess in the Greek church, that (in the churches of the Orient, at least), the hymns are executed by two singers, one of whom sings the hymns, while the other sustains the key note or principal tone only.

This note the singer gives out with regularity and monotony, its only object being to keep the principal singer in bounds and to prevent him from straying away from the key on account of the numerous trills and *fiorituri* which he is expected to introduce into the song.

It may be well to mention here, as we shall not recur to the music of the Eastern Greek church again, that its style of notation, and singing has altered very little, in the course of centuries; it is totally different from that of all other countries, and consists wholly of signs, which are not in any manner measured off into bars, but somewhat resemble the chants of the Catholic church. The notes are only relative in value, and the scale on which the melodies are founded, may be represented thus,—

Re, Mi, Fa, Sol, La, Si, Do, Re.
Pa, Bou, Ga, Di, Ke, Zô, Ne, Pa.

Every embellishment is represented by a character; rising and falling inflections by others, and comparative length of notes by yet others.

It will therefore be seen that although the notation is decidedly complicated, there is a comprehensible system followed, by consulting which, we attain certain information as to one branch of the early church.*

The works found in the old monasteries of the Orient are almost invaluable to the musical antiquary. We believe that many more will yet be discovered among the monks of Mt. Athos, those strange and illiterate custodians of some of the rarest manuscripts in existence, relative to this subject.†

We are sorry that a thorough description of this subject (though full of interest) would demand much space and many engravings. The effect of the singing of this church in its oriental branches is very similar to that of the Hebrews in their services of the present day.

SYRIAN CHURCH.

We now turn to the early Christian church of Syria, founded by the Apostles Paul and Barnabas.

One of the earliest in existence, the church of Antioch soon became the metropolis of Syrian Christianity. Yet it was in this church also that the first heresy took place, by the rise of the

---

* A good explanation of the system is to be found in Fetis, v. 4, pp. 29-56.

† See Curzon's " Monasteries of the Levant," or Proust's " Voyage on Mt. Athos."

Gnostics (disciples of science); one of this sect, named Bardesanes, founded a separate denomination of these, and was the first who composed hymns in the native tongue, and adapted them to melodies. He composed one hundred and fifty psalms in imitation of David.

But greatest of all the musicians of the Orthodox Christian church of Syria, was Ephraem Syrus. He is still called "Harp of the Holy Spirit" in many churches who yet honor him and celebrate his feast.

He was a monk of Syria, born of poor parents, in a village of Mesopotamia. At eighteen years of age he was converted and baptized, and soon retired to a desert spot to practice penitence and piety. It was in this retreat that he composed his voluminous sermons, hymns, etc., all of which have much poetic beauty and oriental imagery.* He wrote fifteen hymns on the "Nativity," fifteen on "Paradise," fifty-two on "Faith," and "The Church," fifty-one on "The Virginity," eighty-seven against "Heresy," and "The Arians," eighty-five "Mortuary," fifteen moral hymns, etc. His writings on the *Peshito* or Syriac version of the scriptures are still of use to the theological student.

He arranged the music to his hymns, and he himself speaks of having arranged sixty-six of them in the style of Bardesanes.

---

*Some excellent German translations of the hymns, have been made by Zingerle, and are to be found in the "Zeitschrift d. Deutschen Morgenl. Gesellschaft.

Many of the songs and prayers in the Syrian liturgy, ascribed to St. Ephraem are spurious. It is related that at the first interview between him and St. Basilius, the former was endowed by the Holy Ghost with sudden power to speak Greek, and the latter Syriac, thus giving them a choice of languages in which to converse.

It is impossible to give a thorough account of the music of the Syrian Church, as although the first instruments mentioned in the Bible (the taboret, a tambourine held in one hand and struck with the other, and Kinnor, a seven stringed triangular harp) are Syrian, yet the people have never, from time immemorial, written down their melodies, but always handed them down orally, father to son, or teacher to pupil.

The mass in Syrian liturgy, is very different in its form, from the Catholic: there is neither *Kyrie Eleison*, *Gloria*, nor *Epistle*, contained in it.

There are two distinct sects in the Syrian church; the first Ephraemitic, or followers of the Orthodox saint; the second, heretical and followers of Jacob Baradaeus, a Syrian monk of the sixth century. These are called Jacobites, and hold Eutychian doctrines.

The music of the latter is ornamented to excess; that of the Ephraemitic rite nobler and plainer.

THE ARMENIAN CHURCH.

The rise of Christianity among the Armenians, goes back to the third century, but they early developed the doctrines of Eutychius, and the Monophysites. At times, portions of the Armenian church have adhered to the Western church, but in its rites it far more resembles the Eastern Greek church. The language is well adapted for song.

Their most ancient religious songs were written by *Sahac,* the great *Katholicos,* or patriarch of the church; the psalms were sung by them to popular melodies.

THE CHURCHES OF AFRICA.

St. Mark is considered as the Apostle of Egypt and founder of the church of Alexandria; the liturgy used by this church is said to have been written by him; but many manuscripts exist which point to St. Basilius as its author, and it bears internal evidence that St. Mark could not have written it, for among the prayers for the dead, it names many saints, martyrs, bishops, etc., *including St. Mark.*

The songs of the early Christians here, as throughout the Orient, were hymns, psalms, and anthems of which the melodies were taken from the popular music of the day.

The Coptic church in its liturgy entirely resembled the Greek church of Egypt, and in looking over its ritual, one continually meets with translations of the liturgies of St. Basil, St. Cyrille, or St. Gregory Nazianzen. In the National Library, of Paris there is also a Coptic translation of the Liturgy of St. Mark.

The music of the Coptic church is very much embellished, and of inordinate length; for, owing to the practice of the singers to vocalise upon one syllable sometimes to the length of *several minutes** the vespers alone, often attain the length of *four or five hours.*

As the rules of worship of the Copts do not allow them either to kneel or to sit down during services, they are obliged to support themselves by placing under their arm-pits, a long crutch, in order not to drop from fatigue.

This race is degenerating fast, and will soon disappear under the despotic sway of the Arabs. Their number is about one hundred and fifty thousand. Few of them understand the Coptic language, and although part of the service is sung in that tongue, it is usually afterwards explained in Arabic. Their modulations in singing are very bold, constant, and fatiguing; so much so, that long before the end of the song, all remembrance of any key-note, is lost.

All writers agree in speaking of their music, as tiresome in the extreme. This proceeds from three causes;—their extraordinary length, their insignificant melody, and the constant repetition of the syllables and vowels of a single word, whereby it is made almost impossible to follow the sense of the text. This fault is not confined to the Coptic sect only, but is largely found in the Greek church throughout the Orient. Fetis gives a strong example of one case, taken from an Eastern Hymnal, it runs as follows,—

Aga-a-a-a-a-aate-e-e-e-e mara ky-y-y-ri-i-i-i-i-ou.

* Paris Histoire Gen. T. 4. p 90

Each of the vowels is given separate from the others, and the effect is ludicrous in the extreme. The Copts do worse than this; after mincing a word into such minute fragments, they go back and re-mutilate the first syllable, then again the second, then perhaps the first two, and so on for a long time before they give the word complete like the Syrians.

The Copts have no musical notation whatever, and it is a most curious fact in music, that they should be able to recollect such lengthy songs, devoid of any apparent melody, or sequence, and hand them down traditionally, from generation to generation; they must possess either phenomenal memories, or an insight to a connection of ideas in their songs, which has escaped European perception. These remarkable descendants of the ancient Egyptians, hate other Christian sects with much more fervor than they do the Mohammedans.

Of the Abyssinian Church we have already spoken (see chapters on " African Music ");— there is little more to add. They have different modes of singing for different grades of sacred festivals. Responses made by the people or the choir, enter largely into their mass. The number of choristers is from eight to twelve, and they have all powerful voices; this is in fact a prime necessity, as at the door of the church, during service, a constant din of drums, cymbals, and sistrums is kept up.

On certain days, the priests and people have a

a grand religious dance, to the sound of these instruments, while the chorus sing a litany and all mark the time by a clapping of hands.

GENERAL SYNOPSIS OF EARLY CHRISTIAN MUSIC.

That the art of music was esteemed among the more educated of the early Christians is very strongly shown by a fresco in the cemetery of Domitilla (in Rome). This painting which seems to be of the first or second century of our era, represents Christ as Orpheus, charming all nature by his music.* It is probably only an allegorical figure, representing his divine gifts, but the figure must be a shock to all who are accustomed to see the face of Jesus, as drawn by the Leonardo da Vinci. Instead of the meek and beautiful form, we see here a lank loosely-built young man, sitting in a very uncomfortable attitude, on a rock, and twanging away at a four-stringed lyre.

Regarding the origin of the present pictures of Christ (although not strictly belonging to our subject) we are tempted to make the following remarks.

It is believed by some scholars that the head of Christ was first copied from the statue of Jupiter (or the Greek Zeus), which was, in the early centuries regarded as the most perfect model of manly beauty. It is scarcely to be doubted that the general model of the Pagan sculptures was followed in the early representations of the

* Rambosson, Harmonies du Son, p. 21.

THE EARLY CHRISTIAN CHURCH. 297

Saviour. But the style of portraits was altered in consonance with the description handed down by good authorities.

A brass medal with a head of Christ on one side, was discovered in 1702, in some Druidical ruins, at Aberfraw, Wales, which although of a later era than that assigned to it, is of great antiquity, and coincides with the pictures of to-day.

There exists a letter ascribed to Publius Lentulus and directed to the emperor Tiberius, which describes Jesus. Although it is apocryphal, yet it was certainly written in the days of the primitive Christians. It is translated as follows,—*

"There hath appeared in these, our days, a man of great virtue, named Jesus Christ, who is yet living among us, and of the Gentiles, is accepted as a prophet, but his disciples call him the Son of God. He raiseth the dead, and cures all manner of diseases; a man of stature somewhat tall and comely, with very reverend countenance, such as the beholders both love and fear; his hair the color of chestnut, full ripe, plain to his ears, whence downward it is more orient, curling and waving about his shoulders."

"In the midst of his head is a seam or partition of the hair, after the manner of the Nazarites; his forehead plain and very delicate; his face without a spot or wrinkle, beautified with the most lovely red; his nose and mouth so formed that nothing can be reprehended; his beard

* King's "Ten Thousand Wonders," p. 241.

thickish, in color like his hair, not very long but forked; his look innocent and mature, his eyes gray, clear, and quick. In reproving he is terrible; in admonishing, courteous and fair spoken; pleasant in conversation mixed with gravity."

"It cannot be remarked that any one saw him laugh, but many have seen him weep. In proportion of body, most excellent; his hands and arms most delicate to behold. In speaking, very temperate, moderate and wise. A man for his singular beauty, surpassing the children of men."

From this letter of the predecessor of Pontius Pilate (?) the two earliest known portraits of Christ (in the Calixtine and Pontine catacombs at Rome) were probably sketched and the model has been followed up to our day.

But there is another description, by St. John of Damascus, which is much more in keeping with the Jewish type, of which he supposes the Saviour probably may have had some trait.

According to him, Christ had beautiful eyes, but the eyebrows meeting; a regular nose, flowing locks, a black beard, and a straw colored complexion, like his mother.

CHAPTER XXI.

THE AMBROSIAN AND GREGORIAN CHANT.

St Ambrose, the first real reformer in the music of the Christian Church, was born A. D. 333, probably at Treves, where his father who was prefect of Gaul, often resided. He is said to have received an auspicious omen even in his cradle; a swarm of bees alighted upon him during his slumber, and the astonished nurse saw that they did not sting him, but clustered around his lips; his father, remembering a similar wonder related of Plato, predicted a high destiny for his son. He was therefore, thoroughly educated in his youth, and soon was sent with Satyrus, his brother, to Milan to study law.

He soon became so eminent in this profession, that he was appointed (A. D. 369) prefect of upper Italy and Milan. In A. D. 374 he was unanimously, and against his will, chosen bishop of Milan.

Once in the chair, however, he ruled with vigor and great sagacity, making numerous and necessary reforms in church regulations and discipline.*

We shall only follow his musical career. Unfortunately, although there are some remains in the

*Marcillac Hist. de la Mus. Moderne, p. 28, and Brendel Gesch. d Mus. p. 9.

Milanese church-chant of to-day, we have but little proof of the nature of his reforms. That it was deeply impressive we have the testimony of St. Augustine who eulogises, without accurately describing it,* but it is certain that his reforms were founded in part upon the Greek music, and that in the Gregorian and Ambrosian chants of the church, we have a legitimate descendant of the ancient Greek music. The reader must remove one impression from his mind; the music of the early Christians, though certainly crude, was by no means simple; on the contrary, it contained many flourishes and rapid embellishments, most of which were of oriental origin. The reform was in the nature of simplicity, and added dignity to a service, which already, in its words, possessed beauty and poetry.

He cast aside much of the cumbrous nomenclature of the Greek modes, and retained of them only what was beautiful and easily comprehended. He did not aim at any sweeping reform, as is evident from his letter to his sister St. Marcellina, wherein he says that he is endeavoring to regulate the mode of singing the hymns, canticles and anthems in his own church,† and St. Augustine‡ says that it was done after the manner of the churches of the Orient.

The modes which he chose for his compositions were the following:—

---

* Confessions, Book IX, Chap. 6.

† Ambros Geschichte der Musik, vol. 2, p. 14. Fetis, Biographie Univ. v. 1. p. 85.

‡ Confess, IX., 7.

First mode:— $\begin{cases} D, & E, & F, & G, & A, & B, & C, & D, \\ re & mi & fa & sol & la & si & do & re \end{cases}$

Second do. $\begin{cases} E, & F, & G, & A, & B, & C, & D, & E, \\ mi & fa & sol & la & si & do & re & mi \end{cases}$

Third do. $\begin{cases} F, & G, & A, & B, & C, & D, & E, & F, \\ fa & sol & la & si & do & re & mi & fa \end{cases}$

Fourth do. $\begin{cases} G, & A, & B, & C, & D, & E, & F, & G, \\ sol & la & si & do & re & mi & fa & sol \end{cases}$

It will be seen that the semi-tones are immovable, and therefore occur in different positions in each mode, by the change of the key-note; being respectively,—

First mode, semitones   2-3, 6-7
Second "   "   1-2, 5-6
Third "   "   4-5, 7-8
Fourth "   "   3-4, 6-7

It was this distinction which gave to each mode its peculiar character.

Not only did St. Ambrose reinstate these modes, but he composed many beautiful compositions in them. Many of the so-called Ambrosian chants and hymns, were not written by him, but after his manner; but some ten of the ancient hymns, including "*Veni Redemptor Gentium,*" "*Eterna Christi munera,*" etc., are from his own pen.

The Cathedral of Milan still uses *Aeterne rerum conditor; Deus Creator omnium; Veni Redemptor omnium; Splendor Paternæ gloriæ; Consors paterni luminis;* and O *Lux Beata Trinitas.**

Some of these are of rare beauty, and remain

---

* Fetis, Hist. Gen de la Mus., v. 4, p. 135.

as monuments of the cultivated taste of this pioneer in church music. The composition of the " *Te Deum Laudamus,*" has been ascribed to St. Ambrose, and St. Augustine; but it was composed nearly a century after their death. Among other persons to whom this beautiful production has been assigned, may be mentioned St. Hilary, St. Abundius, St. Sisebut, and St. Nieat; but it may be safely affirmed that its real author has never been discovered.

The greatest boon bestowed on the church by St. Ambrose was the rhythmical hymn, mentioned above, all of which, and many others he wrote for the Cathedral which he built at Milan.

" The entire accent, and style of chanting as regulated by him. was undoubtedly an artistic and cultivated improvement on that of preceding church services, such as would naturally result from the rare combination of piety, zeal, intellect, and poetical and musical power by which he was distinguished." The Ambrosian chant was eventually merged, but certainly not lost in that vast repertory of plain song, (whether then ancient or modern,) which we now call Gregorian, from the name of the next great reformer of church music, St. Gregory the Great.* St. Ambrose died A. D. 397; it was but a short time afterwards that the great invasion of the northern barbarians took place. The history of the vicissitudes of the ecclesiastical music, during the general disruption of Europe and the western civilization, which

---

* Grove's Dictionary of Music and Musicians, part 1, vol. 1, article "Ambrosian chant," by Rev. Thomas Helmore.

followed, can only be imagined; but scarcely had a calm been re-established, when, at a period when the reforms and inventions of St. Ambrose had not been vitiated or lost, the great reformer of church music arose, and re-instated the art upon a firmer pedestal than ever.

Gregory, the Great, born about A. D. 540, and pope from September 3, 590, to March 12, 604, was of an illustrious Roman family. His father Gordianus, was a senator, and Felix III., one of the early pontiffs, was among his ancestors. He was one of the most remarkable, zealous, and intelligent of the fathers of the church.

We have here only to follow his musical work, but in every branch of work connected with his church, he was most eminent. He founded six monasteries in Sicily alone. He voluntarily resigned an honorable office, to leave the world, and seek retirement in the monastery of St. Andrew, which he himself had founded at Rome. On this occasion he gave to the poor all his wealth, and declining the abbacy of his own convent, began with the ordinary monastic life, about 575.

He wished to attempt the conversion of the Britians, (moved thereto by the well known incident of seeing some beautiful Anglo-Saxon youths exposed for sale in the Roman market place), but was prevented by the clamor of the populace who refused to lose him. Like St. Ambrose, he was called to office entirely against his will, and, on being made pontiff, he seems to have excelled in every department of his administration; thus much, to show that music was but one of the fields in which this wonderful man exercised his talents.

He collected the available church music, he added to it by composing new hymns and anthems, he arranged them for the various special days of the year, he invented or amplified the system of ecclesiastical composition, and took care that the reforms should be permanent, by having most things relative to his musical labors, written out in a lasting manner.*

These reforms he began about A. D. 599. He did not discard the four modes of St. Ambrose, but rather extended them; and yet (through the great personal popularity of St. Ambrose), the Milan Cathedral kept the Ambrosian chant unadulterated, for centuries after the establishment of the Gregorian.

As late as the latter half of the fifteenth century, Franchinus Gafor speaks of the Gregorians and Ambrosians as partizans. Of course, in order to secure uniformity, the rulers of Europe, sought to dwarf the workings of the Ambrosian system, and Charlemagne even ordered the Ambrosian books to be burnt. Although, as above stated, there was nothing antagonistic in the two systems, yet their musical results seem to have had a material difference, for Radulf of Tongern an unimpeachable witness of the fourteenth century, who heard both methods in their purity, says that he found the Ambrosian chanting, widely different from the Roman (Gregorian);

* Ambros Gesch. d Mus., v. 2, p. 43.

the former being strong and majestic, while the latter was sweet-toned, and well arranged.* This distinction is utterly meaningless to us, for the Gregorian chant is certainly majestic and strong, at least to our ears.

Gregory also founded a singing school in Rome, which was large enough to occupy two good-sized edifices. In this he probably taught personally.

There have been shown as relics of his instruction, the couch on which he sat while teaching, and the rod with which the boys were corrected, or awed into giving proper attention to their studies.

The amplification which he made in the Ambrosian scale was the addition of four tones or plagal modes, and also that he totally abolished the difficult Greek nomenclature, such as *para-mese* and *proslambanomenos*, and gave the names of the first seven letters of the Roman alphabet, to the seven notes, A, B, C, D, E, F, G, in the same manner as used to-day. There is no question but that the scale founded by Gregory, had a diatonic character, but as to the number of systems of tones employed, authorities differ, and even the books of music of Gregory's own compilation (one of which was chained to the altar at St. Peters, to fix the standard of tone for ever and ever) do not clear up the difficulty, for the number differs.

But the system gradually settled itself, and eight tones only (our ordinary diatonic scale

---

*Ambros, v. 2, p. 45.

tones) were found practicable for composition and singing.

Gregory's system was founded on the division of the octave into two intervals; a perfect fifth and perfect fourth. The fifth was, next to the octave, the most important interval.

The added modes (called plagal, signifying "oblique, sideways"), were so called to distinguish them from the authentic tones or keys (D, E, F, G, A), a synopsis of the entire set of tones would be as follows,—

A, B, C, D,	E, F, G, A,	B, C, D,
plagal 4,	authentic 5,	plagal 4.

There were four authentic modes, viz.,— D, E, F and G, and four plagal, as follows,—A, B, C and D.

To give a description that would be at all adequate, of the system of Gregory, would require much space, and many plates and engravings. We shall therefore touch but lightly on the tone systems and notations of the early and middle ages. The founding of the scale from a fifth and fourth, led to one grave mistake; these intervals were supposed to be of prime importance, and more perfect than others, and finally were employed in harmonies which were decidedly harsh. But to such an extent did the evil spread that no composition (in the dark ages) was thought to be pure or classic, without containing a series of fourths, fifths, and octaves, and an invariable close upon an empty fifth. Thirds were rejected as totally impure. But these faults are not of Gregory's origination, and he must ever stand as the man who made the connecting link between the old Greek music and our own.

CHAPTER XXII.

MUSIC IN EUROPE FROM THE FIFTH CENTURY.

In proceeding to briefly sketch the curious facts of musical history in the dark ages, we shall necessarily confine ourselves to pointing out only what is chiefly remarkable, and shall not enter into the field of dispute regarding systems and notations, for this period of Musical History is a very hazy one. It is but natural to suppose, that when general barbarism spread over Europe, music was not likely to be either much practised or written about. The last writer on the previous systems was Boethius (the last of old Roman writers), who lived at about the same epoch as Gregory (he was put to death by Theodoric, the Goth, A. D. 525).

In his work, he uses the letters of the alphabet, to designate musical notes, but does not repeat the letters at the octave; his nomenclature therefore does not end at G, but continues on, to *N*, *O*, and P.*

Musical progress was at a stand still from the time of Gregory, until the reign of the Carlovingian kings. Charlemagne at the end of the

* These latter letters may however, only refer to the diagrams, and not to musical notes.

eighth, and beginning of the ninth centuries, took all art and music under his powerful protection. He loved to compare himself with King David, and had in many respects, good reason to, for he possessed both the virtues and the failings of that ancient monarch.

He gathered about him a number of musical and literary friends, and we can judge of the pleasant manner of their intercourse by the names of antiquity which each one was known by. Alcuin, was dubbed Flaccus Albinus; Riculf, Archbishop of Mayence,—Damoetas; Arno,—Aquila; Angilbert,—Homerus, etc.*

In addition to the literary and musical schools founded throughout his empire, in his own palace was one devoted to the education of the children of his servants. Books were read, and music sung to his courtiers, during the hours of dining or other leisure.

The singing at his court, he often conducted himself, and every one was obliged to participate. If a stranger arrived, he was also obliged to stand with the chorus, and even if he could not sing, at least to make the semblance of doing so.

In the conservation of ancient legendary songs Charlemagne was very active, and many which have come down to our day, owe their existence to his wise and thoughtful care.†

In church music he was, most of all, interested, and remarked with much concern, the variations

---

*Epoch men, by Sam'l Neal, p. 48.

†Vie de Charlemagne, Guizot, T. 3, p. 151

between the Gregorian and French singing. To put an end to the matter, he sent to Stephen IV., the reigning pope, for ecclesiastical singers; the latter responded by sending, (in imitation of the twelve apostles,) twelve clerical singers to teach his empire.

But these twelve apostles, turned out to be *all* Judases, for jealous of the rising civilization of France, they agreed among themselves, not to aid in its rise. When therefore, they had been received at the French court with every honor, and were sent to their various fields of labor, it is said, they began to sing in a most wretched manner, and not content with that, they *taught* this abomination to their pupils. But when Charlemagne celebrated Christmas at Tours that year, and in Paris the succeeding year, he heard other Roman vocalists sing in a manner totally different, and lost no time in making complaint to the pope, who, calling back the untrustworthy teachers, punished them, some with banishment, and some with perpetual imprisonment; and in order that a similar deceit might not again be practised, he persuaded Charlemagne to send two French Ecclesiastics to Rome, where under Papal supervision they learned the true Gregorian style of song.*

There also exists another anecdote of the ruling of Charlemagne in church singing, which will

---

*Ambros Gesch d. Mus., v. 2, p. 94. We must remind the reader that "Gregorian" music, does not always refer to the compositions of Gregory, but simply means the singing used at Rome, as the "Ambrosian" means the style used at Milan.

show how high partizan feeling ran in musical matters at this era. It is as follows,—

"The most pious King Charles having returned to celebrate Easter at Rome with the apostolic Lord, a great quarrel ensued during the festival, between the Roman and Gallic singers. The French pretended to sing better and more agreeable than the Italians; the Italians, on the contrary, regarding themselves as more learned in Ecclesiastical music, in which they had been instructed by St. Gregory, accused their competitors of corrupting, disfiguring, and spoiling the new chant. The dispute being brought before our sovereign lord the king, the French, thinking themselves sure of his countenance and support, insulted the Roman singers; who, on their part, emboldened by superior knowledge, and comparing the musical abilities of their great master, St. Gregory, with the ignorance and rusticity of their rivals, treated them as fools and barbarians."

"As their altercation was not likely to come to a speedy issue, the most pious King Charles asked his chanters which they thought to be the purest and best water, that which was drawn from the source at the fountain-head, or that which after being mixed with turbid and muddy rivulets, was found at a great distance from the original spring?"

"They exclaimed unanimously, that all water must be most pure at its source; upon which our ord the King, said, 'mount ye then up to the pure fountain of St. Gregory, whose chant ye have manifestly corrupted.' After this our lord the king, applied to Pope Adrian (the first) for singing masters to convert the Gallican chant; and the pope appointed for that purpose Theodore and Benedict, two chanters of great learning and abilities, who had been instructed by St. Gregory himself; he likewise granted to him *Antiphonaria*, or choral-books of that saint, which he had himself written in Roman notes."

" Our lord the King, on his return to France, sent one of the two singers granted him by the Pope, to Metz, and the other to Soissons; commanding all the singing masters of his kingdom to correct their *antiphonaria*, and to conform in all respects to the Roman manner of performing the church service."

" Thus were the French *antiphonaria* corrected, which had before been vitiated, interpolated, and abridged at the pleasure of every choir man, and all the chanters of France learned from the Romans that chant which they now call the French chant, which is entirely as the Roman except that the French do not execute the tremulus and vinnulas, the bound and staccato notes *(collisibiles vel secabiles voces)*, with facility, and give a rather rude and throaty manner of singing. The best style of singing remained in Metz, and as superior as Rome is to Metz, so superior is Metz to the rest of France, in its school of singing."[*]

[*] Monachus Engolismensis (the monk of Angouleme), an anonymous writer of this era, in his *Vita Carol Magni*. quoted by J. J. Rousseau, in his Dictionnaire de Musique article "Chant," also by Crowest, Mus Anecdotes, v. 2, p. 239; Fetis, v. 4, p. 279; Ambros, v. 2, p. 94, etc., etc.

Both the above anecdotes, although quoted very frequently, must be taken *cum grano salis*, for as Ambros and Fetis well observe, the two singers, if they had received instruction from Gregory, and also taught in the era of Charlemagne, must have been about *two hundred years of age*, which is certainly too old for active service. Another historian gives the names of the envoys as *Petrus* and *Romanus*, and it is certain that one of these did go to Metz, and that a famous school of singing was founded at Soissons about the same time. Both the teachers, also must have instructed the French, in the musical characters then used in notation, and known by the name of *Neumes*.

The *Neumes* which were in use for musical writing from the eighth to the twelfth century were short lines, twirls, and hooks, which were written above the words of a song to denote the melody.

The origin of these marks, is buried in oblivion, for they seem to have been developed, not at one time, but gradually, and from the simplest beginnings. Although we have not space to describe the theories concerning them, a short explanation of them is necessary, for from these Neumes gradually came our modern system of notation. At first these marks were only meant as guides to memory; to aid the singer to sing an air which he had previously learned. Thus the first bar of "Home Sweet Home," would be represented by a *Scandicus* signifying three upward moving tones, the first two short, the last one long.

The exclamation and interrogation point, are in language, what *Neumes* were at first in music, they roughly sketched out the inflection of the voice. The connection between them, and our modern notation is very evident; in our musical notation the requirements of the eye, have been well attended to; not entirely perhaps, as regards the length of notes, but certainly in the matter of ascending and descending passages, etc.;* the old Greek notation, with its upturned and fragmentary letters, meant nothing to the untutored eye; but the *Neumes* of the middle ages, were the first attempt to express a meaning *by their arrangement.* Thus the *tripunctum* (.·˙) would denote three notes ascending, though not which ones; it might mean

C, D, E.   E, F, G,   F, G, A,
do, re, mi, } or mi, fa, sol, } or fa, sol, la, }

etc., the *bipunctum* (.˙) two ascending, or (˙.) descending notes; the *plica ascendens* (⌣) an upward spring of a third, etc.

It being a system which was evolved by slow degrees, it is not astonishing that there are various signs, about which opinions differ. The system though seemingly barbarous, was in reality an improvement; although not developed so extensively as the Greek notation which preceded it, it bore the germ of a more natural style of musical characters.

* It has been suggested by some recent writers on this subject, that even this should be met by forming the notes of various lengths, thus, a whole note ——, a half note ——, a quarter —, etc., but this difficulty can be obviated, in spacing, by any good music engraver, and does not require so radical a change

But the constant change of, and addition to the *Neumes*, bore evidence, that it was but a pathway to a more complete system. The next great reformer in music gave his attention to abolishing the uncertainty which clung around the *pneumata*.

Hucbald, Monk of St. Amand, in Flanders, (born about 840, died 932,) made the first practical effort to fix notes permanently. To him is due the germ of the idea which afterwards culminated in the modern clefs and staff.

He took (unfortunately) the Greek system for his starting point, and this led him into many errors, and much lessened the permanent value of his work. He took the tetrachord (or succession of four notes) as the foundation of music, but he applied it in a most strange manner; his scale was as follows:*

G, A, B flat, C,   D, E, F, G,   A, B natural, C, D,

E, F sharp, G, A,   B, C sharp,

it will be readily seen that the above scale contains some incongruities, which are precisely similar to those noticed in the music of the Hindoos; that is the octave comes out a semi-tone sharp; B natural being octave to B flat, F sharp to F, etc.

Naturally, in singing it is not to be conceived that the singers took any such outlandish system as to substitute this for an octave, but it must have allowed great license to the singers,

* The semitone falling always between the second and third note, is the only regularity apparent.

and the whole must have given rise to much ambiguity.

His improvement in the method of notation consisted (a perfect anticipation of clef and staff) in placing the letters of the notes employed, before each line of the words, and then writing each syllable of the song, opposite to (and level with) the note to which it belonged. As he adopted the clumsy Greek method of lettering (using only four letters, and placing them upright, reversed, backwards, and sideways) we will give an example with English letters.*

A		a -		
G	da -	te	num	
F	Lau -		mi -	de -
E		do -		e
D				cœlis

The words being "Laudate Dominum de cœlis."

The harmony of Hucbald was as peculiar and barbaric as his scale system.

He followed the principle of the ancients in treating intervals of thirds and sixths as *dissonances*, and therefore did not allow them to appear in his works. In common with some of his predecessors, he held that the only pure intervals were fifths and fourths. To us this succession of discords appears most appalling, but it is probable that in the practical use of music it was ameliorated somewhat. At this time when the organ was in such a primitive state that the organist struck the keys heavily with his *fist* in playing,

*Stainer's Dictionary, p. 311.

the left fist was sometimes allowed to hold a tone (in the manner of an organ point), while the right played a succession of tones with the singers. The constant rejection of sixths and thirds as impure intervals, must ever remain a mystery to us; yet the effect of even this harsh and uncouth singing was deep on those who heard it. History tells us that King Canute was deeply impressed on hearing the monks chant, while being rowed in his boat, near a monastery, and a lady upon hearing the music of the first organ erected in France, went raving mad, from excess of emotion.

We will leave the rude harmonies of Hucbald, with a final example showing the succession of fourths used in his *organum* (or art of composing).

The letters T, and S, signify tone and semitone.

		Do-				
T		mini				
T	Sit	oria		in	cula	bitur
S		glo -	Do -	sae -		ta
T			mini		lae -	
T	Sit	oria		in	cula	bitur
S		glo -		sae -		ta
T					lae -	

} etc.

Sometimes four voices were thus written on a staff of fifteen lines. Although this system was so cumbrous, yet the right path had been attained, and the progress was continual; little inventions followed one upon the other, and many of the modern usages in music date their rise to this obscure age of Musical History.

The next great name, in the art, is that of **Guido**

Aretino, or of Arezzo, a monk of the Benedictine order, born at Arezzo. He flourished about A. D. 1030 though the date of his birth and death, is not accurately known. His work has had more influence in shaping modern music, than that of any one before him. Yet much of his life and work belongs to the hazy realm of legend. He attained such celebrity that every invention to which his successors could not find a father, was attributed to him.

Guido's great success lay in the fact that he was a *specialist*. He did not undertake, like Gregory and Ambros, to shine in all art, science, and enterprise; his position precluded that; he says "The ways of Philosophers are not mine, I only occupy myself with what can be of use to the church, and bring our little ones (the scholars) forward."

There was need of such a man; for though music teachers were sought in every country at this time, and those from Italy, Greece, France and even Germany, were highly prized, yet there were many who presumed on this state of affairs, and the consequence was that incompetent teachers were the rule. To remedy this great evil was the aim of Guido's life.

He says some of these would-be teachers, " If they sang in their aimless manner, every day, for a hundred years, they would not invent even the slightest new Antiphon, and he who cannot easily and correctly sing a new song, by what right can he call himself a musician or singer?

"At the service of God, it too often sounds, not as if we were praising Him, but as if we were quarrelling, and scolding among ourselves."

He devoted himself greatly, to the teaching of a most important branch of singing, i. e., *sight reading*, and soon brought his cloister class to such perfection in this that they astonished all beholders. He was not however, as mild-mannered a reformer as his predecessor in art, Hucbald. His bitter sarcasms on his brother monks, soon brought a result, and he found himself though not actually chased from his convent, yet ostracized in it.

But he was well able to sustain such a strife, and continued his work with zeal unabated. His style of teaching sight reading was far in advance of his competitors, for he taught his scholars to sing intervals, not by referring to the monochord, but instead of it to think of some similar interval in any hymn well known to them, thus combining thought, memory and musical ear, in a practical manner.

He was struck with the regularly ascending intervals of the first syllables of each line of the hymn in honor of St. John, and with the inspiration of genius attached the syllables ut, re, mi, fa, sol, la, to the notes, and caused his scholars to memorize each interval, thus forming a new and easily comprehended system of *Solfeggio*. The hymn which inspired this wonderful stride in music runs,

Ut — queant laxis.   *Re* — sonare fibris.
Mi — ra gestorum.   *Fa* — muli tuorum.
Sol — ve polluti.   *La* — bia reati.
         Sancte Johannes.

The fame of his wonderful results in choir-training, soon reached Rome, and the Pope, John XIX.,* sent an invitation to the still ostracized monk, to come to Rome.

Guido is credited with having made many changes in the notation and harmony of his day. The hexachord system is attributed (justly or unjustly) to him. He also is said to have introduced lines of different colors into the staff, for the purpose of aiding the singer to recognize certain notes with more facility. He says in his *Micrologus*† "In order that sounds may be discerned with certainty, we mark some lines with various colors, so that the eye may immediately distinguish a note, in whatever place it may be. For the third of the scale [C] a bright saffron line. The sixth [F] adjacent to C is of bright vermilion, and the proximity of others to these colors, will be an index to the whole. If there were neither letter, nor colored lines to the Neumes, it would be like having a well without a rope—the water plentiful, but of no use to those who see it."

While Guido does not lay claim to having invented the colored lines, it is probable that he

---

* There is some ambiguity regarding the title of this pontiff. Some authorities call him John xx., and the next Jean. (1276), the xxi

† Quoted by Stainer and Barrett, Dict. p. 815.

brought them, by his influence into much more general use.

He certainly invented a modification of the line system of Hucbald. Instead of the inverted letters, and fragments of letters which the latter used, he employed the vowels only, to designate the pitch, thus,—

						u
				tu -		u
	so -				os	o
F	ri -	ri	lis	u -		i
	ve -		ter	ber-		e
Ma -	a		Ma -		a	a

"Maria, veri solis mater, ubera tuos."

Guido, altered Hucbald's *Organum* in so far, that he rejected consecutive fifths, as being too harsh, and substituted a series of consecutive fourths as being milder.

It may not be out of place to remark here, that the present scrupulous avoidance of all consecutive fifths, in modern composition of strict school, is simply a reaction from the rude taste of past centuries, which employed them *ad nauseum;* there is no valid reason for their complete ostracism, any more than there was cause for the banishing of all sixths and thirds from the harmony of our ancestors. To Guido is also attributed the invention of the method of the harmonical hand (Guidonian hand, as it has been named after its supposed originator). This consisted of marking certain notes and musical signs on the tips of the fingers, and by this means more readily committing them to memory. As before stated, many of the inventions credited to Guido, are only adaptations. The Sol-faing system was almost an accidental occurrence; yet only genius can derive full profit from accidents. The hymn which gave rise to it (quoted above), is a most prosaic invocation to St. John to save the throats of the singers from hoarseness, in order that they may fittingly sing his praise. A very diplomatic way of requesting it.

Musical history in the ninth, tenth, and eleventh centuries is at its darkest; hence little is positively known of the life of Guido. It is certain that he was in great favor at Rome, and that other countries applied to him for his musical services to reorganize their ecclesiastical chanting, and also that his health failing, he returned to his monastery, forgetting and forgiving the ill treatment he had received there, and in its cloisters peacefully ended his days.

The date of his decease is not known.

Other names appear in this misty epoch in musical history. Franco of Cologne, Walter Odington, an English Monk, Heeronymus von Maehren, etc., wrote works upon the theory of music, while Adam de la Hale (of Arras, France) wrote music in four-part harmony, about the year 1280. But in the midst of this darkness there came a glorious sunburst in the shape of chivalric bands who elevated music to a broader sphere by adding to the ecclesiastical chanting a secular school of composition, both warlike and lyrical.

CHAPTER XXIII.

THE ANCIENT BARDS.

While Rome and Milan were devoting themselves almost entirely to ecclesiastical music, there had sprung up among the barbarian nations a school of music more consonant to their habits, being warlike in its style, and having for its object the celebration of the heroes of each country, and the inciting of their descendants to similar deeds of glory. From earliest days Wales has possessed a guild of such singers, who were, in fact, the historians of the country, at a time when written books would have been nearly useless. The songs of the Welsh bards have been preserved traditionally by that people; while the songs of the druids who preceded them have been allowed to pass into utter oblivion, the latter having, evidently, not taken deep root in Welsh soil.

At the commencement of the sixth century, the bards of Wales exerted all their energies of exhortation to animate their countrymen in the strife with the Saxon invaders, and when Wales was conquered by Edward I., (1284) he dreaded their influence so much that he is said to have persecuted them and put them to death. The bards in Wales had an organization similar to that which we shall presently find among the troubadours and minne-singers. They were divided into two classes,—poets, and musicians. Each of these classes were subdivided into three divisions. The first class of poet-bards was composed of those who understood history, and dabbled somewhat in sorcery, thus being held in awe as prophets and diviners. The second class consisted of bards attached to private families, whose duties were to chant the praises of the heroes of their particular house. The third class were the heraldic bards, who wrote the national annals and prescribed the laws of etiquette and precedence. These must have exerted a powerful influence on a nation which clung so strictly to ceremony and the privileges of lineage.

The musicians were also divided into three classes, of which the first were harpers, and possessed the title of Doctors of Music; the second class were the players upon the *crouth* or *chrotta*, a smaller stringed instrument; the third class consisted of the singers. Many laws and regulations were made to define the privileges of each class, and the classification of new bards took place at an assemblage called the Eisteddfod, which met triennially, and conferred degrees. The highest degree could only be obtained after nine years faithful study. From the thirteenth century Wales also possessed a class of wandering musicians entitled, "*Clery dom.*" The harps used were various, though the three-stringed one was the national instrument. One variety was made of leather, strung with wire, and is said to have been peculiarly harsh; another called *isyywer* was so small that it could be played on horseback; another was strung with hair. The order of the bards was hereditary to some extent. King Howel Dha issued edicts regarding them (fixing their rank) about 940 A. D., and in 1078 the whole order was reformed and full regulations made by Gryffith ap Conan. In spite of the persecutions to which they were subjected, the order was sustained for centuries, and *Eisteddfods* were held under royal commission down to the reign of Queen Elizabeth.

In Ireland minstrelsy has had a foothold in all times. There is a legend that about the year 365 B. C., there occurred in Ireland the first triumph of poetry and music. A young prince, driven from his throne by a usurper, was so moved by a song which his betrothed wrote and caused Craftine, a celebrated bard, to sing to him, that he resolved on hazarding a supreme effort to regain his crown, and succeeded in driving the usurper from his kingdom.

The Irish claim that they were the originators of the Welsh system of bards, but this statement seems to be founded rather on national pride than upon fact, for it is probable that the borrowing was upon the other side. But it is certain that the Irish have ever possessed musical taste and skill.

Gyraldus Cambriensis (who wrote in the twelfth century) says of them: "The aptitude of this people for performing upon musical instruments is worthy of attention."

"They have in this respect, much more ability than any nation I have ever seen. The modulations are not with them slow and sad, like those of the instruments of Britain, to which we are accustomed, but the sounds, though rapid and precipitate, are yet sweet and soothing."* The harp was, as in Wales, the national instrument. The bards were a hereditary class, and their guild, as in Wales, had three divisions; the *Filedha*, who sang both about religious and martial subjects, and were also heralds to the nobility; *Braitheamhain*, who chanted the laws; and the *Seanachaidehe*, who were the musical and poetical chroniclers and historians. Their influence and privileges were fully as great as those of their Welsh brethren, and they had many valuable possessions of land. Their skill was universally acknowledged up to their conquest by Henry II., but from that epoch the profession began to decline, although noble families still made it a point of honor to keep private bards to sing to them of the deeds of the ancestors of their house.

The influence which these songs exerted in fomenting rebellion was such, that severe laws were promulgated against them in England, and

---

* Topog. Hibern. 3 C. 1.

under Elizabeth all the Irish bards who were captured, were hanged.

The last Irish bard existed as late as the eighteenth century.

Turlogh O'Carolan was born 1670, and died 1737; worthily closing the long reign of the fiery minstrel guild of Ireland.

Scotland's bardism, was similar to that of Wales and Ireland, but the ranks and privileges are less known. The bag-pipe was played as much as the harp, and there was much analogy in the ancient music of Ireland and Scotland. The scale on which the Scotch pieces were founded, bears much resemblance to the Chinese, and to some of the Hindoo modes.

In England there were also bards, but there was not an order, as in the preceding countries, and at a time when these heraldic singers were so highly honored in Wales, the singers and musicians of England were held in very slight social estimation. The irruptions of the Danes, and Norsemen generally, upon England in the ninth, tenth and eleventh centuries, brought a taste of the forcible Northern *sagas* along with them, and when King Canute held the throne, bards and " *gleemen*," were protected and favored, for King Canute was very fond of song. He, himself, wrote a song which was for a long time the favorite ballad of England.

The circumstances which prompted it were as follows:—

He was being rowed near the Monastery of

Ely, in the evening, when the sound of the monks singing their vesper chants, came across the water; he was greatly moved by the beauty of the song, which, with the accessories of the tranquil evening, the rippling water, and the measured stroke of the oars, caused him to improvise upon the spot, a song which soon spread among the peasantry as well as the higher classes.

Only one stanza has been preserved of this interesting effusion,—

> "Merie sungen the muneches binnen Ely,
> Tha Cnute Ching, reu ther by
> Rowe cnihtes, næw the land,
> And here we thes muneches sæng,"

which may be rendered in English thus:—

> "Sweetly sang the Monks of Ely,
> As King Canute rowed there by,
> Row men, nearer to the shore
> And hear we these Monks' song."

The minstrels of England from the first, took a more peaceful and religious turn than those of Wales and Ireland. The most of the really authentic pieces of their era, take the shape of Christmas carols.

CHAPTER XXIV.

THE TROUBADOURS AND MINNE-SINGERS.

We now come to an era in music, where the most cultivated minds gave their attention to the art; and where it is no longer confined to the narrow channels of ecclesiastical, and even heraldic and martial use, but finds a broader outlet in the subjects of Love, and Nature. The troubadours were gentlemen (often knights), who held themselves totally distinct from those musicians who wrote for pay. The rise of chivalry in the middle ages, elevated woman from an unjustly low position, to an absurdly high one. She was held to be the arbiter of Fate; the Queen to whom all service was due; and was almost religiously worshipped. From this exaggerated devotion arose the school of troubadour and minne-singer composition. When knights racked their brains, as to what new offering they could bring to their lady, it was but natural that they should find, in the combination of poetry and song, a series of never-ending tributes with which they could pay homage to their chosen one.

It is easy to imagine that once launched into

this fertile field, they would not wholly confine themselves to Love, but that an occasional poem on Nature, or War, would attest their versatility so that even the puerile "Courts of Love," of the chivalric age, brought a general onward impulse to art; it was not to be expected that the knights could step at once from a condition of rudeness, to a state of culture, and it is not surprising to see a vast exaggeration of politeness, where little had been before.

In the beautiful country of Provence (South France), this branch of art took its rise. The lyrical songs of the troubadours were written in the Provencal tongue, which soon became, for all South France the court language for amatory poetry. It was called also the *Langue d'oc* (from the affirmative "*Oc*," or "yes"), to distinguish it from the *Lingua di Si* (Italian) and the *Langue d'öil* (North France); the name afterwards was attached to another province of France. The Trouvères, were the poets and minstrels of North France, and wrote in the *langue d'öil*. They wrote chiefly epic poetry, (fables, tales and romances), while the lyrical school was left to their southern competitors.

The troubadours composed and sang their own songs, but did not play their own accompaniments; that branch of music was turned over to hired musicians, called *jongleurs*.

Celebrated troubadours had often several *jongleurs* in their employ. Those who made music a means of gaining a livelihood, were classed much lower. All in fact who did not invent ("*Trobar*," to find, or invent, whence comes the word trobador) their own songs, but sang or accompanied others, were called *jongleurs*, which was about as ordinary a trade as that of our perambulating "jugglers;" whose name is only a corruption of the more ancient calling.

The troubadours had a position which was even better than that of the bards of Wales or Ireland. They also made a livelihood of music, but in a far more genteel way than their humbler assistants, who were proscribed for so doing. The first thing the troubadour did, on practising his art was to seek out some person on whom to bestow his heart. This person was almost invariably a married lady. To her, he would then dedicate all his lays; he would (bestowing upon her, an assumed name), sing of her beauties, and entreat her favors; he would sneer at the charms of other dames, and sometimes satirize them.

The feelings of the husband during all this can "better be imagined than described."

Yet often the dame, may have been totally indifferent to his ardor. We feel sure that at times this was the case, for husbands are known to have begged their wives to accept the troubabour's flattery, and keep him on, with slight encouragement.

Meanwhile the singers went on from Court to Court, received as equals, by the highest; flattered and sought for by the most brilliant circles, and fairest ladies. Often they attached themselves to some particular prince, and gained his favor and enriched themselves by singing *sirventes* (songs of service) in his honor, and in derision of his enemies.

The nobles and kings of that era, also took up the Troubadour's lyre, at times. Richard L, Alfonso X., William IX. Count of Poitiers and others were famous for their efforts in this line, and they richly patronized such troubadours as sought them.

The gifts with which a successful song was rewarded, were of course influenced by the liberality of the giver. Horses, richly caparisoned, elegant vestments, and money, are mentioned in this connection.* Meanwhile the troubadours occasionally display the utmost contempt for their assistants, the before mentioned *jongleurs*, and reproach nobles, in some verses, with receiving such persons (who play at village fairs, dance on the tight rope, and exhibit performing monkeys), into their castles. Yet not all of the poets shared in this feeling, for Boccaccio tells us that Dante loved to associate with the musicians who set his *canzone* to music. In the thirteenth century, Guirant Riquier (called the "last of the troubadours") complains to the king of Castile, Alfonso X., of the decadence of the troubadour's art, and attributes it to the indiscriminate mixing of troubadours and jongleurs, in popular estimation. He says — "You know that all men live in classes differing and distinguished from each other.

* "The Troubadours," F. Hueffer, p. 61.

Therefore it seems to me that such a distinction of names ought also to be made amongst the joglars; for it is unjust that the best of them should not be distinguished by name as well as they are by deed. It is unfair that an ignorant man of small learning, who knows a little how to play some instrument, and strums it in public places, for whatever people will give him, or one who sings low ditties to low people about the streets and taverns, and takes alms without shame from the first comer,—that all these should indiscriminately go by the name of joglars . . . for joglaria was invented by wise men to give joy to good people by their skill in playing on instruments. . . . After that came the troubadours to record valiant deeds, and to praise the good, and encourage them in their noble endeavor. . . . But in our days, and for some time past, a set of people without sense and wisdom have undertaken to sing and compose stanzas and play on instruments,"* etc.

The poor troubadour desired the king to classify them, and to title the best. The king's answer is extant, wherein he endeavored to do so, but as the real essence and life had departed from the whole institution, it was unavailing.

The troubadours often had poetical combats, when they would indulge in a verse-battle about some "Law of Love," and the judges were selected from the fairest and wittiest of the noble dames. These were called the "Courts of Love."

---

* Quoted by Hueffer, "Troubabours," p. 72.

The muse of some of them seems to have taken a most curious turn, for there are still in existence some " *Essenhamens*," or books of etiquette for young ladies, which emanated from these lyrical pens, which are of the quaintest description. We reproduce a quotation from one, written by " Amanieus des Escas, called God of Love."*

In this treatise we are supplied with a minute account of the accomplishments expected from a well educated young lady, and of the bad habits most prejudicial to her character. The poet is supposed to be addressing a noble damsel living at the court of some great baron, as a sort of 'lady help' to his wife; this being a not unusual, and undoubtedly a most efficient method of polite education in Provence. The young lady has accosted Amanieus on a lonely walk, asking for his advice in matters fashionable. This the poet at first refuses to tender, alleging that " you (the damsel) have ten times as much sense as I, and that is the truth!" But after his modest scruples are once overcome, he launches forth into a flood of good counsel. He systematically begins with enforcing the good old doctrine of 'early to rise,' touches delicately on the mysteries of the toilet, such as lacing, washing of arms, hands, and head, which, he sententiously adds, ought to go before the first mentioned process, and, after briefly referring to the especial care required by teeth and nails, he leaves the dressing room for the church, where a quiet undemonstrative attitude is

* Hueffer. ٿ 274-5.

recommended; the illicit use of the eyes and tongue being mentioned amongst the temptations peculiarly to be avoided.

Directions of similar minuteness assist the young lady at the dinner table; the cases in which it would be good taste, and those in which it would be the reverse, to invite persons to a share of the dishes within her reach are specified; and the rules as to carving, washing one's hands before and after dinner, and similar matters, leave nothing to be desired. 'Always temper your wine with water, so that it cannot do you harm,' is another maxim of undeniable wisdom.

After dinner follows the time of polite conversation in the sala (drawing room), the arbour, or on the battlements of the castle; and now the teachings of Amanieus become more and more animated, and are enlivened occasionally by practical illustrations of great interest. 'And if at this season,' he says 'a gentleman takes you aside, and wishes to talk of courtship to you, do not show a strange or sullen behavior, but defend yourself with pleasant repartees. And if his talk annoys you; and makes you uneasy, I advise you to ask him questions, for instance:—'Which ladies do you think are more handsome, those of Gascony or of England, and which are more courteous, and faithful, and good? And if he says those of Gascony, answer without hesitation; Sir, by your leave, English ladies are more courteous than those of any other country. But if he prefers those of England, tell him Gascon ladies are much better behaved, and thus carry on the discussion, and call your companions to you to decide the questions.'"

We also give two extracts from the poems of that famous troubadour, Bertrand De Born. He was a poet far more given to martial songs, than to the lyrical muse. His enemies dreaded his pen as much as his sword. He describes his belligerent qualities without any exaggeration, for he was literally never contented except when at war with some of his neighbors. One of his poems (addressed to a lady) begins smoothly enough, but before he is half done, he breaks into an abrupt praise of fighting.

In the following, he warns Williams of Gordon, against Richard of Poitou, and hurls invective at the latter.

"I love you well," Bertran says, "but my enemies want to make a fool and a dupe of you, and the time seems long to them before they see you in their ranks." "To Perigeux, close to the wall, so that I can throw my battle axe over it, I will come well armed, and riding on my horse, Bayard; and if I find the glutton of Poitou* he shall know the cut of my sword. A mixture of brain and splinters of iron he shall wear on his brow."

Here follows a frank avowal of his delight in war.

"All day long," he says, "I fight, and am at work, to make a thrust at them and defend my-

---

* Richard.

self, for they are laying waste my land, and burning my crops; they pull up my trees by the roots, and mix my corn with the straw. Cowards and brave men are my enemies. I constantly disunite and sow hatred among the barons, and then remould and join them together again, and try to give them brave hearts and strong; but I am a fool for my trouble, for they are made of base metal."

We cannot better take leave of the troubadours than by giving two additional specimens of the writing of Bertrand de Born.

The first is an ingenious poem. He has quarreled with his lady, and as a means of reconciliation he borrows from all the famous beauties of his time, their special charm, and gives them all to his love. The second song will explain itself.*

> Domna, puois de mi no us cal,
> E partit m'aretz de vos, &c.

> Lady, since thou hast driven me forth,
>   Since thou, unkind, hast banished me,
> (Though cause of such neglect be none,)
>   Where shall I turn from thee?
>   Ne'er can I see
> Such joy as I have seen before,
> If, as I fear, I find no more
> Another fair, from thee removed,
> I'll sigh to think I e'er was loved.
>
> And since my eager search were vain,
>   One lovely as thyself to find:

---

* Taylor's "Lays of the Minnesingers," p. 229.

A heart so matchlessly endow'd,
   Or manner so refined,
      So gay. so kind,
So courteous, gentle, debonair, —
I'll rove, and catch from every fair
Some winning grace and form a whole,
So glad (till thou return) my soul.

The roses of thy glowing cheek,
   Fair Sembelis, I'll steal from thee;
That lovely smiling look I'll take,
   Yet rich thou shalt be,
      In whom we see
All that can deck a lady bright,
And your enchanting converse, light,
Fair Ellis, will I borrow too,
That she in wit may shine like you.

And from the noble Chales, I
   Will beg that neck of ivory white,
And her fair hands of loveliest form
   I'll take; and speeding, light,
      My onward flight
Earnest at Roca Choart's gate,
Fair Agnes I will supplicate
To grant her locks, more bright than those
Which Tristan loved on Iseult's brows.

And Audiartz, though on me thou frown,
   All that thou hast of courtesy
I'll have,—thy look, thy gentle mien,
   And all the unchanged constancy
      That dwells with thee.
And Miels de Ben, on thee I'll wait
For thy light shape so delicate,
That in thy fairy form of grace
My lady's image I may trace

The beauty of those snow-white teeth
  From thee, famed Faidit, I'll extort,
The welcome, affable and kind,
  To all the numbers that resort
    Unto her court.
And Bels Miraills shall crown the whole,
With all her sparkling flow of soul;
Those mental charms that round her play,
For ever wise, yet ever gay

  Be in play lo douz temps de paseor
    Que fais fuelhas e flors venir;
  E play mi quant aug la baudor
    Dels auzels que fan retentir
      Lor chan per lo boscatge;
  E plai me quan rey sus els pratz
    Tendas e parallos fermetz;
  Quan rey per campanhas rengatz
    Cavalliers ab carals armatz.

The beautiful spring delights me well,
  When flowers and leaves are growing;
And it pleases my heart to hear the swell
  Of the birds' sweet choruses flowing
    In the echoing wood
And I love to see, all scatter'd around,
Pavillions, tents, on martial ground;
    And my spirit finds it good
To see, on the level plains beyond,
Gay knights and steeds comparison'd.

It pleases me, when the lances bold
  Set men and armies flying;

And it pleases me, too, to hear around
  The voice of the soldiers crying;
    And joy is mine
When the castles strong, totter and crack;
  And I see the foemen join,
On the moated floor all compass'd round
With the palisade and guarded mound.

Lances and swords, and stained helms,
  And shields dismantled and broken,
On the verge of the bloody battle scene,
  The field of wrath betoken;
    And the vassals are there,
And there fly the steeds of the dying and dead;
And where the mingled strife is spread,
    The noblest warriors care
Is to cleave the foeman's limbs and head,—
The conqueror less of the living than dead.

I tell you that nothing my soul can cheer,
  Or banqueting or reposing,
Like the onset cry of "charge them" rung
  From each side as in battle closing,
    Where the horses neigh,
And the call to "aid" is echoing loud;
And there on the eárth the lowly and proud
    In the foes together lie;
And yonder is piled the mangled heap
Of the brave that scaled the trench's steep.

Barons! your castles in safety place,
  Your cities and villages too,
Before ye haste to the battle scene,
  And, Papiol! quickly go,
  And tell the lord of "Oc and No,"
That peace already too long hath been.

TROUBADOURS AND MINNE-SINGERS. 341

The Trouvères, were, as before intimated, the poet-musicians of North France. They wrote in a much more matter-of-fact manner than the troubadours, and wrote in the *Langue d'öil*, while the latter wrote in the *Langue d'oc;* two tongues as dissimilar as French and Italian, or English and Dutch.

There existed lady troubadours and trouvères; the works of some of them are extant, and do not in any way compare unfavorably with those of the other sex. Of course there are several solitary cases where the Norman poet would write a love song, and the Provencal a fable, but the general tendency was as above indicated.

Contemporary with the troubadours and trouvères, there arose in Germany, a similar order of singers, whose productions have been preserved, even more copiously than those of the southrons.

The minne-singers began their career in Germany, under the glorious reign of Barbarossa, (Frederic I.) in the last half of the twelfth century. The first name which we meet with is Henry of Veldig, yet it is a singular fact that he, the first of a new order of singers, begins by complaining of the decadence of the true minne-lied (love-song.) The word minne-singer means simply love-singer, i. e.—singer of love-songs. We give here, a verse of this early love-song, and have endeavored to give a translation, preserving the original metre (as nearly literal as possible) below it.

"Do man der rehten minne pflag
　Da pflag man ouch der ehren;
Nu mag man naht und tag
　Die bosen sitte leren:
Swer dis nu siht, und jens do sach,
　O we! was der nu clagen mag
Tugende wend sich nu verkehren."

"When true love had its proper sway,
　Then honour too, was nourished
But now by night and day
　All evil ways are cherished,
Who knows the past and present way,
　Oh Woe! how well complain he may
Since every virtue now has perished."

Almost all the lays of the minne-singers were written in the Swabian dialect which was then the court language of Germany. As a rule, their grace and elegance of diction was superior to that of the troubadours. They did not, like the latter, hire accompanists, or jongleurs, but played their own accompaniments on a viol. As in the South, emperors, princes, and knights, were proud to be known as minne-singers.

There exists a little epigram (ascribed to Frederic II.,) which we are tempted to reproduce, as it gives an insight to the qualities which were esteemed at that time.

"I like a cavalier Frances,*
　And a Catalonian dame;
The courtesy of the Genoese
　And Castilian dignity

* French.

> The Provence songs,*my ears to please,
> And the dance of the Trevisan;
> The graceful form of the Arragoneze
> And the pearl of the Julian; †
> An English face and hands to see,
> And a page of Tuscany." ‡

The love songs of the Germans were not so fiery as those of Provence; while the adoration of the troubadour for his love went all lengths, the German knight rendered to his own a much quieter, (and chaster) species of homage. There were not such criminal passions (often ending in murder at the hands of the outraged husband) as in France. In epic poems this school was very successful, and that stateliest of German poems, "The *Nibelungen-lied*," dates from about this time, although its author is not known.

The preservation of many of the songs of the Minne-singers is due to Rudiger of Manesse, a senator of Zurich (fourteenth century). To those who are desirious of seeing the main part of his collection we cannot do better than to recommend the excellent work of F. von der Hagen, *("Minnesänger," Manessische Sammlung)*, in which all the gems of this early growth of mediæval poetry are given. One peculiar species of their songs were called "*Wacht-lieder*" (Watch-songs), and represent the pleading of the knight, with the watchman of the castle, for admittance to his love; or the warning of the watchman to the lover

---
*Those of the Troubadours
†This line is vague in its meaning
‡Taylor's "Minne-singers," p. 98.

in the castle, to avoid discovery by leaving while it was yet dark. We present the reader with a specimen (author unknown).

> Vor tags ich hort, in liebes port, wohl diese wort,
>   Von wächters mund erklingen;
> Ist jeman ji, vorborgen hie, derachte wie,
>   Er mog hindannen sprengen, &c.

> I heard before the dawn of day
>   The watchman loud proclaim;—
> "If any knightly lover stay
>   In secret with his dame,
> Take heed the sun will soon appear;
> Then fly, ye knights, your ladies dear,
>   Fly ere the day-light dawn.

> "Brightly gleams the firmament,
>   In silvery splendor gay,
> Rejoicing that the night is spent,
>   The lark salutes the day:
> Then fly, ye lovers, and begone!
> Take leave before the night is done,
>   And jealous eyes appear."

> That watchman's call did wound my heart,
>   And banished my delight;
> "Alas, the envious sun will part
>   Our loves, my lady bright."
> On me she looked with downcast eye,
> Despairing at my mournful cry,
>   "We tarry here too long."

> Straight to the wicket did she speed;
>   "Good watchman spare thy joke!
> Warn not my love, till o'er the mead
>   The morning sun has broke:

Too short, alas! the time, since here
I tarried with my leman dear,
   In love and converse sweet."

"Lady, be warn'd! on roof and mead
   The dew-drops glitter gay,
Then quickly bid thy leman speed,
   Nor linger till the day;
For by the twilight did I mark
Wolves hyeing to their covert dark,
   And stags to covert fly."

Now by the rising sun I view'd
   In tears my lady's face;
She gave me many a token good,
   And many a soft embrace,
Our parting bitterly we mourn'd;
The hearts which erst with rapture burn'd,
   Were cold with woe and care.

A ring, with glittering ruby red,
   Gave me that lady sheen,
And with me from the castle sped
   Along the meadow green;
And whilst I saw my leman bright,
She waved on high her 'kerchief white;
   "Courage! To arms!" she cried.

In the raging fight each pennon white
   Reminds me of her love;
In the field of blood, with mournful mood,
   I see her 'kerchief move;
Through foes I hew where'er I view
   Her ruby ring, and blithely sing,
   "Lady, I fight for thee."

But the glory of the minne-singers was but short; the emperors of the house of Swabia, had fostered the art, by allowing an unheard-of liberty of speech and thought; with the downfall of that house (1256 A. D.) the church regained a continually-increasing ascendancy, and this liberty was again fettered. Song and poetry, especially of an amatory or frivolous (?) character were condemned, and the place of the pleasant school of minne-singer poetry was usurped by paraphrases of the Scriptures, hymns or legends, written either in very weak German or bad Latin; the school of German poetry took a very long retrograde step. Before leaving the minne-singers, a word must be said of their fables and tales; in these we find many modern ideas in a quaint and ancient dress, proverbs abound, and many tales of Roman History. "Don't set the wolf to guard the Sheep," "Never borrow trouble,"

"The king must die,
And so must I,"

and many other sage thoughts.

The tales are sometimes very prettily told. We have thought it worth while to translate one, which we believe, has not yet been seen in an English dress.

As far as possible we have adhered to the abruptness and quaintness of the original.

"At one time there was a king, who had but one son, who was very dear to him; the son demanded leave of absence from his father, and said that he wished to see the world, and wished to make friends. Then the king spoke " that pleases me well; but see that you do not have your labor in vain." The son was made ready for his journey, and remained seven years away; after that he returned to his home and his father, which pleased the father very much, and he said, — " Dear son: how many friends hast thou earned in these three years? Then the son answered "only three; the first I love better than myself; the second as much as myself; and the third, not as well as myself." The father said " It is well to have friends, and it is well to try them; I counsel you to kill a hog, and put it in a sack, and go in the night to your friends and say, you met an old enemy on the street and killed him, and are afraid that if the dead body should be found on you, it would cost you your life, and beg him that he should, in such extremity, help you, and that he will allow you to bury the body in his house, that it may not be found on you; so you shall find out if you have good friends."

This advice pleased the son well, so he went back again to the city where he knew he should find his friends; and killed one night, a hog, and did as his father had advised him to, and came to the friend whom he loved better than himself. When this one had heard his story, he said:— " you killed him yourself, so suffer for it yourself; if it were found by me it would cost me my life; but because we are good friends and comrades, when you are caught, and when they are about to kill you, I will go to you, and will console you.

and will buy many ells of cloth for you, wherein they may wind you and bury you; because you loved me more than yourself." When he heard this, he answered nothing but went to the other friend whom he loved as much as himself, and knocked at his door with the same tale as he had told to the first; this one said:—"Dear one! do you suppose I am such a simpleton that I want to die for you? If it is found here then I must die; but if they kill you, then I will comfort you, because that we are friends, and will do it the best I can, since we must all die." When he heard this, he parted from him, and came to the third friend whom he did not love as well as himself. This one asked what was in the sack, which he came with. He said:—"I can not say well, but I need help in this day; yet know that it has been my fate to kill a man, and I carry his body on my back, and if it is caught by me, then I must die, therefore I call on you for counsel; This one spoke;—"Give me here the body, and let me carry it myself, for I will even die for you," and when he opened the sack he found that only a dead hog lay therein. After that the son went home and told the whole story to his father."*

The end is of rather startling abruptness; we should have liked to have heard of the rewards and punishment, *a la* modern novel.

One song took its rise at this time which is even to-day a popular one, the world over. We refer to

---

* Fabeln und Erzehlungen aus d. zeiten d. minne-sanger. Von Bodmer und Breitinger Zurich, 1757, p. 247.

the music of the song now known as, "We won't go Home till morning," or "For he's a jolly good fellow;" and known in France as "Malbrook s'en va-t-en Guerre." This was a favorite air at the time of the crusades, and the crusaders often made it resound before Jerusalem.

The Arabs first knew the melody and have retained it to this day. The Arab fellahs will listen apathetically to the whole repertoire of a European orchestra; but the moment that the above tune is played, the whole aspect changes, and instead of a lifeless audience, the performers have the most enthusiastic of listeners.* In the course of descent from the Crusaders and ancient musicians, the tune has become a little quicker but is not changed in any material respect.

Some time after the decline of Minne-singing, an attempt was made to revive its glories, by musical competitions, somewhat similar in style; but the essence of the real "Minne" was gone; it was no longer the knight singing to his love, or telling in unaffected verse, the beauties of Nature. Instead of this, there was a competition of burgers and tradespeople, affecting a passion foreign to their nature, and caring far more for a stilted style of verse, than for the subject of it. Such were the Meister-singers;† Nuremburg was their chief seat, and like all the tradesmen of that age, they made their Guild a very close one. No one could be admitted as a Master, unless he

*Rambosson, Harmonies du Son, p. 46.
†Anglice—Master-singers.

invented a new style of rhyme. Almost all the members came from the lower classes, and the result of such tyros endeavoring to strike out paths which would have been difficult even to genius, can be imagined.

Hans Sachs (a Nuremberg shoe-maker) and a couple of others, were probably all that sang with real poetic feeling.

Their songs were also accompanied with music. There was a severe set of rules regulating the poetical and musical contests; and the Guild spread over all Germany; the last vestige of it did not disappear until as recently as 1839.

But while this stultified mode of music was going on in Nuremberg, a truer musical plant was growing beside it: at this time the Volks-lied (folk song) took its rise in Germany.

The first form of the volks-lied was religious, and it was of a simplicity which adapted it to the wants of the people. The pedantry of the Meister-singers had an excellent effect upon this class of composition, for it added counterpoint and harmony (even if driven to excess) to a class of music which was able to bear it.

Another order of music was that connected with the miracle plays, where scriptural events were represented upon the stage, with music. Much of this music was taken bodily from the ecclesiastical chants of the period.

With the commencement of the reformation, the music of Germany was lifted to a very elevated sphere, in being applied to the stately chorals which came into general use, through the efforts of Luther, who himself composed some of them. Luther had a most musical nature, which left its imprint upon his whole epoch.

It is related of him, that he spent the largest part of the night before he appeared to define his doctrines before the Diet of Worms, playing on his lute, in order to give composure and firmness to his thoughts.

He ranked music next to theology, and said: — "I am not ashamed to acknowledge, that next to divinity there is no study which I prize so highly as that of music."

With the reformation, the epoch of modern music may be said to begin. Of course there was both crudity and pedantry in the art, but the Meister-singers, although they yet existed centuries later, had ceased to exert an influence.

There are but few curious facts, which are not generally known, from that age, to our own. Yet we think a brief sketch of the growth of some branches of our music, will not be uninteresting to the general reader, even if the facts have lost the relish of novelty.

CHAPTER XXV.

CURIOSITIES OF THE OPERA.
MODERN COMPOSERS, AND CONCLUSION.

Our series of sketches now draws towards its close. The rise of the many-voiced harmony in Italy, France, Germany, England, and the Netherlands, the contrapuntal works of Palestrina, Dufay, De Lattre, etc., come rather under the head of the history and science of music, than within the scope of a work which only endeavors to collect the curiosities of the art, and things not generally known. But in the rise and progress of the opera, we find some interesting facts which belong to our subject, and which bring our chain of sketches down to the music of our own times.

The opera was the legitimate offspring of the Miracle plays of the Middle ages, which were only sacred operas or oratorios, wherein some events in the life of a holy personage were represented with songs and acting. The first opera (being exactly like a "mystery play," except that the subject was a secular one) was "Orpheus," by Angelo Poliziano, and was performed in Rome in 1480. The libretto was by Cardinal Riario (nephew of Pope Sixtus IV.)

Pope Clement IX., wrote seven librettos for operas. All was not sung in these: they were rather tragedies with choruses.*

In 1500 the popes possessed a theatre, with decorations and machinery. The paintings in this edifice were by Balthazar Peruzzi, who may be said to be the father of scene painting. His scenery is said to have been very realistic.

Julian de Medicis, brother of Leon X, on being proclaimed a citizen of Rome gave public plays, and had a comedy of Plautus presented for two days, the music of which was much admired.

In 1574. Claudio Merulo, organist at St. Mark's, composed music to a drama, which was performed in the presence of Henry III., of France.

Vincent Galileo, father of the astronomer, and Giovanni Bardi invented the recitative at about the same time.

Peri and Caccini, two of the best musicians of Florence were engaged by two rich noblemen to write for them a complete opera; *Dafne*, produced in Florence (1597,) was the result, and was the first complete opera in modern form; these composers were therefore the originators of the opera.

An opera by the same writers was given at the wedding of Henry IV., and Marie de Medici. Rinucci, the author of the *libretti* of both the above was silly enough to imagine that Marie de Medici loved him, and followed her into France

---

*L'Opera Italien. Castil-Blaze, p. 20.

the ridicule which he received for his conceit soon sent him back to Italy.

The score of "Orpheus," by Monteverde, 1608, allows us to see the construction of his orchestra.

There were,—
- 2 Clavichords,
- 2 Lyres, or Grand Viols (13 strings),
- 10 Violas,
- 3 Bass Viols,
- 2 Double Bass,
- 1 Double Harp (2 rows of strings),
- 2 Small French Violins,
- 2 Great Guitars,
- 2 Organs (wood),
- 4 Trombones,
- 1 Pair of Regals (small organ),
- 2 Cornets,
- 1 Small Flute,
- 1 Clarion,
- 3 Sourdines (muted trumpets).

These instruments gave to each chorus and character a different effect, thus the double basses accompanied Orpheus; the viols, Euridice; the trombones, Pluto; the regals, Apollo. The shepherd's choruses were accompanied by flute, cornets, sourdines and clarion, and most singular of all, Charon sang to the light tones of the *guitar*.*

In Italy, from this time forth, opera followed opera.

In France it was not known till much later

---

*L'Opera Italien. Castil-Blaze, p. 28.

plays " with songs " were known however, and one of these, " in the Italian style," was performed in Paris, before the King and Royal family, on the occasion of the victory of the Duke of Guise at Calais, 1558.

The chief representations for years after, lay rather in the direction of ballets, than of operas. Religious plays also still were given at Paris, but after the ordinance, of 1548, that no Catholic ceremony should be represented on the stage, they disappeared.*

The theatres, tnat is those which were public, were at this time very poorly appointed, but through the constant festivities of the court, many inventions came into use.

The Court of France had always a *penchant* for music, the drama, and dancing. Henry IV., was very fond of the latter.

Louis XIII., cultivated music with much success, he composed many airs, and several motets which he had performed in his Chapel. Music was his ordinary recreation when he could not go hunting. At the siege of La Rochelle, there being no musicians or singers with the army, he himself wrote out the vespers for Pentecost, that they might be ready in time. Three weeks before his death, and after he had received the extreme unction, feeling himself somewhat better, he begged Nyert, his first *valet de garderobe* to sing a paraphrase of David, which he had set to music, to **give thanks to God.**

* Curiosites Theatrales, Fournel (Paris), p. 17.

Saint-Martin and Campeforte who were present, each sang a part, and thus made a concerted piece which they sang around the bed, the king from time to time joining in with his own voice.

He also wrote a " *de Profundis,*" which was sung over him after his death.* The words still exist which were written by him for his now well-known " Amaryllis;" they were written for Madame de Hauteforte, and one of the verses runs:—

> Tu crois, o beau soleil!
> Q'ua ton eclat rien n'est pareil;
> Mais quoi! tu palis
> Auprès d'Amaryllis.†

Tallement speaks of a concert given once where one of his songs was sung four times, the king beating the measure. To these gatherings he would admit none who were not musical, and no women whatever, " for" said he, " *they cannot keep silent.*"‡

Under Louis XIV., the opera became well known in France, nor was it any longer a borrowed spectacle, for Lulli in 1664 associated himself with Moliere in writing; the latter furnishing the *libretti*, which were in themselves of the best order. In 1672 he built a permanent opera house, (Academie Royale de Musique) and thus gave to France, what it had never before possessed,—a national opera.

There were, to be sure, a few French operas,

---

* Bibliotheque de Poche, v. VIII., p 345
† Ibid vol. II., p. 311.
‡ Historiette d. la Marechale de Themines, book 5, p. 196.

befcre his enterprise; one given at Paris, by Cardinal Mazarin, in 1645; one entitled "Akébar, King of Mogul," by the Abbeé Mailly and "La Pastorale en musique," by Cambert,* but these do not deprive Lulli of the claim of being the "founder of French opera."

La Fontaine tried to write some *libretti* for Lulli, which were total failures, and declined by the musician.

The King (Louis XIV.), was passionately fond of Lulli's music, and would hear scarcely any other.

About this time, the idea of *whistling and hissing* to show disapproval, was invented. It is said that Corneille's "*Baron de Fondrieres*" has the questionable honor of being the first play that ever was hissed.

The hiss, spread rapidly, but on some one having injudiciously hissed the opera of Orpheus, by the sons of Lully, the hiss was interdicted by law in 1690.†

The repression was not very effectual, and innumerable epigrams (some of which still exist),‡ showed the derision of the public.

The singers of Lulli's operas had all the faults of their later brethren. Dumenil, the tenor, used to steal the jewelry of the *prime donne*, and get intoxicated with the baritone. He is said to have drank six bottles of champagne every night, and only the sixth deteriorated his performance.

* Edwards' History of the Opera, vol. 1, p. 15.
† Curiosites Theatrales, Fournel, p. 161
‡ See Annals Dramatiques, VII., p. 165

Marthe Le Rochois, another of the troupe, on being accused of too much intimacy with the bassoon of the orchestra, exhibited a promise of marriage from the fond performer, written on the back of an *ace of spades*.

Mlle. de Maupin was the wildest scapegrace the stage ever saw: her adventures read like the most improbable sensational novel, and would take as much space to reproduce.

England's first opera was performed in 1656. It was entitled the "Siege of Rhodes," and was composed by five persons in collaboration. Musicians and players were at this time held in low esteem, and were liable to arrest as vagabonds at almost any moment.

England possessed in Henry Purcell (1658-1695) a musician of whom any country might be proud. This composer soon turned his pen to the writing of operas; the music to "The Tempest" was excellent, while his "King Arthur" contains music which is still loved by Englishmen everywhere.

Now that opera was established firmly, the rivalries of the singers at once began.

In 1726 a bitter rivalry sprang up in London between Cuzzoni and Faustina Bordoni, in which the whole town took part. It lasted over two years, and was throughout causeless, as the styles of the two were entirely dissimilar, Bordoni being unapproachable in the lightness and rapidity of her runs and embellishments, and Cuzzoni excelling in the pathetic quality, and breadth of her tones.*

But to follow the absurdities which constantly arose in the rivalries of the various composers, singers and performers, would require, not one, but very many volumes by itself; we need only allude to the disputes and rivalries between Gluck and Piccini (in the composition of operas,) the singers Mara and Todi, in France, and Billington and Mara in London.

The names of those who have established a reputation as wonderful operatic singers, also make a formidable list. Among the very greatest may however be mentioned Farinelli (male soprano) Catalani, and Lablache, and among the most successful of operatic writers, Gluck, Mozart, Meyerbeer, Rossini, Verdi, Gounod. Of course many names could be added, but these may stand as representatives.

It is not singular that the great masters, Händel, Beethoven and Mendelssohn failed in this branch of composition. None of them had the ability to stoop to the musical *finesses*, and *coups de theatre*, which were necessary to make a successful opera. They might have succeeded, if the pure style of Gluck, with *libretti* taken from the Greek tragedies, had continued, for these were in their vein. But the public demanded a more spicy operatic diet which they were not able or desirous to finish.

It is well that it was so, for to this fact **we owe** our grandest oratorios.

*L'Opera Ital. Castil-Blaze, p. 128.

Händel had trouble enough with opera, before he finally left it. He had a temper which was simply frightful (and an appetite which was the same), and when he came in contact with the conceited and irascible singers of his day, an explosion was sure to follow.

Cuzzoni (who had the sweetest of voices, and the harshest of tempers), was the hardest of all for him to get along with.

One day she refused absolutely to sing a part which he had assigned to her; his patience, small at the best, gave out totally, and he was going to throw her out of the window, when she hurriedly gave her consent to sing.

Händel's losses and trials as operatic manager, temporarily drove him crazy.

Rossini also had his troubles in the operatic field. Once a manager, whose *libretti* he was bound by contract to set to music, took offence at some action of the composer, and sought to revenge himself by writing a wretched opera for him. The result nearly brought both to ruin, for Rossini retorted by writing a terribly poor score to the words; in the overture, during an *allegro* movement, the violins were arranged so as to stop at every bar, and tap the tin shades of their lamps with their bows. The audience nearly demolished the theatre. The "Barber of Seville" was a failure at its first performance.

There is a note to be made here, of a passage in one of his operas, which is of interest to conductors.

The overture to "William Tell" had been played from its first representation, August 3, 1829, for more than thirty years, with a major trill in the violincello at the cadence of the first part; (the andante at the beginning of the work), but on the 16th of November, 1861, the piece was played before the composer, who stigmatized as " a great fault," the major trill in the third measure of the cadence.* "It should be minor" he said. And since that date it has been played so. But it is very uncertain whether the abrupt remark was not a mere whim of the composer. The trill is more satisfactory with G sharp, than with G natural; the earlier editions have none of them any mention of a minor trill and it is scarcely possible that "a great fault" like this, should have escaped notice so long.

Meyerbeer, was in all respects, a person well calculated to popularize opera. He knew how to work up dramatic effects, in which he was well seconded by his French librettists, and he did not hesitate at any innovation to ask if it were classical, or belonged to pure art; and he succeeded far better than the martinets who condemned him.

At the first representation of his "*Robert le Diable*," an accident occurred which nearly resulted in disaster. In the last act, Bertram, the tempter, has to descend to the infernal regions, alone; Levasseur (who performed the character) leaped down the trap, and Robert (represented by the tenor Nourrit), who should have remained on

* Deldevez. Curiosites Musicales, p. 215

earth, saved by the prayers of Alice,— after a moment of indecision (not remembering the denouèment) *leaped after him.*

There was general consternation on the stage, for all thought that Nourrit was injured. In the audience they must have thought that the opera had a rather immoral ending, since Bertram, the tempter, had triumphed over the prayers of Alice.

Fortunately the mattresses had not been removed; and Bertram was vastly astonished to find that he had bagged his victim after all; he asked Nourrit in amazement.—"Has the plot been changed?" but Nourrit recollecting his mistake, hastened back to the stage, where the audience were astonished to see him reappear, but soon grasping the situation burst into loud applause.

The curiosities of the opera of to-day are even greater than those of twenty years since, for the world has found an iconoclastic composer who is endeavoring to reform all that went before him, by pulling it to pieces. Yet he has done opera precisely the service which it at present needed, in showing composers the importance of bestowing a greater attention upon the libretto, and elevating the orchestra as well as the scene painter to their proper places; his idea that an opera should be a "perfect chrysolite," a complete picture in all its accessories, is the true one, though his mode of effecting it may not be.

His zeal has allowed him to commit a ludicrous "curiosity of music" in attacking almost all that the Jews have ever done in music, and endeavoring to depreciate the most prominent talent of that race; a talent which has been acknowledged ever since the days of the Babylonian captivity.

Yet a still greater curiosity (and the most recent of all) has been written by one of his defenders. Of course his attacks upon all who differed from him, provoked retorts innumerable; these have been collected and published in a compact form, and the work is entitled "A Dictionary of Impoliteness."

With this "curiosity" our catalogue appropriately ends. We have not mentioned some of the great names in music (Haydn, Cherubini, Palestrina, Schumann, Schubert, etc.), and have touched but lightly upon others. They did not seem to come within our scope.

The incidents in the lives of the musical giants have all been sought out by persons possessing facilities which no American writer can have, and are generally so well known that they can no longer be called curious. We have endeavored to show that music is a very uncertain and fickle art, and continually changing, and that there never can be *absolute* laws laid down in this free art, as if it were a fixed science. If we have done this and amused our readers at the same time, we consider our work brought to a satisfactory conclusion.

THE END.

INDEX.

Abyssinian Music	270
Æschylus	74
African Music	251
Amanieus, troubadour	334
Amaryllis	356
Ambrosian Chant	299
Ancestors, feasts of	186
Aristotle	57
Armenian Church	292
Bamboo Instruments	153
Banquet Music, Egyptian	17, 24
Banquet Music, Grecian	53, 57
Banquet Music, Japanese	213
Barbarians, Music of	229
Bards, ancient	323
Bardesanes	291
Bells	148
Bertrand du Born	336
Bœthius	308
Bongo Songs	267
Brahma, legend of	8
Caligula	99
Canadian, curious song	234
Canute	328
Caste of musicians, Chinese	131
Caste of musicians, Egyptian	18
Chant, Ambrosian	299
Chant, Gregorian	303
Charlemagne	308
Cheng	155
Chinese ceremonies	162
Chinese compositions	162
Chinese music	114
Chinese a musical language	160
Chinese music resembles Scotch	166
Chinese songs, earliest	115
Chinese songs	158
Chinese theatre and plays	173
Chinese whistle	149
Chorus, a terrible	74
Chorus, Greek	74
Christian, early customs	287

INDEX.

Christian, early music 280
Christian churches of Africa 293
Chun, Song of 121
Clavichord in China 137
Confucius 124
Conservatories in ancient Egypt 25
Coptic Hymns 294
Crusaders' songs 349
Cuzzoni 358, 360

Dances, Australian 234
Dances, Bushmen 256
Dances, Chinese 176
Dances. Egyptian 21
Dances, Fiji Islands 248
Dances, Grecian 79
Dances, Roman 97
Dances Savage 234, 277
Dances, Tasmanian 238
Dances, War 241
Destruction of musical instruments 133
Dictionary of Impoliteness 363
Drums, African 265
Drums, Chinese 143
Drums, used to mark the hour 144
Drums, Javanese 243
Drums, water 256

Egyptian music 15
Egyptian Muses 16
Egyptian banquets 17
English Bards 327
Essenhamens 334
European music in China 135

Female musicians, Chinese 129
Female musicians, Greek 51
Female musicians, Troubadours 341
Festivals, Chinese 170
Festivals, Theban 21
Fiddle, Chinese 156
Fiji Islanders, Music 248
Flute, Chinese 139
Flute, Egyptian 23
Flute, Grecian 41, 42, 43, 59
Flute, Kaffir 255
Flute, Roman 86
Flute, Prehistoric 232
Flute-playing at Grecian Games 41
Foang-hoang 116

INDEX. III.

Fo Hi, the Chinese Noah................................ 116
Folk Songs... 350
Funeral music, Chinese................................. 173
Funeral music, Egyptian................................ 19
Funeral music, Japanese................................ 207
Funeral music, Roman................................... 88

Games of Greece.. 35
Goura—African Instrument............................... 257
Greek Church, music of................................. 288
Greek music, ancient................................... 35
Greek Hymns.. 35
Greek Scale...36, 55
Gregorian Chant.. 303
Gregorian Chant in France.............................. 310
Guido d'Arezzo... 318
Guitar, African.. 263
Guitar, Hindoo... 14

Handel... 360
Harmony, Egyptian...................................... 19
Harps, African... 255
Harps, Egyptian.. 23
Harps, Hebrew.. 26
Hebrew music... 26
Hebrew music, resemblance to Negro..................... 33
Hermes, Egyptian god................................... 15
Hindoo music... 8
Hissing, when first began.............................. 357
Hucbald.. 315
Hymns, Christian, ancient......................281, 294
Hymn, Chinese.. 164
Hymn, Greek.. 35

Instruments, African..............................257, 259
Instruments, Chinese................................... 142
Instruments, East Indian............................... 13
Instruments, Egyptian.................................. 24
Instruments, Greek..................................... 59
Instruments, Hebrew.................................... 29
Instruments, Hindoo.................................... 13
Instruments, Japanese.................................. 202
Instruments, Kaffir.................................... 255
Instruments, Roman..................................... 89
Irish Bards.. 325
Irooa, Japanese.. 204

Japanese music... 201
Jews, music of modern.................................. 27
Jewsharps in Africa.................................... 258

INDEX.

Jongleurs 331
Julian, reforms of Emperor 100
Kaffir songs 251
Kin, Chinese 150
King, Chinese instrument 147
Kithara, Greek instrument 57
Laborers' songs, Egyptian 18
Lamia 61
Laws relative to music, Egyptian 20
Legends of music, Chinese 116, 119
Legends of music, Egyptian 15
Legends of music, Hindoo 8
Legends of music, Japanese 215
Legends of music Javanese 244
Louis XIII 355
Louis XIV 357
Malay music 243
Meistersingers 349
Melody, Hindoo 12
Melody, an old 348
Meyerbeer 361
Military music, African 262
Military music, Chinese 131, 169
Military music, Greek 47, 60
Military music, Japanese 219
Minnesingers 329, 341
Mode, Ambrosian 301
Mode, Gregorian 365
Musical Buildings 44
Musical course Roman 86
Music as a means of inspiring fear 276
Music boxes in Africa 269
Music boxes, Chinese 175
Nero, musical history of 101
Neumes 313
New Zealand, Harmony in 233
New Zealand songs 240
Nose-flutes 248
Notation 313, 316, 317, 321
Nyam-Nyams, Music of 258
Olympic Games 89
Opera 352
Orchestra, an old 354
Organ, ancient Rome 89
Organ, Chinese 155
Organ, Hebrew 28, 30

INDEX.

Pantomimes, Chinese	195
Pantomimes, Roman	97
Pantomimes, Javanese	243
Persecution of musicians	126
Philosophers and music	53
Pindar	65
Pianoforte in Japan	227
Poems of the Troubadours	338
Power of Music	9, 10
Power of Music in Africa	274
Processional music, Egyptian	22
Processional music, Japanese	218
Processional music, Roman	92
Processional music, Savage	263
Provençal songs	330
Psaltery	30
Ptolemy	62
Pythagorus	53
Pythian Games	41
Quarrel between choirs	311
Quarrel between singers	358
Ragas, Hindoo	9
Religious music, Abyssinian	269
Religious music, Chinese	162
Religious music, Christian	280
Religious music, Greek	35
Religious music, Hebrew	26
Religious music, Japanese	205
Religious music, Roman	86
Rhythm, Egyptian	20
Rhythm of savage nations	229
Riquier, Guirant	332
"Robert," accident at first performance	361
Roman, ancient music	85
Roman Empire, music of	99
Rossini	360
Royal dancers	193
Royal musicians	99, 100, 102, 115, 232, 355
Salaries, ancient Greece	61
Salaries, Chinese	187
Salaries, Nero	105
Sappho	61
Savage music	229
Scale, Chinese	167
Scale, East Indian	11
Scale, Grecian	36, 55
Scale, Hindoo	11

Scale, Japanese	201
Scale modern	320
Scale, Religious, Greek	289
Schofer, Hebrew horn	27
Schools of music, Egypt	25
Schools of music, Rome	86, 190
"Selah!" meaning of	81
Signals, musical Chinese	123, 173
Simonides	63
Sistrum	22
Skolion	57
Societies, or Guilds of Musicians, Roman	87
Songs, Chinese	158
Stesi-chorus	49
Stones, musical	145
Stringed instruments	149
Syrian Church	290
Tales of the Minnesingers	346
Terpander	45
Theatre, Chinese	176
Theatre, Greek	67
Theatre Japanese	219
Theatre, Javanese	245
Theatre, Roman	95
Timbrel	30
Time marked by bells	120
Time marked by drums	120
Tone-picture, Grecian	59
Treatises on music, Chinese	135
Triumphs, Roman	92
Triumphal Odes, Greece	62
Trumpeter, a great	40
Trumpets, African	265, 261
Trumpets, Chinese	120, 157
Trumpets, pre-historic	231
Trumpets, Russian	157
Troubadours	329
Vina, Indian instrument	13
Violin, Hindoo	13
Volkslied	350
Wagner	362
War Song	284
Watch Song	344
Welch Bards	324
"William Tell," an error in	361
Wood instruments of China	151
Yu, Chinese musician	132

University of California
SOUTHERN REGIONAL LIBRARY FACILITY
305 De Neve Drive - Parking Lot 17 • Box 951388
LOS ANGELES, CALIFORNIA 90095-1388

Return this material to the library from which it was borrowed

SD - #0019 - 031023 - C0 - 229/152/20 - PB - 9781330653296 - Gloss Lamination